FOUR FACES OF ANGER

Seneca, Evagrius Ponticus, Cassian, and Augustine

Gertrude Gillette

Foreword by George Lawless

University Press of America,® Inc.
Lanham · Boulder · New York · Toronto · Plymouth, UK

**Copyright © 2010 by
University Press of America,® Inc.**
4501 Forbes Boulevard
Suite 200
Lanham, Maryland 20706
UPA Acquisitions Department (301) 459-3366

Estover Road
Plymouth PL6 7PY
United Kingdom

Library of Congress Control Number: 2010925375
ISBN: 978-0-7618-5169-1 (paperback : alk. paper)
eISBN: 978-0-7618-5170-7

To my Monastic Community
who daily witness to me the love of Christ

CONTENTS

ABBREVIATIONS

Common Series:

CSEL: *Corpus Scriptorum Ecclesiasticum Latinorum*
FC: *Fathers of the Church*
PG: *Patrologia Greca*
PNF: *Post-Nicene Fathers Series*
PL: *Patrologia Latina*
SC: *Sources Chretiennes*

For Evagrius:

Ant. : Antirrhetikos
Cnsl. : Counsel to Monks / Exhortations to Monks I-II
Ep. : Letters
Eul. : To Eulogios
Fnd. : Foundations of the Monastic Life
Gn. : Gnostikos
KG : Kephalia Gnostikos
Mon. : Exhortation to Monks / Ad Monachos
Prak. : The Praktikos
Pray. : Chapters on Prayer
Skem. : Skemmata / Reflections
Th. : On the Various Evil Thoughts
8Th. : On the Eight Thoughts / On the 8 Spirits of Wickedness

For Cassian:

Conf. : Conferences
Inst. : Institutes

For Augustine:

Conf. : Confessiones
Div. quaes. : De diversis quaesitionibus LXXXIII.
En. in ps. : Enarrationes in psalmos
Ep. : Epistula
MA : Miscellanea Agostiniana I
Mor. Eccl. : De moribus ecclesiae catholicae
Obj. : Obiurgatio (Ep. 211.1-4).
Op. Mon. : De opere monachorum
Serm. : Sermones

FOREWORD

A pagan philosopher, an anchoretic monk, a cenobitic monk, a fifth-century bishop make interesting bedfellows. Their cumulative lives range from four years before Christ to some four-hundred-and-thirty years after Christ, specifically, c. 4 B.C. to 430 A.D., from the birth of Lucius Annaeus Seneca, the philosopher to the death of Augustine, the bishop of Hippo. John Cassian of Marseilles outlives Augustine by a few years.[1] Evagrius of Pontus dies in 399 A.D. The impact of their written legacy is immediate. These ancient authors are read today by widely divergent special interest groups in their original language and translations of recent vintage. Evagrius of Pontus writes in Greek.

Seneca the Younger

...was a worthy rival to Cicero in transplanting Greek philosophical vocabulary to the West. Both authors frequently found it necessary to employ two Latin words to express the meaning of one Greek word. Seneca conveys the impression of being less attracted towards the hard stuff of logic, epistemology, cosmology and meta-physics. His attention is drawn, principally though not exclusively, towards the area of moral behavior and ethics. He was more philosopher than rhetorician, unlike his father of the same name. Both disciplines permeate his twelve *Dialogues* on themes such as "Consolation," "Clemency;" "Leisure," "Tranquillty," "Providence," and kindred topics. His *Dialogues* and *Epistles* were once thought to have been cobbled bits and pieces of ethical interest from his Greek predecessors, without adding any substance to them. Recent scholarship demonstrates that this criticism is unfair.

In Canada, the United States and Europe since the second half of the 20th century there has been a remarkable reassessment and resurgence of scholarly interest in Seneca's ethical writings. The sophistication, subtleties and complexities of Stoic philosophy ought not to be underestimated.[2] A professor of Hellenistic philosophy and literature has felicitously catalogued at least nine species of anger in the Graeco-Roman world: 1) the generic word, *orgē*; 2) incipient anger; 3) swollen anger; 4) anger that breaks out suddenly; 5) anger that awaits the right time for vengeance; 6) anger that longs for things to go badly for someone, with eager intensity; 7) anger that longs for things to go badly for someone for his own sake; 8) anger that bides its time and does bad things; 9) anger that stores itself up for a long time, *mēnis*.[3] In each of the above instances the author identifies the original Greek word. This last sample, the "wrath of Achilles" is the first word of the *Iliad*, where Homer recounts in epic magnitude "the blood, sweat, toil, and, tears" resulting from one man's anger. Also worthy of note, "...[The] Stoics' most important contribution to political thought are [sic] in their account of the therapy of excessive attachments to *money, power, and honor,* and of the related therapy of *anger,* and other socially divisive passions...."[4]

Evagrius of Pontus

. . . was a well-educated prominent thinker much influenced by Origen, not just an Origenist. From the year 533 A.D. onwards his reputation suffered from the condemnation of Origen by the Second Council of Constantinople. His writings surfaced surreptitiously and sporadically under the respectable names of Nilus of Ancyra, Basil of Caesarea and others. A partisan individual possibly substituted the names of orthodox non-Origenist authors as the putative source of such writings. Fruitful results of textual criticism, through the centuries, have correctly identified Evagrius as the authentic author of works erroneously attributed to Nilus and to others. For the above reasons scholars did not turn their attention to Evagrius until early decades of the 20th century.

Evagrius is distinguished as the first monk to have written extensively on ascetical and mystical spirituality. He is "the first theoretician of Christian mysticism,"[5] and the first primary textual witness to the doctrine of the eight "thoughts" which aim to deter an individual from his/her pursuit of asceticism.

These "thoughts" (*logismoi*) antedate by a century-and-a-half John Cassian's revision of the same materials (1) by adding *envy*, (2) by combining *vainglory* with *pride*, (3) by amalgamating *listlessness* with *sadness* into a single category, called by Pope Gregory the Great *melancholy*, but called by his successors *acedia*. In this manner the so-called Eight Deadly Sins or Capital Sins, when reduced to seven become pride, envy, anger, acedia, avarice, gluttony and lust.

In the fourth century, this register of human failings was construed by Evagrius as "thoughts" (*logismoi*) which generically identify the passions (*pathē*), another Greek word which Cicero translated into Latin as "disturbances of the mind" (*perturbationes animi*), unreasoning ways of responding to and coping with the waywardness of the human condition. This helps explain why the metaphor of soldier, or wrestler, or athlete punctuates the pages of monastic and ascetic literature.

It is important to understand that these eight "thoughts" are involuntary: they are not vices or sins as such. Sin implies consent. The phrase "process of thought" or in contemporary terminology "psychosomatic impulses" offers a more accurate description of the phenomenon. The word "capital" is likewise misleading. Vices are called "capital," not because they are grave, but because they lie at the root of sins or they give rise to sins.

Evagrius commented on the Book of Proverbs in sententious phraseology, a trademark of his writings, reminiscent of 3rd and 4th century Hellenistic non-Christian literature. His *Sentences to a Virgin* and stimulating treatise *On Prayer* are noteworthy accomplishments in these genres. His exegesis is philosophically

reflective and at the same time reinforced with singular]
Scripture. Scholarship these last forty years demonstrate
Chadwick was both perceptive and prophetic: "the title ⌣.
of spirituality,' which Henri Bremond reserved for Cassian, sɴᴏ⌣
Evagrius."[6]

John Cassian

If I were invited to have Cassian as a conversation partner and were permitted
to ask him one question only, I would ask: "Is there anything you know about
monasticism that you failed to include in your *Institutes* and *Conferences*?" I like
to consider the *Institutes* and the *Conferences* of John Cassian as documentaries of
5th century monastic life, a source book and a minefield of information. While there
are many overlapping areas and repetitions in the two works (the *Institutes* were
written for "beginners," *renunciants*, and the *Conferences* were designed for practi-
tioners in an advanced stage of monastic life), both works represent a monumental
achievement in their time and place.

There is a subtle tonality throughout the *Conferences*. The didacticism of the
Institutes has been softened. The role of the spiritual director becomes heightened.
While the twenty-four speeches are rhetorical artifices consciously composed as
such by their author, the reader never loses sight of the sincerity and seriousness of
purpose with which a monk who is writing for monks endows his script.

Cassian's itinerary from either "ancient Scythia Minor or more recently
Dobrudja, a part of modern day Romania,"[7] then to Bethlehem, to Scetis, Kellia,
and, Nitria in Egypt, to Constantinople, to Rome, and lastly to Marseilles, largely
accounts for his bilingualism and marks him as a monk well-connected with both
the local episcopate and monasticism, east and west.

The conclusion to Book Four of the *Institutes* (IV, 43) summarizes the words
of Abba Pinufius to a novice in what we may correctly call a ladder of perfection
in ascendant and inverted order of the original spoken words. The structure of the
ladder metaphorically facilitates step-by-step an understanding of Cassian's intent,
by accentuating and identifying purity of heart as the goal of both a solitary life and
common life.

> Purity of heart,
> flowering of the virtues,
> expulsion of the vices,
> mortification of desires,
> humility,
> renunciation,
> salutary compunction,
> the fear of the Lord
> is the beginning of wisdom
>
> (Ps. 110:10, Prov. 9:10, Sirach 1:14,16,18 Vulg.)

That the second triad of the six requirements for *friendship* waves the red flag of *anger* reiterates Cassian's seriousness of purpose in his juxtaposition of the two diametrically opposed themes. Entirely absent from *Conference* 16 is any resonance of Pythagoras, Plato, Aristotle, or Cicero, each of whom is reflected, for example, in the urbanity of Augustine's understanding of friendship. Cassian, meanwhile, never conceals his preference for the *fuge, tace, et quiesce* motifs of desert monasticism; Augustine, but once only, as far as we know, "had meditated taking flight to live in solitude."[8] He repudiated the thought. The word "hermit" never belonged to his vocabulary.

In contrast, however, to the wider Graeco-Roman eclecticism on the matter of friendship, Cassian like Seneca generally adopts the uncompromising stance of early Stoicism.[9] For example, section 14 of *Conference* 16, *De amicitia,* offers insightful illustrations of the distinctions between *love* and *affection.* Cassian uses the Greek words *agapē* and *diathesis,* respectively. These distinctions are upstaged in the second half of *Conference* 16 by the theme of anger (secs. 15-28).

As a strict constructionist of early and middle Stoicism, Seneca had raised the question in *Letter* 9 whether one who strictly adheres to the rubric, *secundum rationem,* ought to have any desire or need for friendship. The ideal prototype of the Stoic way of life is the individual who puts up with privations: "The one who desires more, not the one who is lacking, is poor."[10] Does the moral rigor of Stoicism extend to the cultivation of friendship?

On the one hand, I understand the estimate of Professor Robert Markus: "Thus the Stoic ideal of friendship found its fulfillment in monasticism."[11] On the other hand, the observation of a Cistercian monk is not without equal merit: "John Cassian's *Conference* on friendship would have been better entitled *De concordia in claustro.*"[12] Both perspectives are defensible. Nonetheless, is it somewhat offputting that Cassian nowhere in his oeuvre cites the "twin precept of love," *praeceptum caritatis geminum,* from any of the Synoptic Gospels? (Mt 19:19, Mk 12: 31, Lk 10: 27) The absence of the "twin commandment" is possibly occasioned by the fact that Cassian's optic on *amicitia* prejudices the life of the anchorite over the life of the cenobite.

Afterlife

The incredible surge of interest both in Stoicism and in John Cassian from independent wellsprings during the last quarter of the 20th century, notably in the anglophone world, augurs well for the future study of this 5th century monk. Like a cat, Cassian has nine lives. His first reincarnation is attested in the oldest extant manuscript of the monastic *Rule* (*Praeceptum*) of Augustine, Paris BN lat. 12634. It is found in the Bibliothèque National, Paris, written probably in Italy in the late 6th century or early 7th century. The second half of the manuscript contains a series of forty-four extracts from monastic *Rules*, for example, the *Rule* of the Master, the *Rule* of Saint Basil, the *Rule* of Pachomius, and other monastic legislators, some of whom remain anonymous. Nine extracts derive from Cassian, chiefly from the

Institutes 4,9 on spiritual direction; *Inst.,*2,15-16; 3,7; 4,12 on prayer; 4,16 on amendment for sins; *Inst.* 4, 18 comportment at common table; *Conl.* 12,2 and 12,7 on chastity.[13] A *Regula Cassiani* derived from the first four books of the *Institutes* circulated in the post-patristic era and was incorporated by Benedict of Aniane in his *Codex Regularum monasticarum et canonicarum* of the 9th century.[14]

In the last chapter of his *Rule* Benedict of Nursia makes both Cassian's *Institutes* and the twenty-four *Conferences* required reading for all the monks (RB 73, 5).

In his exposition of "unceasing prayer" (1 Thes 5:17), Benedict assigns Ps. 69 (70):2 "God, come to my assistance. Lord, make haste to help me," as the invocation to each of the hours in the Divine Office. This "devotional formula"is repeated sixteen times in Cassian's *Tenth Conference* on Prayer at X,2-13, intercalated with singularly apposite petitions, a rubric that is honored in the liturgical life of the Catholic Church to this day.

The following forecast at mid-20th century was neither sanguine nor exaggerated: "The honor belongs entirely to Benedict to develop and to propagate in the West the true monastic tradition of Casssian."[15]

Finally, "Like the Rule of Saint Benedict, [Cassian's] work was a protection against excess, and a constant recall to that primitive simplicity where Eastern spirituality meets Western."[16]

Augustine of Hippo

Chapter six of Augustine's *Rule* has much to say about anger. Interestingly, the chapter lacks any mention of either the superior (*praepositus*), or the priest. The entire chapter dealing with the escalation of anger into hatred (*ne ira crescat in odium*) is directed towards all members of the monastery. In an unusual collocation of ideas, Augustine melds a dictum from Cicero, "hatred is inveterate anger," (*odium ira inveterata*)[17] with Mt. 7:3-5 where simple anger is described as "straw" (*festuca*), and inveterate anger becomes the "beam" (*trabs*).[18] Evidently, anger presented a serious threat all year round to the litigious temperament which characterized many north African people. Among the "sermons to the people" the bishop's Lenten preaching urged laity, clergy, religious men and women "to fast from quarrels and discord" (*ss.* 205.3; 208.2; 209.1; 210.12; all of 211). Twice within this chapter six the bishop insists upon the promptness[19] with which forgiveness for offenses, such as "insults, abusive language, or even an incriminating accusation,"[20] is to be extended to the injured party. It is worth noting that "quarrels" is the first word of chapter six, also that no less than eight extended commentaries by Augustine on the "Lord's Prayer" constitute the undergirding of chapter six. With sound psychological insight the author of the *Rule* contrasts the individual who is prone to anger, yet hastens to beg forgiveness as "better (*melior*) than another who is less inclined to anger and less likely to ask pardon." He regards with severity the individual who absolutely refuses to ask pardon, or does so without meaning it, as one who is without meaning it, as one who is entirely out of place in the monastery (*sine causa est in monasterio*), even if he is not dismissed.

It is not uncommon to find references to grumbling or murmuring in monastic documents. The *Rule* is no exception.[21] Mention is made of brothers/sisters who are unhappy with the clothes they are wearing (V,1), those who refuse to accept the advice of a physician (V,5), and the librarian, the steward of the general storeroom, and the custodian for the storage of clothing who begrudge members of the community (V,9). Such people are vividly portrayed elsewhere as the "wheels" of a cart that cannot stop creaking (Sirach 33:5), and in like manner "a bucking horse in harness not pulling its weight but further damaging the rig with its hooves."[22]

On three occasions when invited to oblige a third party, Augustine intervened to settle quarrels in monasteries of men and women. One of these interventions took the form of two letters (210 and 211.1-4) addressed to quarreling nuns at Hippo, who were disenchanted with their Mother Superior and determined to replace her. A second such endeavor responded to a request from the metropolitan bishop of Carthage. Aurelius urged Augustine to rebuke refractory monks in the environs of that city, because they refused to cut their hair but, more importantly, because they were citing totally irrelevant verses from Scripture (Mt 6:25-26) in defense of their conduct and refusal to work.

The third call for Augustine to act as an arbitrator came from Hadrumetum (modern Sousse in Tunisia), where disputatious monks denied both the necessity for grace and the need for authority in the community. Augustine generously and irenically answered with three letters (214, 215, 216A), and two books, *Grace and Free Will* to the Abbot Valentine and the monks who were with him, also *Correction and Grace*.

Sermon 302 describes Augustine's reaction to a riot where members of his congregation took the law into their own hands by lynching an unpopular government official identified as a soldier (*miles*), very likely a custom's official at the port of Hippo.

In the Spring of 411 the bishop himself aroused the anger of his congregation by refusing to ordain to the priesthood a Roman aristocrat named Pinianus who was resolutely refusing ordination. Perhaps Augustine had in mind his own ordination exactly twenty years previously in similar circumstances. It was clear to the bishop that his parishioners were coveting Pinianus' enormous wealth, with the hope that such largess would be directed to the Church at Hippo. Shouting and tumult erupted intermittently. Augustine hesitated to leave the basilica for fear that the irate dense crowd might harm Bishop Alypius and himself. An intemperate letter (now lost) from Albina, the mother-in-law of Pinianus subsequently posted to Augustine blamed him possibly unfairly for his inaction during the fracas and his "quasi-connivance" with a money-grubbing community (*Letters* 125-26).[23]

A bizzare exhibition
While on "church business" at the bidding of Pope Zosimus in Caesarea Mauretania (Cherchel in western Algeria), Augustine then age 65 addressed a gathering of men (fathers, sons, brothers and neighbors) fighting one another in a savage ritual of blood-letting called the *Caterva*, which is the Latin word for "mob."
Each fighter was at liberty to kill whomsoever he could by pelting one another with stones. Augustine intervened in the melee and spoke in the grand manner of Roman rhetoric, which he rarely invoked, and in that same elevated manner of speech he mollified the mob. The random throwing of stones at one another ceased and civility was restored. The occasion was a pagan religious festival with excessively violent tactics in honor of Mars, the Roman god of warfare.
At the time of dictating *Christian Doctrine* the bishop recalled the incident with great satisfaction: "By the grace of Christ, nothing similar has been attempted there for eight years or more" (4.29.53). In this classic book on ancient Christian rhetoric the bishop of Hippo demonstrates the superiority of speech and reason over basic human instincts gone awry.

* * * * * *

Sister Gertrude Gillette, o.s.b. enables the reader to examine the nasty business of anger in writings from ancient Rome, the desert of Egypt, the southern coastline of the Mediterranean, specifically, ancient Gaul, Marseilles, Lerins and the seaport city of Hippo (Annaba in Algeria). The disciplines of anthropology, philosophy, psychology, and Sacred Scripture are prominently represented and resonate with the ring of modernity. Each author's voice is communicated through a variety of media: essays, sermons, conferences, short staccato sentences, maxims, epistles and oral teaching.
The fragile world of today has much to learn from the anthropomorphic phrase, "wrath of God" in the Bible, interpreted as an instrument of divine pedagogy; the sour notes of discord which disrupt the rhythms of married and monastic life; the many strategies for the appeasement of anger in political life; and the positive contributions of ancient Stoicism and Christianity towards an understanding of the passions.

George Lawless, o.s.a.

Notes: Foreword

1. The date of Cassian's death is a matter of conjecture, mid-430s. C. Stewart, *Cassian the Monk* (New York: Oxford University Press, 1998) 24.
2. See note 9 below.
3. M. Nussbaum, *The Therapy of Desire. Theory and Practice in Hellenistic Ethics.* (Princeton, NJ: Princeton University Press, 1994) 404, note 1.
4. M. Nussbaum (1994) 319-320, note 6[italics added].
5. A. de Vogüe, *Dizionario di Istituti di Perfezione* 6 (1980) 1454.
6. O. Chadwick, *John Cassian.* Second Edition (Cambridge: Cambridge University Press, 1968) 86.
7. Stewart, C., *Cassian the Monk,* (1998) 4.
8. *Confessions* 10.43.70; tr., H. Chadwick.
9. Stoicism was not monochrome in its development. *Early stoicism*: Zeno of Citium founded the school, c. 315 B.C. Chrysippus c. 280-204 B.C. systematized Stoic doctrine. Cleanthes succeded him as head, c. 330- 231 B.C. *Middle Stoicism*: Panaetius of Rhodes, c.180-c.110 B.C. and Posidonius of Apameâ in Syria, c.135-51 B .C. *Roman Stoicism*: Seneca the Philosopher c. 4 B.C.-A.D. 65. Epictetus c. 60-140 A.D.. Marcus Aurelius 161-80 A.D.
10. *Non qui parum habet, sed qui plus cupit, pauper est.* Seneca, *Ep. ad Luc,* II, 6. Ed., Préchac, Budé (1969) 7.
11. *The End of Ancient Christianity* (Cambridge: Cambridge University Press, 1990) 80.
12. Cf. Brian Patrick Mc Guire, "Friendship and Community: The Monastic Experience 350-1250," *Cistercian Stidies,* 95 (1988) 78-81.
13. Verheijen, Luc , *La Règle se Saint Augustin.* I. Tradition manuscrite (Paris: Études Augustiniennes, 1967) 113-14.
14. Stewart, C. *Cassian the Monk* (1998) 24-25.
15. Lorié, L. Th. A., *Spiritual Terminology in the Latin Translation of the Vita Antonii* (Nijmegen 1955) 162-3.
16. Chadwick, O., "Foreword" in *John Cassian Conferences.* Translation and Preface, C. Luibheid. The Classics of Western Spirituality (New York: Paulist Press, 1985) 36.
17. *Tusculan Disputations* 4. 9. 21.
18. Verheijen , L., "The Straw, the Beam, the *Tusculan Disputations* and the *Rule* of Saint Augustine – On a Surprising Augustinian Exegesis," *Augustinian Studies 2* (1971) 17-36.
19. *sine disceptione,* 6. 2; *inpetrare festinat,* 6. 2.
20. *convicio, vel maledicto, vel etiam criminis objectu,* 6. 2.
21. Bonner, G., Augustine of Hippo, *The Monastic Rules* (New York: New City Press, 2004) 86-91.
22. *Exposition of Psalm* 132, 12.
23. S. Lancel, *St. Augustine* (SCM Press, Eng. tr., Canterbury, 2002) 312-314.

PREFACE

This work had its beginning in classes on the *Rule of St. Benedict*. Studying under Sr. Aquinata Böckmann o.s.b., I came to realize that the horizontal vision of community in Benedict's *Rule* owes much to St. Augustine's vision of communi-ty relations found in his own monastic *Rule*. Intrigued and desiring to delve deeper into his concept of community, I began to do further research into Augustine's *Rule*, aided by the expertise of Fr. George Lawless, o.s.a. who suggested that I explore the topic of "Anger in the Rule." I was at first taken back, being inclined as I was to a more positive approach to fraternal relationships within community, but after some reflection I realized that anger was a very good place to start in coming to comprehend a community living in Christ. Although the initial ideas, expressed in abstractions and ideals, are important foundations for communal living, the genuine work of building a loving and unified community is realized in the concrete strug-gles of human nature striving to overcome the tendencies of individualism and egoism. Anger, as a force which often breaks down and prevents the growth of com-munity, must eventually be squarely faced and–according to our monastic authors– the sooner the better.

From the initial study of anger in Augustine's *Rule* and monastic writings, this work expanded to his sermons and to several episodes in his own spiritual journey, and then to anger in three ancient authors who were possible sources of his own thoughts on the subject.

The three authors chosen are broadly representative of the classic views on anger in the tradition: Seneca, the first century A.D. Stoic philosopher whose moral teaching won the admiration of pagans and Christians alike, even that of the irasci-ble Jerome; Evagrius, who represents the monastic anchoretic tradition of the desert and its emphasis on the spiritual growth of the individual; and finally Cassian, who– trained in the same desert–shaped this tradition to speak to cenobites in the West. We have confined ourselves to presenting each author's basic teaching on anger with the broadest of strokes. This assuredly does not due justice to the authors' full treatment of the subject, but I trust it will offer ample reflection to many while encouraging a few to further study.

The research revealed that each author has his unique approach; although there is some overlapping of ideas (especially between Evagrius and Cassian), never-theless each author brings his own insights and experiences to bear on the subject. So, even though there are the inevitable repetitions inherent in studying the same topic in several authors, there is also much that sets them apart both in approach and in content. The reader will find the section on Augustine disproportionately longer than the others, due both to the amount of material at the researcher's disposal as well as a personal desire to situate his remarks on anger and community life within the context of all his monastic writings. I trust that other monastics and non-monastics alike will glean from these pages the essentials of community life in its various forms. The whole of this work is offered to the reader as a step towards creating and building a community in Christ, according to ancient Christian wisdom.

Sister Gertrude Gillette, o.s.b. Ave Maria, Florida
January 25, 2010 Feast of the Conversion of St. Paul

ACKNOWLEDGMENTS

Since gratitude and integrity are very closely intertwined, I wish not only to acknowledge the many ideas contained in this work which were culled from others (and duly noted in endnotes) but I wish to thank these authors as well for their insights and observations, not least of all, the four authors whose wisdom is the focus of this work (I trust the good Lord will pass on my gratitude to them). As for my own contributions, I wish first of all to thank the Father of Our Lord Jesus Christ from whom every good idea proceeds, as St. Augustine never tired reminding us of, citing St. Paul: "What have you that you did not receive? If then you received it, why do you boast as if it were not a gift?" (1 Cor 4:7). I wish also to thank Fr. George Lawless, O.S.A. for his patience in reading many drafts of this work and for his invaluable advice along the way. I thank those other scholars who have read portions of this work including, John Rist and Sarah Byers for their very helpful comments on chapter 1, and two fellow monastics, Jeremy Driscoll O.S.B. and Columba Stewart O.S.B., for their encouraging comments on chapters 2 and 3. I also wish to express my gratitude to Sr. Mary Joseph McManamon, O.S.B. for her proof-reading expertise and to Brian DeRocco at University of America Press for his kindness in responding to my queries regarding the more technical side of bringing this publication to birth. And finally, I thank my Benedictine Consorellas for allowing me the time and space that this work required without ever making me feel any less a part of their lives in our common pursuit of God.

I would gladly extend my gratitude to the Arts et Métiers Graphiques for permission to reproduce the drawings of the ecclesiastical quarters of ancient Hippo in Appendix III (pp.138-139), except that no present trace of them can be found. They apparently went out of business in 1972 and I have been unsuccessful in tracking down a possible inheritor of the rights to the publication, *Monuments Chrétiens D'Hippone: ville épiscopale de Saint Augustin* by Erwan Marec (Paris) 1958. If any reader can enlighten us on this subject we would very gladly pursue a request for permission.

CHAPTER 1

SENECA: A STOIC APPROACH

Life

Lucius Annaeus Seneca was born in Spain around 4 B.C. and taken to Rome as a mere child where he received an education in rhetoric and philosophy. He entered into a senatorial career where his gifts as an orator brought him renown. His popularity aroused the jealousy of the emperor Caligula and he escaped death only because his poor health convinced the emperor that he would soon die a natural death. He outlived Caligula, only to fall on the wrong side of the emperor Claudius who banished him to Corsica. Eight years on this lonely island were spent writing some of his early philosophical essays as well as his tragedies. His treatise *De ira* was most likely penned in this period.[1] Seneca's fortune changed when he was recalled from exile by Nero's mother, Agrippina, who made him tutor to the fledgling-emperor. Under Nero, his influence and power (not to mention his wealth) were at first considerable, but with years his influence had less and less effect on the emperor, until the relationship soured completely and he retired from public life. When he was implicated in an attempt on Nero's life, he was forced to commit suicide which he did with Socrates-like valor.[2]

Philosophical Background

The *De ira* is not a systematic work, but it makes up in vividness and personal sincerity what it lacks in organization. The genre is loosely that of a dialogue, in which the author puts forward his own ideas in response to an interlocutor who represents an alternative position. Thus two different attitudes towards anger are seen in the text and generally speaking represent the two prevalent views at the time, viz. the Platonic/Aristotelean view on the one hand which sees anger as sometimes good and sometimes evil, depending on whether it is under the control of reason, and the Stoic position which condemns anger absolutely.

For Plato and Aristotle, the soul is not a simple entity, but one with parts. Reason functions in one part, while the emotion, passion or affection (all three terms refer to the same phenomena) resides in another part.[3] The real or responsible self is identified with the reasoning part. Thus, for these philosophers, anger is a response in the form of an agitated feeling that arises "when we have a strong sense of having been unjustly treated or slighted in some significant way, quite independently of what we *think* or how we judge at the time about whatever it may be that has occurred."[4] In this view, the emotions are not willed, rather they are involuntary responses and indeed they are sometimes difficult or impossible to control. The challenge that faces anyone who wishes to act like a responsible adult, i.e. living in accordance with one's own judgment, is to train oneself in self-discipline so that one is always in control of the emotive part of the psyche, at least to the extent that the reaction to external situations is not excessive.[5]

The Stoics strongly disagree with this explanation. They agree with Plato and Aristotle that a person is responsible for his actions and that he must be self-disciplined, but they go further and consider that a person is also responsible for his *reactions* to a situation. The reason for this lies in the Stoics[6] belief that the soul is not a divided entity consisting of a reasoning and a non-reasoning part, but a single whole which is governed by reason. Passion, far from being something contrary to reason, is rather rational in the sense that it is the product of assent.[7] They believe that reason actually yields "a certain authority to the passions"[8] which gives them their power and control. Once a person has ceded the reins over to them, so to speak, the passions take a person where they want and the person has no grounds for complaint since it is the individual's fault that he assented to their demands. If the passions are thus empowered by an assent of reason, they are likewise also *unempowered* and made subject to discipline by the same reason, when it refuses to assent or give in to their destructive demands.[9]

Furthermore, the Platonic-Aristotelian view admits that at times the emotive reaction might be the proper one especially when functioning moderately. The Stoics again strongly disagree. How could a non-rational response be correct? That is, how could a non-rational response possibly express a correct judgment of how things really are?[10] In their world-view, the Stoics were Platonic.[11] What the senses communicate to the self are appearances, things which are only partially true. This being the case, the only truth for the soul is to turn inwards, not outwards, and to cultivate its own growth which lay in virtue. The pursuit of virtue is what gives value to life and renders it a consistent whole.[12] All else is mere appearance and not worth a response which would grant the external more value than it has in reality. Even the word for passion or emotion: *pathos* in its root means what one suffers, what one is enduring from the outside, i.e. what one feels due to an external influence. In this view, any response which would disturb the soul is considered excessive. Disturbance, perturbation, agitation, etc. are not only signs of weakness but they are evils that jeopardize the good of the soul. Anger therefore must be shunned totally. It is not only possible to be free from these *pathē*, it is likewise a moral imperative.[13] Through the proper use of reason, a person can achieve an equilibrium of soul which admits of no irrational or negative impulses. The goal of the wise man, the true philosopher, is then to cultivate *tranquillitas animi*. Of this tranquillity, Seneca writes:

> What we are seeking, therefore, is how the mind may always pursue a steady and favourable course, may be well-disposed towards itself, and may view its condition with joy, and suffer no interruption of this joy, but may abide in a peaceful state, being never uplifted nor ever cast down. This will be "tranquillity."[14]

Let us now turn to Seneca's treatment of anger. The material will be divided into four parts. First we will present Seneca's definition of anger, what it is and what it is not; then its relationship to human nature. In the third part we will deal with how anger behaves, i.e. what stimulates it and what are its characteristics. Finally we will turn to the remedies for curing this vice or disease of the soul. A concluding paragraph will mention briefly the benefits to be gained from banishing the evil of anger from one's life.

I. WHAT IS ANGER?

Anger is the desire to repay an injury.[15] The injury may be real or imagined, physical or mental, namely anything which one perceives as an offence. Seneca gives Aristotle's definition and agrees that it differs little from his own: "the desire to repay suffering"[16] but disagrees with the great Athenian philosopher because he advocated control or regulation over anger rather than its complete eradication from the soul.

As mentioned above, the difference between the two views is rooted in two diverse concepts of anger. For Aristotle[17] and Plato, anger seems to be a force against a perceived evil–which could get out of control, but need not. The force is not in itself evil, but it can become evil when employed for evil purposes. As a force springing from the emotional and thus non-rational part of the soul, it is at times useful, e.g. in rousing an army to fight an enemy (129).

Quite different is Seneca's concept. For him anger is always a mental sin: a *peccatum*,[18] something blameworthy. This follows from the Stoic view that all the functions of the soul–including anger–are by nature acts under the aegis of the mind. To think otherwise, they believe, is to grant impunity to all sorts of actions under the excuse: "I couldn't help myself." No, they argue, anger is a passion precisely because it contains a *lack of control* due to the mind's capitulation to the emotion. It may at first seem strange that anger is described as both out of the control of reason and the fruit of a mental decision. The following analysis of what happens when someone becomes angry shows clearly how the mind surrenders its power to anger:

1) First there is what Seneca calls a pre-passion or a shadow of passion.
The soul experiences some slight or superficial movement as a reaction to an impression of injury (II.2).[19]

2 a) The mind then makes a judgment about the perceived offence, deciding
      that it is a true insult.
   b) The emotion is stirred up further since the soul now feels "indignant,"
      i.e. that it has not been treated with proper dignity or worth.
   c) The mind condemns the act
3) and decides to seek revenge whether or not one has the right to (II.2-5).

The first step is an involuntary (emotional) response, with no culpability. It is
amoral. Seneca gives several examples to illustrate the difference: "Sensations that
do not result from our own volition are uncontrolled and unavoidable, as for example, shivering when we are dashed with cold water" or the dizziness which follows "when one looks down from a precipice."[20] The feeling aroused in the body
due to an impression of injury is assigned to the same category.

In the next step (2a-c) the soul is conscious of the insult and is stirred up
against the perpetrator. What turns the mere feeling into a passion is the mind's
surrender to the feeling which leads (in step 3) to the decision to give uncontrolled
reign to anger. This very surrender is an act, and therefore cannot be dismissed as
a passive thing happening to the mind. In this act, the mind admits the impression
of injury and approves of it, accepting the injury into itself, so to speak, thus allowing the agitation or disturbance to enter the soul.

However, according to Seneca, the decision reached in the third step must be
followed by a true surrender to the feeling, leaving the mind without control, otherwise it is not yet "passion" or vice. A person who decides to act is still to some degree under the control of his reason and could be persuaded not to avenge himself.
"A man thinks himself injured, wishes to take vengeance, but dissuaded by some
consideration immediately calms down. This I do not call anger, this prompting of
the mind which is submissive to reason;..." Anger, rather, occurs when the mind
abdicates its control and allows free rein to the emotion: "...anger is that which
overleaps reason and sweeps it away....the tumult of the mind proceeding to revenge
by choice and determination."[21] When the mind chooses and determines to take
revenge it believes it has the *right* to do so, whether it actually does or not. This
means that the mind has closed itself off from its own reasoning power, intent only
on its object. Once anger has reached this point, it will not obey reason (175).[22]
Actually, anger and reason are two sides of the same soul, going in two different
directions: "these two do not dwell separate and distinct, but passion and reason are
only the transformation of the mind toward the better or the worse."[23]

Anger's lack of control is likened to the state of a man thrown off a cliff:

> Once the mind has been aroused and shaken, it becomes a slave of the
> disturbing agent. There are certain things which at the start are under
> our control, but later hurry us away by their violence and leave us no
> retreat. As a victim hurled from the precipice has no control of his body,
> and once cast off, can neither stop nor stay, but speeding on irrevocably,
> is cut off from all reconsideration and repentance and cannot now avoid
> arriving at the goal toward which he might once have avoided starting,

so with the mind–if it plunges into anger, love or the other passions, it has no power to check its impetus; its very weight and the downward tendency of vice needs must hurry it on, and drive it to the bottom.[24]

Since Seneca wants to underline the irrationality of the passion of anger, making it the essential element which turns emotion into vice, he has to admit that the agitation which is still under control is not truly anger. Naturally, the sooner the process is checked, the less effect the impression of anger has on a person. For one given to *tranquillitas animi,* any agitation is to be avoided. Assent to an injury need never happen. Eradication is possible. Why let it in at all? Why contaminate the soul with any evil? What does virtue have to do with vice? In response to the measured or regulatory advice of Aristotle, Seneca insists: "Virtue needs not the help of vice."[25] If this is true for all the vices, it is especially true for anger, the worst of all the passions (251, 261). Thus Aristotle's teaching on a controlled anger is, for Seneca, a contradiction in terms.

2. IS ANGER NATURAL OR USEFUL?

The stance that anger has no rightful place in the soul leads us to the question of anger's apparent rootedness in human nature. By now, we can be sure that–to the question "Is anger in accordance with nature?"–Seneca will respond with a definitive "No!" (119) In every way it is contrary to nature.[26] It may seem as if anger has an element of "basic honesty," i.e. a certain genuineness or simplicity in its favor, but our philosopher responds that angry people are not being "forthright" (*simplices*) but reckless (*incautos*) (202). Another element in favor of its "natural-ness" is its very prevalence–it's everywhere. Yet even if it does permeate society like an epidemic,[27] that is not a sufficient reason to designate it as an essential part of human nature. Rather, precisely because it is *not* part of human nature it can be excluded, although it may require some real effort: "Yet nothing is so hard and difficult that it cannot be conquered by the human intellect...[with discipline]....How great a blessing to escape anger!"[28]

There were also those who thought that anger added a note of nobility to the soul, or at least that it seemed to be concomitant with some noble souls. The exam-ple given is that of two peoples whom the Romans never subdued, the Germans and the Scythians. They were free, brave, sturdy and prone to anger. The litany makes anger look like one of their lofty gifts. But, as Seneca explains, their innate vigor makes them prone to anger (199) just as certain temperaments –e.g. the choleric–are more prone to anger than the others. Therefore, it is not a quality of human nature but a proneness of certain types of personalities. Furthermore, he questions the whole premise of calling these people "free." Are they who have never been con-quered by the Romans, by that fact "free"? In unsubdued barbarians, what is called freedom is rather wildness. True freedom lies in proper restraint: "No man is able to rule unless he can also submit to be ruled."[29] The implication is that anger is not only not natural (and certainly not noble), but it belongs to a nature which is wild and unsubdued by discipline.

Concomitant with an inquiry into anger's "naturalness" is the question of its necessity. Anger would seem an appropriate response to real crimes and injustices for two reasons:

i) the very baseness of some deeds naturally evokes a forceful, if not downright violent, disgust.

ii) certain evils require correction; when anger accompanies correction it often causes fear in the evil-doer which leads to a reduction of the deed's recurrence.

Concerning the first, Seneca produces the worst-case scenario: "What then?... will the good man not be angry if his father is murdered, his mother raped before his eyes?"[30] Even here, in the extreme cases, the Stoic response is "no." He must defend a person in danger, and if someone dies unjustly, it is his duty to avenge this person's death, but all must be done without anger. And so, no matter how great the evil, it has no "right" to enter the soul and disturb its calm ability to act and think clearly and reasonably. Even a judge administers justice[31] with a calm but determined countenance (149).[32] So, whether the vile deed has been done against you or against someone you love, or against society, anger is not justified. Defense, or some other proper action, may need to be taken, but even then it must be with the intent to help the person, not for the sake of revenge. Any other action, according to Seneca, involves the soul in vice. This is consonant with his view that an angry man hurts himself (cf. 233).

The second question which we left hanging, viz. "Are there not times when anger moves another to act correctly?" is related to the usefulness of anger. Interestingly, Seneca here allows for a mock show of anger (203). Anger itself is never justified, but at times, its imitation is permissible. Orators, for example, sometimes pretend to be angry in order to persuade a juridical body to make a proper decision.[33] This seems permissible presumably because the feigned anger is only external and is not causing any internal disturbance to the orator himself. It is not passion and therefore not anger in the proper sense.

This feigned anger is also justified in dealing with certain kinds of individuals: "sometimes we must strike fear into the hearts of those with whom reason is of no avail,"[34] namely, those who are "sluggish in mind" (197). The criterion for the allowance of such anger again is presumably that the anger is only an outward show without in any way afflicting the interior calm of the acting person, nor does it arise from a revengeful spirit.[35]

We conclude this section with an observation from the arena of conscience: "The greatest punishment of wrong-doing is having done it."[36] Convincing a person of wrong doing would therefore be a good start on the road to his (or her) improvement.

3. HOW DOES ANGER BEHAVE?
We now turn to the causes of anger, internal and external and to a description of the characteristics of this vice.

1. The Causes or Stimuli of Anger

i) *External Stimuli.* These are not true causes according to Seneca, for external things may stimulate anger but are never responsible for it. The real cause lies within the human heart. Nevertheless, it is part of wisdom to know what things excite a person to anger. As we have seen, the only real values in life are virtues of the soul; external things are illusory and of little value. Therefore, if anyone is angry at externals–such as a difficult-to-read manuscript, clothes no longer liked, or an improperly cleaned wine goblet–then this person is being aroused to anger by mere "trifles" and "petty things" to which he has attached too much value.[37] To get angry over such is sheer folly: "it is madness to get mad at things!"[38] The "thing" which by far stimulates anger more than anything else is money. The Roman law courts abound to decide which man's greed has a more just claim.[39]

Another type of stimulus is that which afflicts our bodies. Internal to the body, they are still external to the soul, and are therefore external stimulants. Among these are hunger and thirst, or the more serious irritants of sickness and old age. The latter in particular tends to weigh on the soul, making the mind irritable.[40]

Of greater irritation, however, are other people. When the provocation is unintentional, they are more like the external things that annoy us: perhaps more favor has been shown someone else (329) or the over-confident behavior in another gets under our skin (153). These things as well are mere trifles which we have overvalued. As for those who provoke our wrath wittingly, even this is not a true cause. It is a mere stimulus, an external inciter of our wrath. We are still free to respond to the perceived injury calmly or with anger.

ii) *Internal Stimuli.* We are now at the real causes of anger which exist in the human soul. The causes are in the mind and are formed by the way it perceives itself and reality. Seneca assigns two causes to anger: arrogance and ignorance.[41] Ignorance refers to the lack of proper value placed on things and situations by the mind. Regarding arrogance:[42] the mind feels that our dignity has been wounded because we have not been treated as we deserve...all calculated from the mind's own perspective. Thus, self-worth has been exaggerated. If ignorance is a lack of seeing other things according to their real value, arrogance overestimates (and is therefore a kind of ignorance) our own value or dignity in the larger realm of society.

In summary, of the categories which arouse anger, the external causes are only stimulants which irritate an already diseased soul. The only real cause is the soul itself which has an arrogant or ignorant attitude toward the world which causes it to respond with negative emotion towards all injuries, perceived or real. Anger– even when not active–is still then in the soul in the form of a negative defense-mechanism which does not allow it to live in peace. We now turn to the characteristics of anger.

2. Characteristics of Anger

We have already noted that anger is inhumane, because it is a degeneration and destruction of what is truly human, and that it is irrational, because the mind has in allowing it entrance abdicated its ability to rule with rational discretion. Therefore, anger does not simply excite the mind, it overthrows it (255) and sweeps it away (173) like a hurricane pushing one headlong (259) into a state of temporary madness[43] (107). Without the guidance of reason, anger is suspicious (cf. 283) and insists that everything is lawful (cf. 287). In short, an angry man is insane (107-109).

Perhaps the most characteristic element in anger is its violence. It is fierce (153), reckless (201), and destructive for all parties concerned: "With what fury he rushes on working destruction–destruction of himself as well and wrecking what cannot be sunk unless he sinks with it."[44] Anger involves assault (173), is rash, unbalanced (153), dangerous (243) and precipitous (153); its power comes upon one suddenly and completely (251). The violence is nothing but a show of power which lends itself to exaggeration (283) and overconfidence (153). It is hostile (119) and is often cruel (177).[45]

Since violence is a show of power, and not true power, it is a cover for the soul's impotence (cf. 189). Anger in itself is of no enduring strength (151 and 161), being petty (267) shallow (193), and silly (189). The only real power it has is for its own harm (261). Along with the show of power goes a certain obstinacy, which seems like strength, but is rather its counterfeit. Seneca believes that this obstinacy or willfulness is anger's chief characteristic (129). Once it has decided on a particular stance, it is persistent (cf. 153), refusing to admit wrong or to be ruled (157). In the extreme, obstinacy is totally blind:

> We obey our first impulse; then, although we have been aroused by mere trifles, we continue to be angry for fear that we may seem to have had no reason to be so from the first, and–what is more unjust–the very injustice of our anger makes us the more obstinate. For we hold on to it and nurse it, as if the violence of our anger were proof of its justice.[46]

Anger is besides: haughty (161), mean in its desire for revenge (123). It is accompanied by sadness (179) and is ugly and repulsive (191). These characteristics of anger naturally dwell within a human agent: the angry man. Of the latter, Seneca adds these qualities: he is bitter, harsh and captious (117), verbally abusive (cf. 157), and has a shallow (193) and narrow mind (267); he is not free (263), and is afraid (191) while being himself feared and contemptible (189). He is a sick man and as irresponsible as a child or a lunatic (319). In short, he is a monster, destroying his object and himself in the process (259). Seneca's vivid descriptions of an angry man are sometimes comical and would even be hilarious (cf. 109 and 245) except that they are sadly true to life. One also cannot help feel that the author's personal association with Caligula and Nero[47] marks the mad depictions with horrific sobriety.

4. HOW IS ANGER CURED?

We have now arrived, I believe, at the purpose of the entire treatise: the presentation of what Seneca calls *remedia*.[48] The ugly litany of anger's characteristics is for no other reason than to move the reader to have nothing to do with anger, to flee from it totally. Having moved his audience, the author now offers concrete suggestions on how to banish this evil vice from its life or at least to restrain it as much as possible. Although the Stoics denounced anger absolutely, there was the practical realization that the struggle against this vice took time and effort.[49] The suggestions fall into: general rules; those which appeal to the mind in order to (re)form its conception of reality and thus form character in a person,[50] and those which we could call techniques or behavioral skills to be learned.

The General Rules

These "rules" (*praecepta*) form an introduction to the whole discussion of anger therapy. As Augustine will later do, Seneca begins with two fundamental principles: 1) do not fall into anger 2) if you do, do not sin (203).[51] To these two correspond two methods to ensure the desired outcome: to the first: repel it, to the second, restrain it. As for repelling it totally, the treatment is divided into the early training for children and the instruction appropriate for adults.

a) *For children*: anger is eradicated from their lives through proper instruction and formation with a balance between freedom and restraint, i.e. enough freedom so as not to blunt their young spirits and enough restraint so as to prevent anger from developing (209). Children need encouragement, but not so much that they are elated (211). Our philosopher believes that a wealthy environment leads to pampering which in turn cultivates a tendency to anger, so this must be tempered with denying things of the child–otherwise the little one will not be able to withstand rebuffs (211). Neither should he gain anything by anger (213).

The child must also–and this is very important for Seneca–be educated in the truth. Therefore, he should not be flattered, should be corrected when he is wrong, and must always show respect to his elders (213). It would be good to give him a tutor who has a quiet disposition, because a child imitates the behavior he sees. As for his companions, it is important that a young person develop a sense that they are his equals, which means that his life style should be simple and resemble theirs (213).

b) *For adults*: since the advice given is not restricted only to repelling anger, but includes restraining it as well, Seneca's neat categories break down at this point.[52] Regardless, the multifarious remedies presented throughout the text fall into: i) those which try to appeal to the mind in order to reform it and ii) those which suggest techniques for developing behavioral skills in order the better to cope with a number of given situations where anger is likely to occur.

i) *Reform of the Mind*

As noted earlier, the role of the mind is essential for Seneca in the development of anger.[53] Although the first movement towards anger starts as a slight reflex feeling of being wounded, it becomes a vice and receives its power from the mind's assent to the aroused emotion, and fuel is added to the fire by the mind's consequent justifying and desiring the revenge. A solution then must be found in educating the mind so that at the moment of decision, it is equipped with counter reasons why it should not acquiesce to the first feeling of being injured (*species iniuriae*).[54] If the mind is strong enough to resist, no anger will occur. This is the ideal, and as we have seen, Seneca thinks it is not only possible, but a moral duty.

There are two directions to turn in this reform: towards the object and towards oneself. As regards the first, it is clear that if the mind knows that things are mere appearances, then "one can discount the shocks [first movements] as mere symptoms of the appearance."[55] Furthermore, knowing what is under control and what is not, gives a person certitude about what to try to control.[56]

As for the self, the age-old wisdom of Delphi is evoked: Know yourself. In the quest for self-knowledge each is to look anger squarely in the face and see it as it is. The characteristics noted earlier then confront the honest observer in all their ugliness. If an individual truly does this, he will shrink from anger and want no part of it. Therefore, Seneca advises: educate yourself on the faults of anger and contemplate them. If anger is already in your heart (I presume, past or present), then drag it into the open as if it were a court room and convict it (265).

Then, from the realm of general psychology, know that what angers you in another is in you![57] (229) By being so frank, you will learn to know yourself and your weaknesses, and in recognizing your soft spot you will then be able to take the necessary precautions. Seneca draws a parallel to persons prone to alcohol. Some of these tell their friends to remove the wine from their place at table prior to festivities so that they will not be tempted (289). So too with anger: knowing your weakness is the first step in preventing an unfortunate mishap. We shall come to some practical steps that can be taken towards prevention in our next section.

Inner frankness also allows a person to examine his or her overall moral rectitude. Perhaps I feel that I do not deserve this particular injury, but am I really totally innocent? (Cf. 227) What about other times? What about the discretions of my own youth? (317) And if my actions do not condemn me, what about my thoughts? And have I ever subtly encouraged others to sin? The purpose of these questions is to challenge our concept of injury: injury comes from thinking we have been unjustly wronged, so if we have a less exalted idea of our own innocence, the remark or act against us will appear less an injustice and more like the truth. Indeed, we will even realize that we deserve much more.[58]

Another advantage to educating the mind is that it will be more attentive and therefore less likely to be taken off guard, resulting in a weak excuse like "I didn't think" which is a terribly shameful response. An educated mind is fortified against surprise attacks: "think of everything, expect everything."[59] Perhaps Seneca is thinking that the sting of an injury is less powerful and therefore less apt to arouse anger when it is known or half-expected beforehand.[60]

To know yourself also means to know the distinction between your needs and your wants. Anger is sometimes aroused through comparing ourselves to others who seem to have more. If we know our needs, and are content with providing for them, then what others have will not be a cause of anger or resentment in us (329).

A corollary of self-knowledge is knowledge of human nature. We have already had reason to mention Seneca's view that we are all sinners,[61] and even worse: we are all examples of vice to each other (187). Even wise men like Socrates fail sometimes, and if such unevenness of character appears from time to time even in good people, then this should make us indulgent towards all (235 and 317). Seeing that the disease of vice is so rampant, is reason for dealing with it in a detached professional way, as a physician does in treating an illness. What physician is angry at the disease? So too, no one should be angry at the mistakes of men (cf. 321ff). The solution or remedy par excellence is to forgive mankind at large, to grant indulgence to the human race.[62] It is also sobering to realize that we are all capable of everything (321).

The same remedy applies equally to individuals who have hurt us personally. If we look at the character of the offender, we will find in each case a reason to excuse, submit or to ignore the situation (231). *Forgiveness* is then the perfect remedy against anger, whether human nature in general or the individual in particular is being considered. If this were practiced, there would be true concord on earth: "Only one thing can bring us peace–the agreement of mutual willingness [to forgive]."[63]

ii) *Behavioral Skills*

The *De ira* has many practical suggestions for avoiding anger. These fall into precautionary steps which one can take before an inflammatory situation arises and techniques one can use on the spot which become skills when they are repeated with a degree of control.[64]

Precautionary steps

These in turn include both positive steps to take and negative situations to avoid. The first positive step is to choose calm companions to live with. Since, as our author says, we adopt the behavior of those with whom we associate, we will remain calmer ourselves and therefore be less provoked to anger....and when we are aroused, these calm folks will be more likely to endure us (275). The second positive step is a good exercise which the Christians will later call an examination of conscience: "Ask yourself upon retiring: what bad habit have you incurred today? In what respect are you better? Anger will cease and become more controllable if it finds that it must appear before a judge every day."[65] Seneca reveals that he was in the habit of reviewing his day in this way in order to try and improve himself.[66] The passage merits quoting at length:

I avail myself of this privilege, and every day I plead my cause before
the bar of self. When the light has been removed from sight, and my
wife, long aware of my habit, has become silent, I scan the whole of my
day and retrace all my deeds and words. I conceal nothing from myself,
I omit nothing. For why should I shrink from any of my mistakes, when
I may commune thus with myself? "See that you never do that again; I
will pardon you this time. In that dispute, you spoke too offensively....
In the future, consider not only the truth of what you say, but also
whether the man to whom you are speaking can endure the truth...."[67]

Two other positive attitudes to develop are to refuse to believe gossip and to
plead the cause of the absent (231). Until the truth is known, it is better to presume
well of others.

On the negative side, Seneca offers advice on the kinds of situations to avoid,
especially if one is prone to anger. Since they need little comment, we will simply
list them. We ought to:
– avoid wine and gluttony (207) since presumably these lessen attentiveness and
  discipline.
– avoid the company of those who provoke us! (275)
– restrain the tongue by checking liberty of speech and check impulsiveness (279).
– avoid being overly inquisitive (281).
– if one feels the conversation is heading in a dangerous direction, check it before
  it develops momentum (277).

Immediate remedies

When one is actually in an inflammatory situation, the following skills can
check an angry response:
– delay tactics: "The best corrective of anger lies in delay."[68] Delay not only helps
  the wounded get some perspective on the situation, it also may help the
  offender regret his indiscretion.
– feign ignorance. Pretend not to hear the remark or notice the offence (239).
– keep externally calm. Changing the symptoms helps change the interior agitation:
  "Let the countenance be unruffled, let the voice be gentle, the step very slow
  and gradually the inner man conforms to the outer."[69]
– do not react and try some reverse psychology: "...challenge him with kindness.
  Animosity, if abandoned by one side, forthwith dies; it takes two to make a
  fight.... If someone strikes you, step back; for by striking back you will give
  him both the opportunity and the excuse to repeat his blow."[70]
– forgive the person. We have already mentioned the need to forgive in order to
  restrain anger. A practical way to help the process is to remember good things
  about the antagonist (243).
–finally, in the last resort, we may simply have to grin and bear an injury (cf. 297
  and 355).

Interestingly, forgiveness is advanced as a noble and salutary way of controlling anger. It never seems to occur to Seneca that a person may need to ask forgiveness for his past outbursts. A man examines his own conscience and convicts himself in the privacy of his own room, but the remedy of apologizing (which is indeed a healthy and powerful corrective to anger) is not mentioned. Did such a degree of humility come in only under Christianity?

Conclusion: the Benefits

Much energy is exerted in the *De ira* in identifying the problem, listing the ill effects and reeducating the reader to the remedies of anger. Very little is said about the final benefits to be gained if one follows through with the whole therapeutic process. That is the topic of another treatise, *De tranquillitate animi*, probably written after our treatise in the 50s. There are however, hints of the benefits to be gained even in the *De ira*. Besides such practical benefits such as "a reputation for forbearance" and "useful friends" (243), the more important benefit is what the discipline does to the inner life: "so great a reward awaits us–the unbroken calm of the happy soul."[71] A fuller description is found in expounding the virtues of "greatness":

> There is no surer proof of greatness than to be in a state where nothing can possibly happen to disturb you. The higher region of the universe, being better ordered and near to the stars, is condensed into no cloud, is lashed into no tempest, is churned into no whirlwind; it is free from all turmoil; it is in the lower regions that the lightnings flash. In the same way the lofty mind is always calm, at rest in a quiet haven; crushing down all that engenders anger, it is restrained, commands respect and is properly ordered.[72]

Thus, for the first century non-Christian seeker-after-wisdom, the highest goal that one could expect in this life was to possess an inner unshaken–and even divine[73]–peace obtained through a life dedicated to the pursuit of virtue through self-discipline. Let us keep this goal of personal fulfillment in mind as we trace the concept of anger through our next three Christian authors.

Notes: Chapter 1

1. The rather harsh remarks on Caligula in the *De ira* point to a time after the latter's death in 41 A.D. and the ascription of the work to Seneca's older brother, Novatus, indicate that the work was written before his brother adopted the name of his patron, Junius Gallio, which he did sometime before 51 A.D. As a provincial governor, his brother would have had "more reason than most to reflect upon anger and to learn self-control: a great deal of the therapeutic part of the treatise makes better sense when one remembers that it is being addressed to an administrator with virtually unlimited power over non-citizens in his jurisdiction." Brad Inwood, *Reading Seneca: Stoic Philosophy at Rome*, Clarendon Press, Oxford

(2005): 153. Incidentally, this brother Gallio is the same mentioned in the Acts of the Apostles (18:12-17), as the governor of Achaia before whom St. Paul was arraigned. The governor comes across ambivalently: as having the sense to dismiss the charges brought against Paul by the Jews as beyond his juridical competence, but also as somewhat weak in not defending or preventing the beating of an innocent man. One source says that he "was to be remembered for his sweetness." John M. Cooper and J.F. Procopé, *Seneca: Moral and Political Essays*, Cambridge University Press (1955): 16. Gallio suffered the same fate as his brother.

2. It seems the brave philosopher was more successful in imitating the wise Socrates in his death than in his life. Although he lived a disciplined life, his "career displays a certain duplicity" especially as regards his relationship to the court. See J.N. Sevenster, *Paul and Seneca*, E.J. Brill, Leiden (1961): 16.

3. Cooper, 5-6.

4. Cooper, 6

5. Thus the philosophy of personal "self-control" had long been in existence before the Stoics. See William V. Harris *Restraining Rage: The Ideology of Anger Control in Classical Antiquity.* Harvard University Press, Cambridge MA and London England (2001), especially chapter 5: "A Tradition of Self-Control": 80-87.

6. Seneca's adherence to Stoicism is presumed throughout this thesis. There has been much debate on just how faithful Seneca is to the traditional Stoic view of the passions. Most recently, Brad Inwood has defended Seneca's adherence to the main tenets of Stoicism, (against the charge of psychological dualism or eclecticism), while pointing out his areas of innovation. Inwood, "Seneca and Psychological Dualism" (chapter 2) in *Reading Seneca*. For some earlier discussions on the subject, I refer the reader to H.B. Timothy's *The Tenets of Stoicism: Assembled from the works of L. Annaeus Seneca.* Adolf M Hakkert Publishers, Amsterdam, 1973; Janine Fellion-Lahille's *Le De Ira de Sénèque et La philosophie stoïcienne des passions.* Études et Commentaries 94. Klincksieck Publishers, Paris, 1984; and John M. Rist's "Seneca and Stoic Orthodoxy" in *Aufstieg und Niedergang des Römischen Welt*, vol. 2.36.3. Berlin (1989): 1993-2012.

7. Inwood, *Reading Seneca*, 55.

8. Inwood, *Reading Seneca*, 49.

9. As "products of the human reason," they are thus "subject to control by that reason." Inwood, *Reading Seneca,* 43. See Seneca, *De Ira*, 2.1.

10. Cooper, 8-9.

11. Timothy, p.111 quotes from Seneca's Ep. 58.26 where his acceptance of Plato's teaching on appearances is clearly demonstrated.

12. Anna Lydia Motto, *Seneca*, Twayne Publishers, Inc. New York (1973): 50.

13. Harris: *Restraining Rage*, 110.

14. *On Tranquillity of Mind/De tranquillitate animi*, II.4 (*Moral Essays* II, Loeb, 215).

15. Ira est cupiditas ulciscendae iniurias. This definition occurred in a lost section of Seneca's treatise, but was fortunately preserved by Lactantius in his *De ira Dei*, 17. See n.e, p.110 Loeb edition. The normal word for anger is ira. Seneca distinguishes it from iracundia which the Loeb edition translates as "irascibility." Villy Sørensen believes their common element is "aggression" but then distinguishes the two thus: "iracundia [is] aggressiveness as an involuntary urge common to animals and men, and ira [is] the aggression of which only human beings can be guilty." Seneca: the humanist at the court of Nero. Canongate Publishers, Ltd. and the University of Chicago Press, Chicago (1984): 100.

16. [A]it enim iram esse cupiditatem doloris reponendi. I.3.3 (115). Numerical citations without further reference in this chapter refer to Seneca's *De ira*: the Roman numeral refers to one of the four books which make up the *De ira*, while the Arabic numbers refer to the chapter and section within the book. The numbers in parenthesis refer to the page number of the English translation in the Loeb edition.

17. It seems, however, that Seneca is not fair to Aristotle: "When one compares, for example, the thorough and persuasive discussion of ὀργή in the *Nicomachean Ethics* (4.11) with the seemingly silly statements that the *adversarius* mouths [in the *De ira*], it is easy to realize that Seneca had no intention of tilting seriously against Aristotle." William S. Anderson, *Anger in Juvenal and Seneca*. Classical Philology 19, No.3. University of California Press, Berkeley and Los Angeles (1964): 154.

18. For example: ...ut Plato ait, nemo prudens punit, quia peccatum est, sed ne peccetur; revocari enim praeterita non possunt, futura prohibentur. I.19.7 (159).

19. Loeb 170.6. Also: primus motus non voluntarius II.4.1 (174). The idea of first movements may have originated with Cicero, who speaks of "bitings and certain little contractions of the soul" (*Tusculan Disputations* 3.83) which "in no way involve the will (voluntarium)": John M. Rist: "Seneca and Stoic Orthodoxy." *Aufstieg und Niedergang des Römischen Welt*, vol.2.36.3. Berlin (1989): 2001. Seneca's purpose in developing them is for the sake of determining the mind's control over these first movements. See "Seneca's Defence: First Movements as Answering Posidonius" in Richard Sorabji's *Emotion and Peace of Mind: From Stoic Agitation to Christian Temptation*. Oxford University Press, Oxford (2000): 66-75.

20. Omnes enim motus, qui non voluntate nostra fiunt, invicti et inevitabiles sunt, ut horror frigida aspersis....sequiturque vertigo praerupta cernentis. II.2.1 (169).

21. Putavit se aliquis laesum, voluit ulcisci, dissuadente aliqua causa statim resedit. Hanc iram non voco, motum animi rationi parentem; illa est ira, quae rationem transsilit, quae secum rapit....concitatio animi ad ultionem voluntate et iudicio pergentis. II.3.4-5 (172). It is the uncontrollable aspect of the third step which defines the passion: Cf. "The uncontrolled form of this (*tertius motus*) is the passion of anger." Inwood, *Reading Seneca*, 62.

22. This is admitted also in I.8.3: Reason relinquishes its power or authority when it admits anger into the soul (127).

23. Non enim, ut dixi, separatas ista sedes suas diductasque habent, sed affectus et ratio in melius peiusque mutatio animi est. I.8.3 (127). See Inwood, *Reading Seneca*: "Reason in its corrupt form *is* passion" (p. 49).

24. Commota enim semel et excussa mens ei servit quo impellitur. Quarundam rerum initia in nostra potestate sunt, ulteriora vi sua rapiunt nec regressum relinquunt. Ut in praeceps datis corporibus nullum sui arbitrium est nec resistere morarive deiecta potuerunt, sed consilium omne et paenitentiam irrevocabilis praecipitatio abscidit et non licet eo non pervenire, quo non ire licuisset, ita animus si in iram, amorem aliosque se proiecit adfectus, non permittitur reprimere impetum; rapiat illum oportet et ad imum agat pondus suum et vitiorum natura proclivis. I.7.3-4 (125).

25. Numquam enim virtus vitio adiuvanda est se contenta. I.9.1 (129). In the same vein: "moderate passion is nothing else than moderate evil": ergo modicus affectus nihil aliud quam malum modicum est. I.10.4 (133) and "A man must banish virtue from his heart before he can admit wrath, since vices do not consort with virtues, and a man can no more be both angry and good at the same time than he can be sick and well." [N]ecesse est prius virtutem ex animo tollas quam iracundiam recipias, quoniam cum virtutibus vitia non coeunt, nec magis quisquam eodem tempore et iratus potest esse et vir bonus quam aeger et sanus. II.12.2 (193).

26. Examples of this are: "man is born for mutual help" while "anger for mutual destruction. The one desires union, the other disunion;... [H]uman life is founded on kindness and concord" (119) which is totally at odds with the hostility of anger. Homo in adiutorium mutuum genitus est, ira in exitium; hic congregari vult, illa discedere.... Beneficiis enim humana vita constat et concordia. I.5.2-3 (119).

27. Of vice in general, Seneca attests to its universal application: "we are all examples of vice to each other" (119); "we are all inconsiderate and unthinking, we are all discontented, ambitious....we are wicked" (321) and "innocence is not rare, it is non-existent" (183).

28. Atqui nihil est tam difficile et arduum quod non humana mens vincat....Quantum est effugere maximum malum, iram. II.12.3...6 (193-195). The last line of the translation in the text is abbreviated, the fuller translation takes account of the *maximum malum*: How great a blessing to escape anger, the greatest of all ills....!

29. [N]emo autem regere potest nisi qui et regi. II.15.4 (201).

30. Quid ergo?" inquit, "vir bonus non irascitur, si caedi patrem suum viderit, si rapi matrem?" I.12.1 (137).

31. The criteria used for correcting others is reminiscent of the biblical injunctions (and of Augustine): first one is to correct another in private, next in public, then with public disgrace; if serious enough, exile is to be imposed, or worse: chains and imprisonment. Finally, capital punishment is reserved for the extreme cases (147). There are those extreme cases where amendment is not possible, i.e. where a person is so hardened that he (or she) has become incapable of reform; then the only course of action is to remove the person from society totally, so as not to contaminate the rest. Seneca likens it to killing off sickly sheep lest they infect the whole flock (145). If the person must be put to death (Seneca believes that the thought of death is sweet to these kind), it is as a deterrent to others (159).

32. A corollary issue is the distinction made between the deed and the perpetrator, an idea taken from Plato: "[N]o man of sense will hate the erring; otherwise he will hate himself." [Cf: Non est autem prudentis errantis odisse; alioque ipse sibi odio erit. I.14.2 (143).] Correction then should not be aimed at the *offense*, for that is past and cannot be recalled, but it should be aimed at the *offender* in as much as his improvement will result in less recurrence in the future. This is also from Plato: "A sensible man does not punish a man because he has sinned, but in order to keep him from sin." [U]t Plato ait, nemo prudens punit, quia peccatum est, sed ne peccetur; revocari enim praeterita non possunt, futura prohibentur. I.19.7 (159). Also cf: "[P]unishment shall never look to the past, but always to the future; for that course is not anger but precaution." [N]ec umquam ad praeteritum, sed ad futurum poena referetur; non enim irascitur, sed cavet. II.31.8 (237) The purpose then of punishment is to make someone a better person "for his own sake as well as for the sake of others" (143). This is the reason why judges give different punishments depending on the person, his motives, if the crime was done accidentally or with full intent, etc. If the judge were to get angry with the criminals, he would be correcting wrong-doing with more wrong-doing. [N]on oportet peccata corrigere peccantem. I.16.1 (145).

33. Seneca compares this to the mock anger of the gladiators, but I'm not convinced the parallel is exact. The anger of the gladiators may have the intent to "move" the audience, but as everyone knows a gladiator's anger is an "act," while there is an element of deception in an orator's use of it. Nonetheless, in both cases the "actor" is free of the passion.

34. Aliquando incutiendus est iis metus apud quos ratio non proficit. II.14.1 (197).

35. Our author does not address the issue of the possible consequence of the mock anger in the addressee. To such a one the anger would certainly seem real enough so much so that he could easily form the impression that anger in certain circumstances is quite acceptable.

36. [M]axima est enim factae iniuriae poena fecisse, nec quisquam gravius adficitur quam qui ad supplicium paenitentiae traditur. III.26.2 (321).

37. Inde, inquam, vobis ira et insania est, quod exigua magno aestimatis. III.34.2 (337). Also cf: rising from most trivial things [ex levissimis] anger mounts to monstrous size. III.1.5 (255).

38. The fuller quotation reads: His irasci quam stultum est, quae iram nostram nec meruerunt nec sentiunt! II.26.2 (221).

39. The fuller quotation reads: "law courts resound with din of trials and jurors summoned from distant parts sit in judgment to decide which man's greed has the juster claim." [F]remitu iudiciorum basilicae resonent, evocati ex longinquis regionibus iudices sedeant iudicaturi, utrius iustior avaritia sit. III.33.2 (335).

40. [I]racundiores sunt valetudine aut aetate fessi. III.9.4 (279).

41. Itaque nos aut insolentia iracundos facit aut ignorantia rerum. II.31.4 (233).

42. Also referred to as excessive self-love (233) and an excess of self-esteem (267).

43. Cf. Quidam itaque e sapientibus viris iram dixerunt brevem insaniam. III.1.2 (107).

44. [Q]uantoque impetu ruat non sine pernicie sua perniciosus et ea deprimens, quae mergi nisi cum mergente non possunt. II.3.2 (259).

45. Anger however differs from cruelty in as much as the latter's "purpose in desiring to beat and to mangle is not vengeance but pleasure" (175).

46. Nunc autem primum impetum sequimur, deinde, quamvis vana nos concitaverint, perseveramus, ne videamur coepisse sine causa, et quod iniquissimum est, pertinaciores nos facit iniquitas irae; retinemus enim illam et augemus, quasi argumentum sit iuste irascentis graviter irasci. III.29.2 (327-329).

47. A true statement, even if the *De ira* was written prior to his association with Nero.

48. Quoniam quae de ira quaeruntur tractavimus, accedamus ad remedia eius. II.18.1 (203).

49. For the concept of degrees of progress achieved through continual perseverance and daily training which slowly brings one closer to the goal, see Motto, 52-54.

50. "When he turns his attention to remedies, [Seneca] divides his efforts between character formation (the prevention of irascibility as a character trait) and instruction on how to react under provocation." Inwood, *Reading Seneca*, 145.

51. In III.5.2 (265) Seneca adds a third: to cure anger in others. This however is dealt with almost as an afterthought.

52. In chart form, the program thus far would look like this:

> Method:
>
> 1) Do not fall into anger: Repel it   Advice for < children / adults
>
> Rules: <
>
> 2) If you do, do not sin: Restrain it Advice for <

To be logical, our chart should include advice for restraining anger in children and adults. Seneca may be thinking that children are either too young to learn the skills, or perhaps that anger takes time to become embedded in a person as a full-blown vice and therefore only adults need to learn the skills for restraining it.

53. It was a commonly held conviction among philosophers that "correct reasoning would lead to virtuous behavior." See Harris, chapter 15: "Can you Cure Emotions? Hellenistic and Roman Anger Therapy": 375. The obvious relation between thinking and behaving can be seen in modern psychology's cognitive therapy, where the premise is: if you change a person's way of thinking you will change his behavior. But a person must also *want* to do what is right. It is therefore a mistake to equate knowledge with virtue.

54. Ergo prima illa agitatio animi, quam species iniuriae incussit, non magis ira est quam ipsa iniuriae species; ille sequens impetus, qui speciem iniuriae non tantum accepit sed adprobavit, ira est. II.3.5 (173).

55. Sorabji, 69. Thus the doctrine of appearances is vital to how one reacts to external stimuli. It is at the second step that a judgment is made, which is a misjudgment if the world is judged to be more than appearances. See Cooper, 10. Martha Nussbaum posits the difference between the two (passions and appetites) in that the former embody ways of interpreting the world. It is not only a matter of appearances verses reality, but of the value placed on the item. That is, things which are judged to have higher value (e.g. a coffee mug with sentimental value vs. another replaceable one) will provoke more passion (e.g. grief, sorrow, anger, etc.) when lost or damaged. *The Theory of Desire,* 367-371.

56. This is depicted graphically in Sorabji's account: "It is very steadying when you have a sinking feeling, or your teeth are chattering, your knees knocking, or you have gone white or red in the face, to be able to say to yourself, 'This is not yet emotion, it is only shock.'" *Emotion and Peace of Mind,* 69.

57. "Each man will find in his own breast the fault which he censures in another." Quidquid itaque in alio reprenditur, id unusquisque in sinu suo inveniet. III.26.4 (321). See similar examples in II.28.5-8 (227-8).

58. [S]i modo verum ipsi nobis dicere voluerimus, pluris litem nostram aestimabimus. II.27.4 (225).

59. Omnia puta, expecta. II.31.4 (235).

60. Nussbaum, commenting on a line from Chrysippus, makes the point that when a situation has just occurred which arouses a passion, the "freshness" of the impact adds an irrational element which dissipates with time. *The Theory of Desire,* 381.

61. Needless to say, Seneca's use of "sinners" (*turba peccantium*) is not employed in the Christian sense of that word (Cf. II.10.4).

62. The larger context reads: Ne singulis irascaris, universis ignoscendum est, generi humano venia tribuenda est. II.10.2 (185).

63. Una nos res facere quietos potest, mutuae facilitatis conventio. III.26.4 (321).

64. Harris observes that one notable difference between the ancients and the modern concept of therapy is that the ancients considered habit to be essential to a cure. See Harris, p.389.

65. "Quod hodie malum tuum sanasti? Cui vitio obstitisti? Qua parte melior es?" Desinet ira et moderatior erit, quae sciet sibi cotidie ad iudicem esse veniendum. III.36.1 (341).

66. The practice preceded Seneca; it may have originated with Poseidonius. See Harris, p.372.

67. Utor hac potestate et cotidie apud me causam dico. Cum sublatum e conspectu lumen est et conticuit uxor moris iam mei conscia, totum diem meum scrutor factaque ac dicta mea remetior; nihil mihi ipse abscondo, nihil transeo. Quare enim quicquam ex erroribus meis timeam, cum possim dicere: "Vide ne istud amplius facias, nunc tibi ignosco. In illa disputatione pugnacius locutus es....De certero vide, non tantum an verum sit quod dicis, sed an ille cui dicitur veri patiens sit...." III.36.3-4 (341).

68. Maximum remedium irae mora est. II.29.1 (229).

69. Vultus remittatur, vox lenior sit, gradus lentior; paulatim cum experioribus interiora formantur. III.13.2-3 (287).

70. The fuller quotation reads: Irascetur aliquis? [T]u contra beneficiis provoca. Cadit statim simultas ab altera parte deserta; nisi paria non pugnant..... Percussit te, recede; referiendo enim et occasionem saepius feriendi dabis et excusationem. II.34.5 (245) The same advice to return kindness for unkindness is found in III.27.3: Mansuete immansueta tractanda sunt (323).

71. The immediate context is that of perseverance: Nos non advocabimus patientiam, quos tantum praemium expectat, felicis animi immota tranquillitas? II.12.6 (195).

72. Nullum est argumentum magnitudinis certius quam nihil posse quo instigeris accidere. Pars superior mundi et ordinatior ac propinqua sideribus nec in nubem cogitur nec in tempestatem impellitur nec versatur in turbinem; omni tumultu caret, inferiora fulminantur. Eodem modo sublimis animus, quietus semper et in statione tranquilla conlocatus omnia infra se premens, quibus ira contrahitur, modestus et venerabilis est et dispositus. III.6.1 (269).

73. Note: "But what you desire is something great and supreme and very near to [being a] god–to be unshaken." [Quod desideras autem magnum et summum est deoque vicinum, non concuti.] *De tranquillitate animi* II.3. lines1-2 (213). *Seneca, Moral Essays II.* Loeb Classical Library, Cambridge MA, reprint 1998.

CHAPTER 2
EVAGRIUS PONTICUS: THE DESERT APPROACH

Introduction

From the beginning, the Christian understanding of anger was generally more positive and nuanced than the Stoic's absolute denunciation–as simple and attractive as the latter might sometimes be. The Christian authors' more positive view may owe something to Aristotle's position that the passions in themselves are neither virtues nor vices; they are neutral and everything depends on the use that is made of them.[1] But no one doubts that the greater influence by far on the Fathers of the Church came from the Sacred Scriptures. Besides the numerous exhortations condemning anger, such as: "But I say to you, that anyone who is angry with his brother will be liable to judgement" (Mt 5:22),[2] there are also passages which present wrath–if not as a virtue–at least as having some value. These texts include the attribution of anger or wrath to God in both the Old and the New Testaments,[3] Christ's own display of anger in driving the buyers and sellers from the Temple (Mt 21:12), and the injunction from Psalm 4:4 repeated by St. Paul in Eph 4:26: "Be angry and sin not." These passages did much to cause some prominent Christian theologians to interpret anger in less categorically dismissive ways.[4] In one fine example, we find Pachomius described as: "He did not get angry as men of the flesh do, but if he became angry on occasion, he was angry after the manner of the saints."[5] The author who is the subject of this chapter, the desert father Evagrius Ponticus, falls into this latter tradition of viewing anger in a much nuanced way. This is due to his own dependence both on scripture and on the great exegetes of the East, notably Origen and the Cappadocian fathers.

Life

Evagrius[6] was born in 345 in Asia Minor, near the family estate of St. Basil who enlisted him as a reader.[7] He was tutored by Gregory Nazianzus from his youth and then ordained a deacon by him around 380. When Gregory was called to the capital, he invited Evagrius to join him. The latter's keen intellectual gifts were soon noticed and esteemed, especially at the Council of Constantinople (381) where Evagrius aided Gregory (and the third Cappadocian, Gregory of Nyssa) in promoting Basil's defense of the divinity of the Holy Spirit. When Gregory retired from the city, Evagrius stayed on, enjoying the stimulating cultural environment of the capital. But the city was not without its temptations and before long Evagrius found himself in love with the wife of an important personage in the city. Fearing to be found out (and no doubt fearing to lose the salvation of his soul) he fled the city and went to Jerusalem where he was given hospitality by two monastic founders, Rufinus and Melania. The latter clothed him in the monastic habit and sent him off to Egypt where he learned the art of spiritual warfare from the great ascetics of the desert.[8] He remained in the desert living a semi-anchoretic life until his death in 399. Although posthumously condemned (along with Origen) for his esoteric doctrines concerning the pre-existence of souls and the final restoration, his teachings on the monastic life have found a lasting place in the tradition, forming a solid body of instruction for all those seeking perfection.[9] In more recent years, Evagrius has been quietly rehabilitated, by both scholars and the ecclesiastical authorities.[10]

Evagrius' Teaching on the Evil Thoughts

To help his fellow monks fight temptations in their striving for virtue, Evagrius developed a list of evil thoughts (*logismoi*) concerning which one must be on guard. The term *logismoi* literally means "reasonings;" from this to "thinking process" or simply "thoughts" is an easy step. The term received a negative connotation in the tradition from Origen, who was the first to equate the first movement of passion with thoughts.[11] Origen's source is again scripture, specifically Christ's teaching that out of the heart of man, comes evil thoughts (*dialogismoi*), murder, adultery, theft, etc. (Mt 15:19; Mk 7:21).[12] The term "thoughts" for these first evil promptings changes the focus from the way that the ancients, such as Seneca, had perceived them; there is a movement from feelings to thoughts, or as one author puts it, it shifts "the shock to its cause."[13] Jerome will follow Origen's use of *logismoi* for evil suggestions, and Antony too in attributing *logismoi* to the work of the demons.[14]

What is unique with Evagrius is the organization which he gives to the *logismoi*. He draws up a list of the evil thoughts and shows their interrelatedness. The purpose is to make the monk conscious of how the evil suggestions work and how they affect each other so that he can be on his guard against them. Although the demons are not the only ones responsible for the evil suggestions, Evagrius often makes that attribution, even referring to them distinctly as a demon of lust or a demon of avarice, etc. "We should recognize the different types of demons and discern how the thought came in the first place. We will thus be in a position to address the demons with the most effective words" (*Prak.* 43). The demons are particularly keen on inciting the monk to anger:

> When our incentive power is aroused in a way contrary to nature, it greatly furthers the aim of the demons and is an ally in all their evil designs. Day and night, therefore, they are always trying to provoke it.

And when they see it tethered by gentleness, they at once try to set it free on some seemingly just pretext: in this way, when it is violently aroused, they can use it for their shameful purposes (*Th.* 5).

Awareness is then the first step in combat. Not unlike the Ten Commandments which brought a deeper recognition of sin to the consciousness of the Israelites, so Evagrius' list of *logismoi* made explicit for the monks the temptations which they were already experiencing. One of the primary characteristics of temptations is their subtlety. Where the thoughts come from and what they suggest are often unclear, or presented in a false way. The inexperienced and the not-so-inexperienced can be taken off guard. For this reason, the fact of having a list exposes the evil suggestions for what they are: evil.

Evagrius organizes the various temptations into eight categories: gluttony, impurity, avarice, sadness/dejection, anger, *acedia*/spiritual listlessness, vainglory, pride. Here then is where our study of anger in Evagrius begins. It is one of the deadly suggestions which come to a monk to provoke him to sin. However, before narrowing our study to anger alone, I would like to continue for a moment Evagrius' teaching on the passions in general and how they interrelate.

Of the eight *logismoi*, three of them hold a kind of primary position (analogous to the primary colors) because they are in some way the foundation for other vices. The three are: gluttony, avarice and vainglory. These particular three are considered primary because Christ himself was tempted by Satan in these three areas (Mt 4:3-10). They are thus the "basic" temptations to which everyone is subjected. Christ, as we know, did not yield, but we do; and so Evagrius goes on to teach that certain sins lead to others: anger, for example, is an effect of both avarice and human glory (vanity). If one is not attached to either things or one's reputation, much of the ground for anger disappears. The same chain effect is also expressed in terms of "leading" and "following." Thus: "Some thoughts lead, others follow. Those of pride, lead; those of anger, follow"(*Skem.* 41). And even among those which follow, some of these can go on to cause others to follow them–specifically, anger can cause depression (*Prak.* 10).[15]

For Evagrius, the aim of the monk's life is to grow in virtue, or to replace his vices with virtues. The end result is a totally peaceful state of soul, in which the soul is undisturbed by the passions. This state he calls *apatheia*: a "passionless state," that is, an absence of passion or "freedom from compulsion."[16] The perfect state of *apatheia* is not to be confused with lack of temptations, for the struggle against these continues throughout one's life; nor should it be confused with a lack of emotion. As Origen and Jerome had done, Evagrius taught that one cannot always control one's feelings, especially the initial first movements, but one could prevent any lingering of the thoughts to prevent further disturbance (*Th.* 16).[17] The state of *apatheia* reflects a healthy soul, just as vice indicates a diseased soul. The more health a soul possesses, the more it is in tune with spiritual realities which enable it to have true knowledge; thus to have holiness is to know, while vice is ignorance (*Mon.* 24). All the vices blind the soul, and anger is no exception as we shall see.

Once the *logismoi* are recognized as evil temptations, what can the monk do to combat them? There are many remedies for the individual evil suggestions as well as for their deep seated offspring, the vices. Before addressing the remedies specific to anger, let us mention two general approaches on how to deal with the *logismoi*. The first is to fight one evil suggestion with another. This at first might seem absurd...as if Evagrius were advising the monks to avoid evil by committing evil. But he is not suggesting that one *do* evil, but that an evil suggestion can be used to prevent an evil act.[18] For example, if one is tempted to lust, and yet is still tempted by vainglory, one might think of how fornication will ruin one's reputation and honor. The desire *not* to be so discredited in other people's eyes, can be an incentive to resist the temptation (cf. *Prak.* 58). A far better way to overcome the temptation, however, is by the exercise of the opposite virtue. Thus, avarice can be overcome by almsgiving, pride by acts of humility, *acedia* (boredom or listlessness) by patient fidelity, and anger by gentleness.

Let us now turn to our study of anger in particular. We will first examine Evagrius' definitions and terms, then the causes of anger, the effects both in the monk in general and then, more specifically, its effects on his prayer; finally, we will consider the remedies our desert father offers for curing anger and in particular the role played by gentleness.

I. ANGER: WHAT IT IS

Evagrius employs several terms to express the concept of anger: *orgē*, and *thumos* are the most common, but also *mania* (*Th.* 9), *mēnis*[19] (rancor or malice, *Prak.* 11), *parorgismos* (provocation, *Prak.* 21) and the verb: *erethizo*, meaning to provoke to anger (*Th.* 5). English translators likewise use a variety of words in representing their meanings: anger, wrath, indignation, rancor, the irascible, and the incentive power. The terms are often fluid. Usually *orgē* is translated by anger, and *thumos* by indignation, the irascible [nature] or irascibility. Evagrius himself defines anger (*orgē*) as a species of *thumos*: "Anger (*orgē*) is the sharpest passion. It is said to be a boiling up and movement of indignation (*thumos*) against one who has given injury, or is perceived as having done so" (*Prak.* 11).[20]

An angry man is one who "stores up injuries and resentments (*Pray.* 22)." By its nature, anger is destructive: like fire among chaff in one's bosom (*Mon.* 10), a ferocious beast (*Eul.* 5), a wild boar (*Supp.* 3), a viper's offspring which consumes the heart which gives it birth (*8Th.* 4.17). It is a dangerous state (cf. *Prak.* 54) which causes the monk to fall mightily (cf. *Mon.* 42), and to be banished by God himself (*Mon.* 85 and cf. *8Th.* 4.14). As we shall observe, one of the main characteristics of anger is that it irritates or agitates the soul, destroying its peace (*Prak.* 11).

From its place among the *logismoi* and the definitions above, one would presume that there would be little good in anger. The nature of anger is however more complicated. Evagrius classifies certain *logismoi* as being "contrary to nature" (*para phusin*: *Th.* 5 and *Prak.* 24), because they tempt a person to forsake virtue which is according to nature. This division follows Evagrius' anthropology.[21] Man is primarily *nous*, a spirit, who fell and was given a body as a corrective aid in returning to its original state. The *nous* or rational soul has three "parts": the concupiscible (*epithumia*), from which flows desires of all sorts; the irascible (*thumos*), the seat of anger and courage; and the rational part (*nous* proper), from which flows the soul's ability to conceptualize, make judgments and will.

Thus the irascible part (*thumos*) far from being evil, is a necessary dimension of the human make-up.[22] The translation of "incentive power" for *thumos* shows its positive nature: a capacity which enables a person to stir up a degree of energizing power in order to face and overcome some perceived obstacle. When this energizing power is exercised as a virtue it is synonymous with *courage* (cf. *Prak.* 89). The perceived obstacle or danger often looms "large" and threatening, and so the incentive power as it were expands the inner soul and instills into it a kind of exaggerated "largeness" in order to go against the danger feeling that it is a quasi "match" for the ensuing struggle.[23]

Since for Evagrius the real battle takes place in the spiritual realm, it is "natural" or "according to nature" for the monk to use his irascible faculties or incentive power in his struggle against the vices. Thus anger is to be used for good and has a positive value as such. "Anger (*thumos*) is given us to fight against the demons" (*Prak.* 24). The same appreciation for this type of anger also allows our desert monk to make sense of Psalm 4:4:

> Our incentive power (*thumos*) is also a good defense against this demon [of impurity]. When it is directed against evil thoughts of this kind, such power fills the demon with fear and destroys his designs. And this is the meaning of the text: "Be angry and sin not." It is useful to apply to the soul this medicine [of anger] in temptation (*Th.* 16).[24]

Because of its ability to be used for good or evil, Evagrius compares the incentive power (*thumos*) to a watchdog. As a virtue, a power under our control, anger is a kind of watchdog,[25] trained to attack the wolves (demons). But if the power in anger is misused and turned on other men, then the dog becomes destructive: "So we must keep this watchdog under careful control, training him to destroy only the wolves and not to devour the sheep and to show the greatest gentleness towards all men" (*Th.* 13).[26]

Now if demons are the proper object of anger, our fellow brothers and sisters certainly are not. To direct anger against them is a total misuse of the incentive power. The demons are the ones who suggest that the anger which has been given us precisely to be used against them be turned instead on our fellow man. Evagrius' language is even stronger: The demons "force the indignation against its nature to fight human beings....making it (*thumos*) a traitor to the virtues" (*Prak.* 24).[27] This passage I think makes it quite clear that the incentive power (*thumos*) can be used for good or ill, depending on its object. In *Letter* 30, Evagrius grants this two-pronged power to do good or evil to all three faculties of the soul:

As for me, however, I do not pay any attention to those who introduce evil into created natures and who declare that law is for the inadequate. Since therefore all evil has its existence through the rational, the irascible, or the concupiscible parts (of the soul), these powers being used for good or evil, then it is clear that evil is created from an improper use. If this is so, then it is also true that not a single malady of the soul was created by God (*Ep.* 30.2).

The reason for the absolute prohibition against using *thumos* against human beings will, I hope, become more clear as we proceed.

A corollary to the idea that anger should not be used against our brothers and sisters is found in the teaching on correction. Although correction may be justified, the use of anger in correction is not. "Beware lest while appearing to heal another you do something to make yourself incurable..." (*Pray.* 25). The teaching is repeated more explicitly in the following passage:[28]

> Do not react in anger against a disciple who has sinned, for it is not good to wound yourself for the sake of healing another; but correct him for the good with patience. For a physician heals the disease, but is not irritable towards someone who is unwillingly sick. When a physician applies the knife, he does so without anger; so when a teacher rebukes, let him not mix anger with the rebuke.[29]

Thus we have learned that anger (*thumos*) is a power within us to be used for good or evil.[30] When used in the battle for virtue, it has a positive value. But when directed towards human beings, even to correct them, it is a misdirection of the power and is therefore evil. Whether anger is a mere *logismos* (suggestion or temptation) or has already taken root in the soul and has become a vice, depends on whether the monk is successful or not in overcoming the initial evil suggestions. As we have seen, knowing the origin of the *logismoi* is beneficial in preventing them from going any further. Let us now look at Evagrius' teaching on how the *logismos* of anger arises at all.

II. CAUSES: WHY DOES A MONK BECOME ANGRY?

So where does this "sharpest of the passions" (*Prak.* 11),[31] which strikes like a flaming arrow (*Mon.* 70) and stings like a serpent (cf. *Th.* 5) come from? Although the origin of anger as a tempting thought can come from various sources, most of the blame is given to the demons. As already noted, this does not mean that they are responsible for every suggestion, but they either produce the temptation themselves or make use of those which come from nature or circumstances to incite the monk all the more (*Th.* 1, *Pray.* 46 and 137). Enough has probably been said about them. There are other causes as well; the passions in general are stirred up by the senses (*Prak.* 38), and the flesh (*Pray.* 46), and more specifically regarding anger: pleasures (*Prak.* 99),[32] memories (*Th.* 2), possessions (*Th.* 1), and vices such as: vainglory (*Th.* 1), and pride (*Prak.* 14). Inasmuch as we are made up of the concupiscible and irascible parts of the soul, nature can add its own suggestions in the form of forbidden desires and anger. When this happens, they are "contrary to nature" (*Skem.* 56).[33] As such the desires are fuel for anger (*Pray.* 27). Another natural source is the will when it is weak (*Ep.* 55.2). Naturally, an injustice done by another is a primary source (*Pray.* 137).

III. ANGER: WHAT IT DOES

How anger affects someone can be looked at from the side of both the offender and the offended. In either case, what is important is for the monk to ask himself: how is anger affecting me and how do I deal with it? The latter issue will be treated in our next section when we consider the remedies. As for how this passion affects human beings, the most obvious fruit of anger is the disturbance it causes in the soul. Anger causes the soul "to be savage (wild) all day long" (*Prak.* 11). Unlike its counterpart, courage, the effect on the soul is not an ordered use of energy, but a kind of agitated, wild drive, similar to waves on a stormy sea (*Mon.* 36).[34]

After an incident which has aroused anger, it typically happens that the face of the offender keeps coming to mind. The offended then rehearses the former incident or fantasizes a future retaliating encounter. Both of these fantasy trips perpetuate the evil by reinforcing the anger–an example of anger leading to more anger (*Prak.* 20) –and does nothing to restore tranquility. Since the monk is striving for *apatheia* (passionlessness or the state of spiritual calmness[35]), the disturbance caused by anger is diametrically opposed to his goal. He is like someone who wants to see but pokes his eyes out: "One who has touched knowledge yet is easily moved to anger is like a man who pierces himself in the eyes with a metal stylus" (*Gn.* 5).

And this brings us to another major effect of anger: spiritual blindness or ignorance. In the state of *apatheia*, the soul is in tune with true reality and "sees" and "knows" itself, the world, and God with deep perception. According to Evagrius, "calmness" is equated with "vision" and therefore anger, destroying the calm, also destroys the soul's ability to see. In order to illustrate more clearly what Evagrius is saying, I beg the liberty to draw from another monastic author, Diadochus of Photice, who compares the soul's capacity to see in this state to that of a fisherman on the sea.

> Therefore we must maintain great stillness of mind, even in the midst of our struggles. We shall then be able to distinguish between the different types of thoughts that come to us: those that are good, those sent by God, we will treasure in our memory; those that are evil and inspired by the devil we will reject. A comparison with the sea may help us. A tranquil sea allows the fisherman to gaze right to its depths. No fish can hide there and escape his sight. The stormy sea, however, becomes murky when it is agitated by the winds. The very depths that it revealed in its placidness, the sea now hides. The skills of the fisherman are useless.[36]

Evagrius readily agrees that the turbulence caused by anger clouds one's spiritual vision in the same way as stormy seas hinder transparency, causing spiritual blindness: "Do not give yourself to your angry thoughts so as to fight in your mind with the one who has vexed you... [this] darkens the soul" (*Prak.* 23).[37] What is darkened is the soul's own light or luminosity, one of the fruits of contemplation (*Th.* 2 and *Gn.* 45). We will speak more about this below when we take up the effects of anger on the monk's prayer.[38]

Sadness is another effect which anger brings upon the soul. First of all, it seems that injuries which are continually before the mind keep alive the negative judgement of the offender and add sadness to the hurt: "He who remembers injury, sorrow will grab" (*Mon.* 41 and *Prak.* 10). But more incitefully, dejection, sadness or what we would call depression, is often due to unresolved anger issues which turn the soul into itself in a self-pitying state: "Sadness is a dejection of the soul and is constituted from thoughts of anger, for irascibility is a longing for revenge, and the frustration of revenge produces sadness" (*8Th.* 5.1). And just as an outward show of anger is visible in a person's facial expression, so too its implosion in the form of dejection leaves its mark on the countenance revealing a person caught in the throes of his passions (*8Th.* 5.15).

In several passages, anger is presented in some relation to fear, as in: "An irascible man will be terrified" (*Mon.* 12). Evagrius probably wishes to say that anger produces fear and this could be true not only in the victim of anger, but in the agent as well, for a person can be afraid of his or her anger when it threatens to get out of control. But he may also be signaling a deeper connection between the agitation of a person who has not come to terms with his or her anger and the restlessness present in the emotion of fear. Fear–as an affect of uncontrolled anger–can take on alarming proportions, as the following sad depiction illustrates. In the scenario anger, which has been allowed to linger, grows into deep indignation or resentment; the ensuing blindness now distorts reality to such a degree that the angry man–if he has not lost his reason totally–is at least a victim of some form of paranoia. For his fear causes "disturbances at night [nighmares?], bodily weakness and pallor and attacks from poisonous beasts [hallucinations?]" (*Prak.* 11). The anger in these cases has become bigger than life and has consumed the person so violently that the mind suffers delusions and the physical body cannot even take in proper nourishment. This might seem a literary hyperbole to most of us, but psychologists with experience in mental hospitals would confirm Evagrius' insight.[39]

In its less violent form, the fear caused by anger can make the injured party retreat into an unhealthy protective silence. This retreat is not to regroup one's forces, but is actually an indication of cowardice and weakens a person for the true fight; this troubled irascibility "leads to desertion" (*Prak.* 21). It is the demons who are suggesting flight and solitude (*Prak.* 22), presumably because it continues the separation and disharmony which are the fruits of anger. It is in this context that the scriptures advise: "Do not let the sun go down on your anger" (Eph 4:26). Anger often uses time as a cloak to hide its cowardly behavior, that is, when the offended is too fearful to face the offender and be properly reconciled.

On the other side, the one who has offended someone with anger and perhaps even driven this person away permanently, can be saddled with guilt for the rest of his life: a sad consequence which again results in the monk's loss of much sought-after peace, especially at the time of prayer (*Prak.* 25).

What Anger does to Prayer

Although it might seem almost too basic, our desert instructor warns against using prayer as a vehicle for anger: "Do not use prayer to pray against someone!" (Cf. *Pray.* 103) Just as Benedict includes "do not murder" in his tools of good works,[40] so too Evagrius takes nothing for granted. Monks come to the desert and to the monastery at various stages of the spiritual journey; those who come from semi-barbaric backgrounds might well need to begin with observing the Ten Commandments and learning that prayer is a power for positive growth and not a tool to be used against anyone.

Of particular interest to Evagrius is the effect of anger on the monk's prayer. This is because prayer, being the monk's main "work" at which he spends most if not all of his time, needs to be "done" well and with as few distractions as possible. One can imagine anger as an external force hindering the work of prayer; but its negative effectiveness is better understood as an internal force hindering the *person*. In prayer, the monk stands before the Lord. The prayer is not so much *what* he offers; rather it is that which *disposes* the monk in his offering of *himself*. The passions–which are basically self-centered movements–are therefore diametrically opposed to prayer, and anger is no exception: "A man who stores up injuries and resentments and yet fancies that he prays might as well draw water from a well and pour it into a cask full of holes" (*Pray.* 22). The contradiction between prayer and anger could not be expressed more concretely.

When the monk has no other occupation and settles down to prayer, the very degree of his calmness is a barometer of his whole spiritual state.[41] Whatever is not right in his life surfaces at the time of prayer. If anger is in his heart, "at the time of prayer, it seizes the mind and flashes the picture of the offensive person before [his] eyes" (*Prak.* 11). If the monk then begins to fight in his mind with the one who has vexed him, he defiles his prayer and impedes pure prayer (*Prak.* 23). The novice has to deal with normal distractions which flood his mind when the rest of his body calms down to a posture of prayer. The mind, naturally active, is not accustomed to remaining quiet and so continues to bring an array of ideas and images before the consciousness. Singing the psalms is an aid for it "quiets the passions and calms the intemperance of the body" (*Pray.* 83).[42] But as a monk progresses, even the images brought forward by the psalms are gently put aside while the monk learns to control his thoughts and eventually arrive at "pure prayer." Pure prayer is prayer without any images or conceptions, even those about God, drawn from this world.[43] One reason for this is that "[r]elinquishing every thought and image is necessary in order to behold 'Him Who is beyond every sense-experience and thought'."[44]

Furthermore, this prayer is a state of being "bare" before the Lord, which–in contemporary language–creates in the soul a totally open and surrendering spirit. This bare encounter allows the Lord to work silently and deeply effecting the transformation of the soul (and its union with God) in his own deft and secret way. Evagrius–like all the great spiritual masters–almost pleads with the monks to yearn for this state of pure prayer. He knows that the monk has to fight hard to persevere in this prayer not only because it is naturally difficult to quiet the ever active mind, but also because the passions work against the achievement of this state. Passion drags and tosses the soul along at the time of prayer, so the soul "cannot stand firm and tranquil" (*Pray.* 71). The demons do their bit as well. They are fully aware of the good done in pure prayer and so try their best to prevent the monk from reaching the state of pure surrender (if I may so call it). Anger is one of their tools (*Pray.* 47 and 50). It is the "fiercest of the passions" and therefore needs special attention at the time of prayer. Since we also know in our modern consciousness of the psyche, that anger can be unconsciously repressed for years, when all the forces keeping it "down" have been released–as happens in this vulnerable state of pure prayer–then up from the depths anger rises to hit the monk in the face. As one makes progress in prayer against distractions, then anger surfaces and the soul has to do "an all-out battle" against it (*Prak.* 63). The fact that anger is present in a monk after years of asceticism is not a surprise to Evagrius, who places anger among the "passions of the soul" which are distinct from the "passions of the body." The latter depart more quickly while the former can "persevere until death" (cf. *Prak.* 35-36). In fact, it is almost the vice that is associated with advanced years just as more carnal vices are associated with the young: "Exhort the elders to mastery of anger and the young to mastery of the stomach" (*Gn.* 31). The very presence of anger is a sign that the surrender of self is not complete. It is therefore a sort of measuring stick: "Since I know that wrath is destructive of pure prayer, the fact that you cannot control it shows how far you are from such prayer" (*Th.* 5).

The importance of prayer to the monk or for anyone striving for perfection can be seen in the following quotation. "Here is the reason–that the spirit in this way should become dull and consequently rendered unfit to pray" (*Pray.* 50). Evagrius shows in this passage that the demons' whole purpose for tempting a person to any of the passions is to destroy his or her prayer life: Why do the demons wish to commit evil acts including anger in us? Their main purpose is to weaken or destroy a person's capacity for inner transformation. Since it is mainly in prayer that a person allows his or her heart to be softened and molded by God, the demons will do anything to prevent such an opportunity.

As the texts have intimated, Evagrius is not only talking about the need to curb acts of anger, but thoughts of anger: "The man who strives after true prayer must learn to master not only anger and lust, but must free himself from every thought colored by passion" (*Pray.* 53).[45] The following idea has already been cited in a parallel text (*Gn.* 5), but it merits repetition now in the context of prayer: "No one who loves true prayer and yet gives way to anger or resentment can be absolved from the imputation of madness! For he resembles a man who wishes to see clearly and for this purpose he scratches his eyes [with a sharp metal object]" (*Pray.* 64).[46] And lastly, but not insignificantly, the Lord will not hear the prayer of an angry person: "The prayer of the irascible person is an abominable incense offering; the psalmody of an angry person is an irritating noise" (*8Th.* 4.18); and "God avoids a resentful heart" (*8Th.* 4.14).

The Good of Restraint

Before taking up the remedies, I would like to mention the benefit derived from restraint. By not replying in a provoking situation, "your lips shut in the beast of irascibility;" regarding the other person, he is "bitten by your silence," which may then have the effect of stifling his "fiery lips" (*Eul.* 4.4). Furthermore, "If you restrain your anger, you yourself will be spared and in the process prove yourself too wise a man to indulge in arrogance" (*Pray.* 26). This is an insightful bit of wisdom. This seems to be one of the few references Evagrius makes to arrogance linked with anger.[47] Yet we all know instinctively that there is in anger a certain amount of pride and self-aggrandizement. This is perhaps why such a vice may recur in old age, since age offers no guarantee of selfless surrender of the ego. As a person grows in true wisdom, he or she grows proportionately in humility which restrains any display of anger. Restraint also carries with it a note of mercy which will receive its reward.[48] Mercy may be the key for understanding why Evagrius never allows anger to be expressed against a person. Mercy's opposite is not justice (another virtue), but a meanness that enjoys exacting what is due and a severity which can easily go beyond its limits and become judgmental. The pride inherent in "playing the judge" is but another expression of arrogance which destroys relationships. It would be salutary to remind ourselves at such moments of God's restraint towards us as sinners, which is the foundation for our relationship with others.[49]

Furthermore, a refusal to indulge in anger keeps alive the knowledge of God,[50] which is the fruit of grace (*Gn.* 45). For one who has reached *apatheia*, this knowledge is perceived as an illuminating gentle radiance proper to the *nous*. Our desert sage speaks of the luminosity of the *nous* on a variety of occasions, referring first of all to the soul's own light (*Prak.* 64[51]) or radiance which the soul is graced to see in contemplation–pure prayer–after the passions have been quieted.[52] This light is the image of God which has been stamped on the soul's nature by the Creator. It is Evagrius' insight to realize that this image is essentially light.[53] A few passages present the light as a theophany of God (*KG* 1.35)[54] or the Holy Trinity[55] (*Th.* 42) in the soul. Other passages are more ambiguous and shows Evagrius' caution (e.g. *Th.* 40),[56] for the devil could easily mislead a person in this area (cf. *Pray.* 73) where the boundary between the soul's radiance and God's luminous presence is humanly impossible to discern. Whatever is the source of the light, anger is detrimental to an experience of it, for "anger extinguishes the radiance of the soul" (*Cnsl.* 2).

IV. REMEDIES FOR THE CURE OF ANGER

After a description of what negative anger does to the monk and to his prayer, there should be no doubt that every temptation (*logismos*) should be seriously avoided and if the vice or sin takes root, it should be eradicated with every effort. Interestingly, anger is often so deeply rooted in the human being that it is in need of more remedies than lust (*Prak.* 38). In fact, throughout his oeuvre, our wise instructor often couples these two vices together. For example: "the demon of anger employs tactics resembling those of the demon of unchastity" (*Th.* 16). And both vices lead the *nous* to disaster and destruction (*Th.* 3 and cf. 1 Tim 6:9). Prolonged fasting reduces the temptations associated with concupiscence or lust, [57] but the demon of anger is more difficult to eradicate, and indeed, may involve a life-long struggle. Again, perhaps the phenomenon of repression in some only brings the vice of anger forward later in life as the soul begins to deal with its deeper and more hidden behavioral patterns. Once this vice is acknowledged and there is a genuine desire to deal with it, Evagrius offers various remedies which fall into five categories: reconciliation, virtue, prayer, ascetical practices and the discernment of thoughts.

A. *Discernment of Thoughts*

This last has some claim to be mentioned first for, from a practical standpoint, if we analyze our thoughts (*logismoi*) and see how they get entrance into the soul and what tricks they use in order to entice us, we shall then be in a good position to dismiss them. And–theoretically–we shall never have to worry about rooting out the deeper forms. Life, alas, is not so simple. By the time we learn how to discern which thoughts are good, bad or neutral, we have lived long enough to have allowed a good number of the bad (*logismoi*) to entrench themselves in our soul as vice. The novice has thus a twofold battle: to exert effort in uprooting the evil tree trunks which have taken over the yard as if they owned it, and to be constantly on guard lest other acorns fall on the ground and begin to send down roots. Watchfulness–a monastic catchword–is fundamental for discernment.

Evagrius offers two ways to analyze one's thought. One way is to separate the different components of the evil suggestion: ① the mind which has accepted the thought; ② the idea suggested; ③ the thing as it exists outside of the mind and as part of God's creation (for example, a concrete thing, like gold in a temptation to greed); ④ the passion. Next one asks: "In which of these does the sin consist?" It is then an easy step to see that the fourth element, passion is attracted to the noxious pleasure being presented regardless of the fact that the law of God commands us to reject this pleasure. Evagrius implies here that once passion is seen as an irrational movement, distinct from the mind and from what God created as good in itself, then the evil is exposed as an "alien" contrary to nature and to God's law.

Another method is to wait until the temptation subsides, since during the actual temptation, the intellect is generally too disturbed to exercise any critical discernment. Then, once the thought has been dismissed, the monk should "sit down and recall in solitude the things that happened," namely: where he was, when it happened, why it happened, and why he was able to triumph over the thought (because of real virtue or because the evil suggestion could never be concretely realized). In this way, the monk becomes conscious of his area of weakness where the demon of anger tried to wedge its way in. He must then commit the scenario to memory so that the next time the tempter returns, he can throw into his face the ruse the demon was using to make the temptation so attractive. Exposure then makes the demon furiously retreat! (*Th.* 2,3,8,9)

B. *Reconciliation*

Although watchfulness is a logical first, there is a certain kind of primacy that must go to reconciliation. More often than not, anger involves other people and dealing with anger cannot in a Christian context refer ultimately only to oneself. We belong to a body and although the communal aspect does not loom as large for Evagrius as it does for Augustine, it is nevertheless present and is certainly one of the main elements which distinguishes the desert monk from Seneca.[58] Stressing time and again how necessary it is that all be well at the time of prayer for it to be truly fruitful, Evagrius "frames" his treatise on prayer with two exhortations for reconciliation: "Leave your gift at the altar and go and be reconciled with your brother. Then you will pray undisturbed" (*Pray.* 21); and again: "God does not hear the prayer of a man who is not reconciled with his brother" (*Pray.*147). Within this "frame" is another which echoes and reinforces the outer frame: "If you really try *you will find some way to arrange the matter* without showing anger. So then employ every device to avoid a display of anger" (*Pray.* 24); coupled with: "Unless you forgive the man who owes you a debt, you yourselves will not find forgiveness" (*Pray.* 104). Whether Evagrius was conscious of this literary framework or not is a secondary issue. More importantly, the quotations show his concern for reconciliation.

And when two have fought in anger, who should be the first to seek reconciliation? The one who first "regains sobriety" must take the initiative and "give his hand to the other in an apology" (*Eul.* 7.7). For Evagrius, if one has negatively responded to an angry word, one cannot use the excuse of having been provoked. If a person has responded, this person is at fault; he or she must then focus on his or her own behavior to the exclusion of the other's fault: "If you responded to someone's anger, consider yourself completely at fault...." (*Eul.* 5), a salutary reminder that we are ultimately responsible only for our own actions. One should furthermore even forget the injury, which is possible through prayer. In a more than usual pithy sentence, Evagrius shows how the forgetfulness of injuries is linked to Christ's own work: "Feast of God: forgetfulness of offenses" (*Mon.* 41). This is what the monks celebrated every Sunday.

C. *Virtue*

The next remedy is virtue. As mentioned in the introduction, Evagrius taught that vice is ousted by virtue. If one is tempted to gluttony, one should fast; if tempted to *acedia*, one should double one's efforts to pray; if tempted to greed, one should practice almsgiving. If after a disagreeable encounter, one is tempted to flee and seek solitude: "Give no confidence to such promptings; *on the contrary, follow the opposite course*" (*Prak.* 22). Therefore if a person is angry with a brother, the remedy is not to avoid contact with him, but to seek reconciliation through fraternal exchange. So, besides offering the hand in apology, is there something else that one can do? Yes, the offender can be shown kindness by being invited to a meal: "A gift snuffs out the fire of resentment, as Jacob knew[59].... [A]s for ourselves...we must supply for our lack of gifts by the table we lay" (*Prak.* 26); and even more explicitly: "If a brother irritates you, lead him into your house, and do not hesitate to go into his, but eat your morsel with him. For doing this, you will deliver your soul and there will be no stumbling block for you at the hour of prayer" (*Mon.* 15). The virtue of hospitality, with its source in charity, thus extinguishes anger. There are a number of passages where love is spoken of as the cure for anger, such as: "love...has a cooling effect on boiling irascibility" (*Eul.* 21.23), it is the "bridle of anger" (*Prak.* 38), and in line with offering a meal: "love turns away anger and irascibility; gifts overcome resentment" (*Virg.* 41).

There are other virtues which are also regularly presented as remedies for anger. The most powerful is anger's opposite, the virtue of gentleness (*praütēs*), which is also translated as meekness. Because of its importance, I would like to place it in a position of honor, at the end of our discussion of anger. With an apology for giving it here only a passing nod, we proceed to two other virtues which are also often mentioned as remedies to anger, namely patience and almsgiving. Patience, patient endurance or perseverance, should not surprise us. Anger is often characterized by rashness and a desire to retaliate with a stinging revenge. A reversal would be to accept the inflicted injury with patience. Evagrius is obviously not talking about putting on a show of acceptance while contorting ourselves with a desire for revenge. The virtue of patience (from *passio*: allowing to happen, enduring) means really accepting the perceived mistreatment and in this way putting out the flames of anger and resentment. Perhaps an illustration drawn from the medical world will help to understand the role of patience in curing anger. When something enters the body as a potential threat, the immune system surrounds the "alien" matter in order to destroy the threat. It does this by drawing into itself the diseased area, as if it were digesting the danger. So too patience, absorbing the angry thrust, quietly undoes its stinging power. Virtue is then a real remedy, a cure for vice.[60]

Patience is often listed as a remedy along with other practices: "Turbid anger is calmed by singing the psalms, by patience and by almsgiving" (*Prak.* 15); and a person: "tames the other [indignation] by patient endurance, forgetfulness of injury, and almsgiving" (*Th.* 3).[61] If it seems strange to hear that anger can be cured by almsgiving, one need only to recall that one of the causes of anger is an attachment to possessions (avarice). Voluntary deprivation heals a too-great-attachment to things.

Another remedy is humility (*Ep.* 4.5, *Ant.* 5.23). Its opposite vice, arrogance or pride, is reduced to non-existence by humility. Why this is so is explained by Basil in his homily against anger where he equates pride with an unrealistic opinion of ourselves; the reason we are offended is because of an inflated idea we have of our own persons. If we really considered ourselves as the least of all we would not experience an affront to our dignity.[62] Evagrius would completely agree, since the passions–whether pride or anger or any of the others–blur the spirit's capacity to perceive reality as it is, distorting the vision of the world and ourselves as well. Because of its touch with reality, humility restores knowledge to the soul and acts like an antidote against anger.[63]

The sage desert dweller also realizes that injuries caused by others are permitted by God as a way of testing the soul. At such moments, a person would do well to recall David's humility when Shimei threw curses at him (2 Sam 16:5-14). Instead of responding in anger, David hoped that the Lord would look upon his affliction and repay him good for the curses he endured that day (*Ant.* 5.8).

And finally, Evagrius reminds his monks that their proper role in the battle for virtue is ultimately a secondary one. Their own efforts are not the primary cause of virtue in the soul because the transformation from vice to virtue is accomplished by Christ, the great Physician. "Through acts of mercy (for example, almsgiving), he heals our irascibility," just as "through prayer he purifies the *nous* and through fasting causes concupiscence to atrophy" (*Th.* 3).

D. *Prayer*

As already mentioned, praying for one's enemies leads to forgetfulness of injuries (*Mon.* 14). Perhaps this is because a person cannot pray for someone else without having a certain care for that person. Prayer then makes us think about the good of the other person and not about retaliation. Prayer teaches us to put aside our own hurts and to think more magnanimously of the larger picture: the salvation of souls and what is good for us and for the other in the eyes of God, who is after all, the One par excellence who–in forgiving–forgets our injuries.

As we have also seen, anger can sometimes put a person into a frightening situation. Evagrius conjures up images of armed men and wild beasts which represent in graphic form the danger and fear which grip the soul. What should the monk do? He should first of all pray to Christ:

> When...the demons stimulate the irascible appetite they constrain us to walk along precipitous paths where they have us encounter armed men, poisonous snakes and man-eating beasts. We are filled with terror before such sights, and fleeing we are pursued by the beasts and the armed men. Let us make provision for protecting this power of our soul by praying to Christ in our nightly vigils, and also by applying the remedies we spoke of above[64] (*Prak.* 54).

Prayer as a remedy for anger comes up often in the form of singing the psalms. "In the one singing psalms, irascibility is quiet" (*Mon.* 98); and: "'Psalms, hymns and spiritual canticles' invite the spirit to the constant memory of virtue by cooling our boiling anger (*Prak.* 71). Why might this be so? There are two interrelated reasons which immediately come to mind: first, the very rhythm of the music is a soothing antidote to agitated emotions. The inner lack of harmony caused by anger is exposed to an external pleasant form with a regular rhythm. Music's highly emotional nature penetrates to the deepest levels of the human psyche. When the music is spiritually vibrant it affects the whole person, body and soul, in a calming manner.[65] The second reason is related to the communal nature of the monks' prayer. It is true that some of the monks of the desert were true hermits who would have prayed alone; but there were many, like the semi-anchorites, who prayed the psalms together:

> In Egypt the communities are constructed of many cells. Every brother goes alone into his cell to work with his hands and to pray there. However, they come together to one location for the hour of refreshment and for the hour of prayer, which are fixed in the morning and evening hours (*Ep.* 27.7).

Many monastics today agree that singing the psalms in common has a powerfully unifying effect. There is no reason to believe that it was any different in the desert in fourth century Egypt among the varieties of holy desert dwellers. Even the genuine solitaries were aware that they were in some way one with the whole world through their prayer. Thus, this unifying nature of prayer, even apart from the music, must have been a contributing factor in curing anger.

E. *Asceticism*

The last but certainly not the least remedy in extinguishing the fires of anger are the ascetical practices to which the monk voluntarily subjects himself for the sake of the spiritual benefits derived from these exercises. There is usually some deprivation involved, as for example when St. Benedict advises his monks to deprive themselves during Lent of some food, sleep or excessive talking.[66] Although the ascetical exercises often contain negative elements associated with deprivation (most importantly the denial of self-will), their value lies in the constructive and affirmative effects of the practices in the inner life of the monk. Evagrius believes that ascetical practices are general remedies for curing all the passions,[67] but often one or more will be especially suited for a particular vice. For example, fasting is beneficial in curing gluttony and lust, while almsgiving reduces an unhealthy dependence on things and therefore helps to cure avarice. Since anger often results from an involuntary deprivation of goods or honor (self-esteem, reputation), Evagrius counsels a monk to give alms and to be humble. Other salutary deprivations include going hungry or thirsty (fasting), keeping vigil (deprivation of sleep), and withdrawal from the world (*Ep.* 55.3).[68] Regarding the latter, Evagrius dryly warns the monks to beware of withdrawing from the world (*anachoresis*) while bringing the passions of the world with them. It is not such a great virtue for a monk to leave his relatives, for even the pagans have practiced "detachment" in sacrificing their children to the gods. More importantly, the monk should make sure that he is not leaving his family because anger is advising him to separate himself from them. *Anachoresis* suggested by anger is not a virtuous deprivation and therefore has no power to cure the vice. The remedy lies rather in persevering in prayer to Christ the Physician of our souls (*Ep.* 55.4-5). All of these ascetical remedies help to quiet the irascible and make proper use of it, which is one of the goals of the *praktike*, or ascetic life.[69]

F. *Gentleness*

We return now to the virtue par excellence for combating and anger: gentleness (*praütēs*).[70] What is gentleness? It is a "concrete manifestation of love"[71] expressed in behavior such as mild manners, soothing words,[72] and compassionate gestures. This bodily comportment of a gentle person reveals a tender and compassionate heart which harbors no anger or resentment.[73] The love which lies at the heart of this virtue disarms anger and dissipates its biting power. To those not spiritually astute, gentleness (or its synonym: meekness) may appear as weakness. On the contrary, gentleness is a sign of mature spiritual strength arising from love. [74] It is charity which enables a gentle person to be patient and kind (cf. *Eul.* 11.10). The interrelatedness between gentleness and love is also revealed in the following passage: "For it is through our love that we behold God's love for us, as it is written in the psalm: 'He will teach the gentle his ways'" (Ps 24:9). Since one would have expected a verse from 1 John 4,[75] the use of a text employing gentleness demonstrates Evagrius' quasi equation of the two virtues. If it is the gentle who know God's love and can truly love, then a true lover of God and neighbor will be known by his or her gentleness.

Obviously, Evagrius does not mean that a gentle person loses his ability to stand his ground against real enemies. In the spiritual journey, the monk comes to know when to be gentle and when to fight, as he learns to distinguish his different audiences. "Prepare yourself to be gentle and also a fighter, the first with respect to one of your own race and the second with respect to the enemy...with gentleness and mildness exercising a charitable patience with one's brother while doing battle with the [evil] thought. Let the gentle person then be a fighter, with his gentleness divorced from murderous thoughts" (*Eul.* 11.10).

The great holy ones of the past present our desert sage with models of gentleness. The first is Moses whom the scriptures say "was more gentle (or meek) than all other men" (Num 12:3). He possessed the gentleness of God himself (cf. *Ep.* 56.3), because he was willing to be annihilated rather than allow God to express his anger against the Israelites. "Forgive them or blot me out of the book of the living.[76] Thus spoke the Gentle One!" (*Ep.* 56.6). Moses' compassion for his people and his willingness to endure patiently their punishment—one might say his solidarity with the sinners even though he was himself innocent–were exactly the qualities which soothed the wrath of God. The gentleness of Moses stirred up the gentleness of God. The second example is David: "O Lord, remember David and all his gentleness" (Ps 131:1 LXX). Perhaps because David–the warrior and man of blood–is not usually thought of as a gentle man, Evagrius was hard pressed to expound on this text. The Septuagint translators may be referring to the mercy David had on his enemies on several occasions or perhaps to his ability to repent from his heart. Regardless, the fact that a prominent figure of the scriptures is commended for his gentleness is enough for Evagrius' needs. The final example takes us to the supreme model, Christ; while the other two exhibited the gentleness of God, Christ himself could say: "Learn of Me, for I am gentle and humble of heart" (Mt 11:29).[77]

These then are his models for gentleness. Its counterpart, anger, also has a model. Instead of finding biblical examples, Evagrius offers the monks only one: specifically, the demons. We have seen how anger is the ally of the demons; now he is even more explicit: "Do not consider the demon to be anything other than a human being aroused by anger and deprived of perception" (*Ep.* 56.4). Since demons and humans are not the same beings, perhaps Evagrius means that when a human being is roused to anger, the behavior is so demonic that there is no real difference between the two subjects in regard to the act. This meaning is implied shortly before in the same letter: "No evil makes the intellect into a demon as much as anger through the troubling of wrath" (*Ep.* 56.4).[78] In order to curb the demon of anger, recourse should be made to the development of the interior virtue of gentleness:

> He who has mastery over his incentive power has mastery over the demons. And anyone who is a slave to it is a stranger to monastic life and to the ways of our Savior for as David said of the Lord: "He will teach the gentle his ways" (Ps 25:9). The intellect of the solitary is hard for the demon to catch, for it shelters in the land of gentleness. There is scarcely any other virtue which the demons fear as much as gentleness" (*Th.* 13).[79]

The *Epistle* 56 referred to above is a little exposé on anger and gentleness. At the beginning of the letter, Evagrius explains that the *nous*, being incorporeal, has as its proper object other incorporeals, most significantly God himself. However, the *nous* by its own nature cannot see God, it is rather reserved to the pure *nous*, and Mt 5:8 is quoted in support: "Blessed are the pure of heart for they shall see God." Purity of heart, however, is no easy achievement. It takes a great deal of purifying which comes from *praktike*, the art of asceticism. Now the doorway, so to speak, between *praktike* and contemplation is gentleness. This is because the purified soul in its undisturbed and gentle state[80] now has the capacity to allow the light to penetrate into its depths; without gentleness there is no contemplation.[81] The relation between these last two is grounded in a personal experience in which

Evagrius was lifted out of his cell in a mystical transport and shown the whole world in a single glance.[82] In this state, a heavenly being said to him,

> "Go, be merciful and meek and fix your thoughts directly on God, and you will be the master of all this [world]"....[Evagrius] struggled to obtain these two virtues, as if [with them] he could obtain all the virtues.[83]

In some ways, gentleness, like prayer, reveals the extent to which a monk is making spiritual progress; certainly, the more he harnesses the energies of the incentive power, the more he grows in gentleness. At the same time, if a person notices that his or her ascetical practices are not bearing fruit in a greater degree of gentleness, this person should take note that a lack of growth may be due to deep seated resentment in the soul. Battle needs to be done in order to dislodge the anger, for if it is allowed to remain, the ascetical practices may do more harm than good:

> Do not approve of any abstinence that is far from gentleness. For he who abstains from food and drink, but in whose interior reigns unjustified anger, resembles a ship that finds itself in the middle of the sea, steered by the demon of anger (*Ep.* 56.5).[84]

Conclusion

Although he wrote no treatise on anger, the monk from Pontus has left behind a full depiction of this passion, its dangers, correctives and its positive contribution to human nature. He carefully nuanced against whom (the demons) anger can and should be used and against whom anger can never be utilized. Situations which arise tempting us to be angry with our brothers and sisters are occasions rather for developing virtue. Laying down anger and cultivating the meekness of Christ leads the monk in his journey towards ever greater gentleness. This is perhaps the virtue that is most obvious in the older monks and nuns of today who have faithfully and lovingly persevered in a genuine search for God. Their gentleness and compassion reveal to the younger that they know, in the Evagrian sense of "gnosis," the face of God, and it is a face of compassion and mercy.

Notes: Chapter 2

1. *Nichomachean Ethics* 2.7, and 4.5. *The Basic Works of Aristotle*, Ed. Richard McKeon. Random House, NY (1941): 959-962; 995-997. Plato is not so explicit, but is generally of the same mind: *The Republic* 4. Tr. B. Jowett. Modern Library, NY (1982): 157-160.

2. Other such passages employed by Evagrius are: "Let not the sun go down on your anger" (Eph 4:26 in *Praktikos* 21]; "Cease from anger and put aside your wrath" (Ps 37:8); "Remove wrath from your heart and put away evil from your flesh" (Eccl. 11:10 LXX); "Lift up holy hands without anger and without quarreling" (1 Tim 2:8). The last three texts are found together in *On Various Evil Thoughts* 5.

3. Out of numerous texts, a few representative verses will suffice: Dt 13:17, 29:20; Jer 3:12, 7:20; Mt 3:7; and Lk 3:7. In the last two texts, John the Baptist speaks of "the wrath to come," namely, God's. It is a major theme in the book of Revelation as well: 14:19, 15:7, 19:15. The day of judgment for the Middle Ages became the *dies irae*.

4. Origen implies that anger has its natural measures when it is in accordance with nature in *On First Principles* 3.2.2 (SC 268: 158, especially lines 118-121). English translation: ed. G.W. Butterworth, Peter Smith Publishers, Gloucester MA (1973): 214. Basil expressly states that anger has a positive role in acquiring virtue. We will be drawing on his *Homily* 10 in this chapter. The same is found in Nemesius of Emesa, *On the Nature of Man*, 35, *Library of Christian Classics* 4, Westminster Press, Philadelphia (1955): 348. According to William Harris–to whom I refer the reader for his Christian, pre-Evagrian sources on anger–Gregory Nazianzus and John Chrysostom also permit anger on occasion. *Restraining Rage*, 125-126. Abbot Isaiah is another example. His text begins: "There is among the passions an anger of the intellect, and this anger is in accordance with nature. Without anger a man cannot attain purity: he has to feel angry with all that is sown in him by the enemy." *On Guarding the Intellect*, in *The Philocalia*, vol. 1. Transl. G.E.H. Palmer, et al. Faber and Faber Ltd. London, 1983: 22-28. Also see sections §§25-26. Abbot Isaiah was brought to my attention by Kalistos Ware in: "The Passions: Enemy or Friend? *In Communion* 17, Fall 1999. The author's presentation of Evagrius, however, is not sufficiently nuanced in this article.

5. First Sahidic *Life of Pachomius*, (frag.3.9), quoted by Harris, 399. This translation is substantially the same, but more flowing than the one in *The Pachomian Koinonia*, vol.I, translated by Armand Veilleux, Cistercian Studies Series 45, Cistercian Publications, Kalamazoo, MI (1980): 430. Cf. Veilleux's French translation of the Sahidic life: "Vraiment, à partir de ce jour, il ne recommença plus à s'irriter comme font les hommes charnels; mais s'il lui arrivait une fois de s'irriter, il s'irritait à la manière des saints." *La Vie de Saint Pachôme*, Spiritualité Orientale 38, Abbaye de Bellefontaine (1984): 306. This *Life* was written after 346.

6. For this account, I am relying on John Eudes Bamberger's Introduction to two works of Evagrius which he has translated in: *The Praktikos & Chapters on Prayer*. Cistercian Publications. Kalamazoo, MI (1981): xxxv-xlviii.

7. Basil's influence on Evagrius will be seen in part as we proceed. Note here that Evagrius spent about nine years in Basil's company. Luke Dysinger, OSB, *Psalmody and Prayer in the Writings of Evagrius Ponticus*, Oxford Theological Monographs, Oxford University Press (2005): 9.

8. One author suggests that Evagrius was already a monk by the time he went to Constantinople. Receiving the habit in Palestine would have then been a *return* to the monastic life that he had earlier committed himself to. Although Palladius says that Evagrius received the habit from Melania, this author believes that it was Rufinus–following Melania's idea–who actually clothed Evagrius. A.M. Cassiday: *Evagrius Ponticus*. Routledge, New York, (2006): 9 and 205, n.32.

9. The works of Evagrius are numerous. His main works and those on which we will be principally drawing, include: his trilogy: *The Praktikos (Prak.)*, the *Gnostikos (Gn.)* and the *Kephalia Gnostikos (KG)*, which take the beginner through the ascetic life to the life of contemplation; *The Foundations of the Monastic Life (Fnd.)*, *To Eulogios (Eul.)*, *Chapters on Prayer (Pray.)*, *Exhortation to Monks (Mon.)*, *Reflections* [also known as *Skemmata (Skem.)*] with 3 supplementary chapters *(Supp.)*, *On the Various Evil Thoughts (Th.)*, not to be confused with *On the Eight Thoughts (8 Th.)* [which is also known as *On the Eight Spirits of Wickedness*], and a second *Exhortation to Monks* I-II [also known as *Counsel to Monks (Cnsl.)*]. He also wrote various *Letters (Ep.)*, and commentaries on the Psalms and other books of the Bible *(Commentaries* and *Scholia)*, and the *Antirrhetikos (Ant.)*: a compilation of Biblical verses to be used as weapons at the time of temptation. The letters in parentheses refer to the abbreviated form we will use in referring to these works. Besides the English translations of the *Praktikos* and *On Prayer*, mentioned in n.6, the *Ad Monachos* has been translated by Jeremy Driscoll, O.S.B., *The Mind's Long Journey to the Trinity: The* Ad Monachos *of Evagrius Ponticus.* The Liturgical Press, Collegeville, MN (1993). There are also a few selections of Evagrius in *The Philokalia* vol.I: 31-93. Some of Evagrius' works in translation along with the Greek can be accessed on web, thanks to Luke Dysinger, O.S.B. See www.ldysinger.com/Evagrius. The most extensive translation into English of Evagrius' Greek corpus is that of Robert E. Sinkewicz: *Evagrius of Pontus: The Greek Ascetic Corpus*, Oxford Univ. Press, Oxford (2003). It also contains the Greek text of *To Eulogios.* See also A.M. Cassiday's work in the previous note. His translations include several less known works of Evagrius, among them some letters and scolia. The translations in my text have been culled from the above sources.

10. Dysinger points out (p.17) that Evagrius is now listed among the saints in the most recent edition of *Butler's Lives of the Saints* (1997), with a feast on February 11.

11. Sorabji, 346. The author also treats Origen and the pre-Evagrian writers on anger, but mostly from the perspective of the emotions and first movements. Regarding Origen, see *On First Principles*, 3.2.2, ibid. 214. Rufinus' Latin links the *logismoi* to the *primi motus*, a term of importance for Seneca and the Stoics, as we have noted in the previous chapter. Jerome also deals with the first movements *(propassiones)* but differs from his (one time) master in assigning a degree of impurity, albeit without culpability, to these involuntary movements. See Richard A. Layton, "From 'Holy Passion' to Sinful Emotion." *In Lordly Eloquence: Essays on Patristic Exegesis in Honor of Robert Louis Wilkin.* Eerdman's Publishing Co. Grand Rapids, MI, 2002. Layton also treats of the use of Origen's and Didymus' concept of the first movements in his "*Propatheia*: Origen and Didymus on the Origin of the Passions," *Vigiliae Christianae* 54.3 (2000): 262-282.

12. The term is also used in 2 Cor 10:4, where Paul is speaking about destroying arguments *(logismoi)*, a reference to the kind of subtle Greek reasoning which knows nothing of faith and humility. More to the point is Paul's injunction in the verse which follows: "we take every thought *(noema)* captive to obey Christ." Although the term is different, its sense is very close to what Evagrius means by *logismoi.*

13. Sorabji, 346.

14. Jerome's terms are *cogitatio/cogitationes* and *cogitata*. See his *Commentary on Mt*: 6:28 §29 (PL 26 col 38-39), *Commentary on Ezechiel* 18:1-2. PL 25, col 168-9; *Ep.* 79.9 §506, PL 22 col 731. For Antony, see Athanasius' *Life of Antony,* 5.23 (PG 26, 849A and 877A); and Antony's *Ep.* 6.4.31, Eng. translation by Derwas J. Chitty: *The Letters of Saint Antony the Great*, SLG Press, Oxford (1995):18.

15. The opposite is also true: a depressing word from one person can arouse anger in another (*Skem.* 43). On the relation between sadness and anger in Evagrius, see L. Misiarczyk: "Smutek i zlosc w nauce duchowej Ewagriusza z Pontu [Grief and anger in the spiritual teaching of Evagrius Ponticus]." *Studa Plockie* 30 (2002): 83–96. The article is in Polish, but for those interested, I have an English translation by Michal Mrozek, O.P. Another example often used by Evagrius is of gluttony (one of the primary *logismoi*) leading to lust (e.g. *Skem.* 42).

16. Dysinger (p.34) describes *apatheia* as: "...freedom from the inner storm of the 'passions,' irrational drives which in their extreme forms would today be called obsessions, compulsions, or addictions." Cf. *Mon.* 31.

17. Re: Origen: If the initial *logismoi* are not immediately rejected, then the hostile power "seizing the opportunity of this first offense, incites and urges us on in every way, stirring to extend the sins over a larger field." *On First Principles*, 3.2.2. p. 214. Concerning anger, Origen says: "It is possible when the demon of anger is standing over us not to get angry. But perhaps it is impossible not to get heated." *Comm. on Ps.* 38:4. And: "If one progresses in virtue, the emotional part does not disappear, but it comes to be in a state called sympathy." *Comm. on Ps.* 55:3-5. Jerome writes in a similar vein: "It is allowed to us as humans that we should be moved in the face of anything undeserved, and that like a light breeze it should disturb the tranquillity of our mind. But in no way is it allowed that we should be worked up into swollen whirlpools." *Comm. on Eph* 4:26.

18. In a footnote to *Prak.* 58, (n. 52) Dom John Eudes advices caution in following this procedure.

19. The reader will recall that the *Iliad* begins with the "wrath of Achilles" (*mēnin aeide thea Pēlēiadeō Achilēos*)." *Homeri Ilias*, vol. 1, edited by Thomas W. Allen. Oxford University Press, London/ New York, (original 1931), reprint 2000.

20. Thus anger includes both an inward movement and an outward expression aimed at a perceived wrong (Dysinger, 125). Basil distinguishes thus between *orgē* and *thumos*: "As the words for indignation (*thumos*) and anger (*orgē*) are different, so also are the significations which they bear very different. Indignation is a kind of flaring and sudden ebullition of passion. Anger, on the other hand, nurses a grievance; the soul, itching, so to speak, for vengeance, constantly urges us to repay those who have wronged us." *Homily* 10: "Against those who are prone to anger." *The Fathers of the Church* 9. St Basil: *Ascetical Works.* Translated by Sister M. Monica Wagner, csc. The Catholic University of America Press, Washington DC (1962): 447-461. Quotation is from p. 459. Jerome makes the same distinction for *furor* and *ira* : Furor vero incipiens ira est, et fervescens in animo indignatio. Ira autem est (cujus amaritudo et furor species sunt) quae furore restincto desiderat ultionem, et eum quem nocuisse putat, vult laedere." *Comm. in Ephes.* 3.4.31 (PL 26 col. 516B). Layton believes that Jerome is dependent on Origen's *Comm. in Eph.* Layton, 284 n. 13.

21. For a summary of Evagrius' anthropology and cosmology, see Dysinger, 31-33. Another helpful reference is that of Abbot John Eudes Bamberger, OCSO: "*Desert Calm:* Evagrius Ponticus: The Theologian as Spiritual Guide." *Cistercian Studies Quarterly* 27 no. 3 (1992): 190-192.

22. They were specifically designed to help the fallen *nous* regain its original place before God: "Each...*logikos* [fallen *nous*] is given a mixture of the twin 'helpers' of *thumos* and *epithumia* appropriate to the world it inhabits." They are thus: "therapeutic remedies." Dysinger, 33.

23. Basil also speaks of the irascible part of human nature in a positive light. FC 9, 456. In fact, there are many points of similarity between Evagrius' teaching on anger and Basil's homily. Some of these will be noted as we proceed. Another influence on Evagrius was that of his master, Makarios, as seen in the latter's teaching on anger as a great obstacle to prayer. See Sinkewicz, xviii.

24. Note Basil: "Unless your anger has been aroused against the Evil One, it is impossible for you to hate him as fiercely as he deserves." FC 9, 456. Basil goes on to see in Psalm 4:4 a justification for a proper use of anger: "The psalmist admonishes us: 'Be angry and sin not.' The Lord moreover threatens with condemnation one who lightly gives way to anger, but He does not forbid that anger be directed against its proper object, as a medicinal device, so to speak." Ibid. 457-458.

25. Basil also likens the irascible nature to a sheepdog. FC 9, 457. See following note.

26. Compare Basil's text which continues the first quotation in note 24 above: "For, our hatred of sin should be as intense, I believe, as our love of virtue; and anger is very useful for bringing this about, if, as a dog the shepherd, it follows closely the guidance of the reason and remains quiet and docile to those who are helping it and readily obedient to the call of reason." FC 9, 456-7.

27. Note again Basil's similar words: "Transfer your anger [from men] to him, murderer of men, the father of lies, the worker of sin, and sympathize with your brother." FC 9, 459.

28. If indeed this work is Evagrius? The consensus, however, is in favor of his authorship. See Graham Gould: "An Ancient Monastic Writing: Giving advice to Spiritual Directors. (Evagrius of Pontus, *On Teachers and Disciples)." Hallel* 22, 1997: 96-103. Quotation is from p.103.

29. *On Teachers* 13, translated by Graham Gould in the article found in the previous note.

30. Anger can also be turned against good things which are a hindrance. For example, when the monk at prayer is distracted by good thoughts from practicing "pure" or imageless prayer, he is instructed to turn his anger against his thoughts, dismissing them in a radical way. More will be said on prayer below.

31. A phrase repeated in *On Teachers* 10.

32. A monk may be angry because he is denied some pleasure.

33. And see *Th.* 2: "I do not say that all memories of such concerns (objects) come from demons; for when the intellect is activated by man, it is its nature to bring forth the representation of past events. But all thoughts producing indignation (*thumos*) or desire (*epithumia*) in a way that is contrary to nature [are caused by demons]."

34. Or to a restless lion rattling the hinges of his cage (*8Th.* 4.7).

35. This translation takes into account both the negative and positive sides of *apatheia*. Literally it means: "passionlessness," *a*–to be without, *pathos*–passion. On the other hand, the state which results from the lack of disturbing passions is a state of inner calmness or tranquillity. The positive aspect of *apatheia* has deep implications for the healing of the *nous*: "Impassibility is not, however, a purely negative concept, for it ultimately involves a restoration of [the] two parts of the soul to their proper nature: the concupiscible is turned towards desire for the knowledge of God and the irascible develops an aversion to all evil and an utter hostility towards the demons." Sinkewicz, xxxi-ii. [footnote continues below]

This unruffled state is also captured by other terms: *atarachōs*, which means: 'untroubled by wrath' or 'calm in the face of adversity;' it is "the virtue which protects the monk during demonic or human assaults, and particularly defends against being inwardly disturbed (*tarassein*) by *thumos, or wrath, inspired by demons.*" Dysinger, 75. *A orgēsia*:

freedom from anger, is also used, emphasizing the lack of anger, it is not yet the more positive and exalted state of *apatheia* (Cf. *Gn.* 45.4). Dysinger, 74, n.47 lists other occurrences of this "characteristic virtue of Evagrius' Christian gnostic."

36. *On Spiritual Perfection* 6.26, taken from *The Liturgy of the Hours*, vol. III. Catholic Book Publishing Co, NY (1975): 154. Although this translation flows well, it leaves out the final two lines which I supply here from Janet Elaine Rutherford's text: "This is just what the contemplative intellect comes to experience, most of all whenever the depth of the soul is troubled from unjust anger." *One hundred practical texts of perception and spiritual discernment from Diadochos of Photike*. Belfast Byzantine Texts and Translations, 8. Belfast, Ireland (2000): 37.

37. There are many other references: Irascibility scatters knowledge (*Mon.* 35); Out of rashness, ignorance [is born] (*Mon.* 99); An angry man will not see the light (*Instruction* 56); A strong wind chases away clouds, memory of injury chases knowledge from the mind (*Mon.* 13). In the same vein, "thoughts from anger...chain the mind," meaning that it narrows its ability to perform well and to see the truth (*Skem.* 60).

"Spiritual" blindness does not mean the inability to see only "spiritual realities" but all the realities perceived by the "spirit" or the soul as a spiritual entity. Dysinger (p.124) notes that anger "tends by its nature to dissipate thoughts."

38. Modern psychology agrees that anger distorts reality but for a different reason than the one offered by our author. Evagrius would say that the state of agitation is the cloudy filament preventing vision. But according to the late Fr. Raphael Simon, O.C.S.O., a monk and psychiatrist, anger distorts reality in that it focuses attention on an evil to the exclusion of other reality factors. In this respect, the distortion comes from a kind of concentration which excludes part of the complete picture. I received this information in email communications with Fr. Simon in March, 2004.

39. Evagrius' psychological acumen has been noted by many, notably Dom John Eudes Bamberger, O.C.S.O., who is himself a psychiatrist. See his introduction to *The Praktikos*, lxviii-lxix and his comments on *Prak.* 11, p.18, n. 25.

40. *Rule of Saint Benedict* 4.3. Translated by Luke Dysinger, O.S.B., Source Books, Trabuco Canyon, CA, 1997. Cf. Augustine's treatment of the same, p.111 below.

41. One of Evagrius' most significant and original contributions to spirituality is his teaching that "progress in the spiritual life is progress in prayer." John Eudes Bamberger, "*Desert Calm...*" 196.

42. Singing's medicinal effect on anger will surface later in this chapter in our examination of anger's remedies.

43. Columba Stewart sees in Evagrius' ban on "self-created" imagery in prayer an attempt to "control the encounter" with God ("Imageless Prayer and the Theological Vision of Evagrius Ponticus," *Journal of Early Christian Studies* 9.2 [2001]:192). In the same article, he resolves the apparent contradiction in Evagrius between "imageless" prayer and his use of such images as "light" (cf. Ez 1:26, 10:1) and "place of God" (cf. Ex 24:10–LXX) in the highest levels of prayer by pointing out that such biblical images do not limit or confine God in representing him in this way (p.200).

44. Dysinger, 5. The citation comes from Evagrius' *Letter to Melania*, 27.

45. "Prayer is not only a matter of having the passions under control, but of being free from the representations tied to the passions" (*Th.* 53).

46. The same idea is also found in *Pray.* 145 where he says that if one is still given to fits of anger and yet dares to know divine things or to pray with pure prayer, he is to be rebuked, for he has not yet obtained the proper respect and humility.

47. Evagrius does say that pride can lead to anger (*Pray. 14 and Skem.* 41) but the explicit reference to pride or arrogance within anger is new here. We will shortly learn from Basil why the two vices of pride and anger are often found together.

48. As you judge others, so you will be judged (Mt 7:1).

49. Restraint is also said to "lighten" the heart, perhaps expanding it and making it apt for prayer...or so I interpret: "As water makes a plant spring up, so humiliation of the irascible raises the heart" (*Mon.* 100). As regards judgments, Gabriel Bunge's insightfully remarks that from anger comes the mania to criticize, mistrust, hate, resent and gossip. *Vino dei Draghi e Pane degli Angeli: L'insegnamento di Evagrio Pontico sull'ira e la mitezza.* Edizioni QiQajon, Comunità di Bose. (No date): 43.

50. A parallel case is that of *Gn.*10 where it is implied that restraint of anger brings about greater clarity in the interpretation of scripture.

51. Cf. *Apatheia* leads also to seeing "your mind shine like a star" (*Th.* 43).

52. The incensed soul "is no longer able to welcome in itself the representation *(fantasia)* of its [divine] lawgiver: for such luminosity only appears in the mind *(hegimonikon)* with the deprival of all conceptions *(noēmata)* of objects ("concerns") at the time of prayer" (*Th.* 2).

53. See Bamberger, *"Desert Calm..."* 196.

54. DelCogliano, 412 cites *KG 1.35*: "That God is light" and says: "When the mind is 'naked' before God, who is without form, the *nous* is capable of beholding its own light in God's light and thus God himself."

55. The "Christian" character of Evagrius' state of *apatheia* has sometimes been called into question. In defense of Evagrius' Trinitarian approach to prayer, see Gabriel Bunge, "The 'Spiritual Prayer': On the Trinitarian Mysticism of Evagrius of Pontus." *Monastic Studies* 17 (1986): 191-208. Sinkewicz does not hesitate to equate this light with the Holy Trinity: "In these special moments of prayer then the mind sees itself as luminous, and this light that allows it to see itself is none other than the light of the Holy Trinity" (p.xxxvi).

56. Stewart, 193, n.96.

57. Evagrius himself was not troubled by carnal desires for the last three years of his life. *Palladius: The Lausiac History* 38.13. *Ancient Christian Writers* 34, Westminster MD, 1965: p.114.

58. One author sums up the difference between the Christian and Stoic approach to virtue in this way: The Stoic aims to be utterly *independent* of everyone and everything. The Christian seeks to be free *from* those things that impede love for others and for God." Italics in original. Diogenes Allen, "Ascetical Theology and the Eight Deadly Thoughts." *Evangelical Journal* 13 (1995) 15-21. Quotation is from p.18.

59. The reference is to Jacob's reconciliation with Esau. In order to appease his brother, Jacob sent him an abundance of gifts from among his flocks and possessions (Gen 32:13-15). Interestingly, the first scripture passage in the section dedicated to anger in the *Antirrhetikos* –a work composed to give monks Biblical verses to use as weapons at the time of temptation–is the passage from Gen 33:10-11. Its important frontal position shows how seriously Evagrius considered gifts to be a remedy for dissipating anger. See *Ant.* 5.1 and cf. 5.28.

60. Prudentius matches the vice of *Ira* with the virtue of *Patientia* in the *Psychomachia* (verses 130-131). *Patientia*, in full armor, "waits for Wrath to perish by reason of its own violence." *Prudentius,* Loeb Classical Library, Tr. H.J. Thomson. Harvard University Press, Cambridge, MA (1969): 288-9

61. And: "He who is merciful to the poor destroys irascibility" (*Mon.* 30).

62. Basil, *Homily* 10 (460). The parentheses refer to the page number in the FC edition.

63. The same might be applied to the monks of today whose pride is probably coming from another source than Evagrius' fellow desert dwellers. Bamberger points out that "most pride that one must deal with in counseling monks is *defensive*; the problem is a lack of confidence due, usually, to a combination of a weakly developed ego and the presence of a somewhat negative self-image. It does not express a desire for domination but a sense of outrage at what is felt as a lack of respect or appreciation." "*Desert Calm...*" 194. Whether it is an inflated ego or an undeveloped one, reality has been distorted. Humility, and the refusal to grasp after false images of the self, is therefore a healthy corrective.

64. Namely: singing the psalms, patience and almsgiving. See *Prak.* 15.

65. We also recall that singing the psalms "quiets the passions and calms the intemperance of the body" (*Pray.* 83). The effect of music on the body and the emotions was commonly known in the ancient world. On the therapeutic role of music in Evagrius and his predecessors, see Dysinger, 124-130. The whole of his chapter 4: "Psalmody as a Spiritual Remedy" is apropos here (pp. 104-130).

66. *Rule of St. Benedict,* chapter 49.

67. Evagrius, I believe, would completely endorse the following analogy which compares the role of asceticism to corrective lenses: "The eye condition known as astigmatism prevents all the light rays the eye admits from being focused. As a result the sufferer cannot see properly. However, a corrective lens can focus the light correctly, insuring proper vision. Likewise various ascetic practices, such as prayer, fasting, reading, almsgiving are intended to enable us to gain sufficient mastery over ourselves so that we can bring our entire self into focus." Allen, 19.

68. A similar list is given in *Ep.* 4.5: Against the passions, including anger, the monk should practice: abstinence, humility, vigils, withdrawal from the world, constant prayer, strengthened by the reading of Scripture.

69. Jeremy Driscoll, "Gentleness in the *Ad Monachos* of Evagrius Ponticus." *Studia Monastica* (1990): 295-321. The reference is to p. 301.

70. Initially, this combat takes the form of restraint: "[A]nger [is restrained] with the help of meekness." *Ep.* 19.2. Casiday, 62.

71. Bunge, 152.

72. Even a person's silence may be "a certain sign of...meekness." Bunge, 151.

73. Cf: "Merciful compassion (*eleēmosúnē*) and gentleness (*praütēs*) diminish indignation" (*Prak.* 20).

74. Cf. Bunge, 51.

75. For example: God is love, he who does not love, does not know God (vv.7-8). or: "...if we love one another, God abides in us, and his love is perfected in us" (v.12).

76. Evagrius here condenses Ex 32:32.

77. Hoti praüs eimi kai tapeinos tē kardiai. Mt 11:29. History reveals the consequences of not taking Christ's words seriously, as Bunge observes: "How different would have been the history of the Church, founded on 'He who is meek' if his members, both bishops and people, would have taken to heart with greater honesty this 'humble teaching.' Undoing the effects of disunity calls for new efforts, but always with gentleness: "Only with firmness... united with gentleness toward the erring, is it possible to eliminate the 'hardness of the neck of the enemy' and restore 'unanimity in the Church' (cf. *Ep.* 24.2)." The citations are from Bunge, 159 and 160.

78. Another possible interpretation involves Evagrius' anthropology: A demon, like human beings, was originally a pure intellect or *nous*. Because their fall was great, they fell into bodies which are even more "dense" than those which humans are strapped with in this life. So, although we would not refer to the demons as "human beings," in Evagrius' system, they belong to the same cosmological phenomenon of fall from an original state of happiness to a descent into bodies; the only difference is one of degree of guilt and the consequential position on the ladder of descent. If this is the correct interpretation, then more significant is the allocation that they can be defined by their anger. This shows how truly demonic anger is. Dysinger refers to the demonic nature as "a sort of freezing rage" (pp.120-1).

79. The passage goes on to present Moses, David and Christ as again models of gentleness. Also note: "Teach your brothers this gentleness, so that they give themselves to anger only with difficulty" (*Ep.* 56.3).

80. An obvious reference to *apatheia*, "the throne of passionlessness" (*Mon.* 81). Also note that Evagrius defines the "gentle" as those who are resting in their souls from the fight against anger [and the other passions]. *Commentary on Ps* 24:4.

81. See: Driscoll, "Gentleness...." 304. The image of gentleness as a door between *praktike* and contemplation comes from this article. Also note: "The most obvious virtue of contemplation is...meekness." Bunge, 58. If knowledge is a way of perceiving, then in the text: "Out of gentleness, knowledge is born" (*Mon.* 99), "vision" could be substituted for knowledge with little change of meaning. Also: "Gentleness is the mother of all knowledge." *Ep.* 27.2. The "gnostic" for Evagrius is the contemplative who "not only speaks of God, but knows him through interior familiarity." Bunge, 58.

82. St. Benedict had a similar vision towards the end of his life: "the whole world was gathered up before his eyes in what appeared to be a single ray of light." *Dialogues II* , 35. *Life and Miracles of St. Benedict,* by Pope St. Gregory the Great, transl. by Odo Zimmermann, OSB and Benedict R. Avery, OSB. The Liturgical Press, Collegeville, MN (no date): 71.

83. Cited from Bunge, 147 who refers to *Vita J.*

84. When abstinence is undertaken without love, one may suspect the presence of rage: "Abstinence alone is like a foolish virgin...where this oil (love) is lacking, there is rage" *Ep.* 28.1.

CHAPTER 3
CASSIAN: ANGER & FRIENDSHIP

Our trek through the writings of our authors, which began in Rome (Seneca) and moved to the Egyptian desert (Evagrius), now takes us back on the road going West, this time to Gaul, via Constantinople and Rome. Our author brings with him a rich monastic tradition, indebted to his masters not the least of whom is our friend Evagrius. In fact, his life and works cannot be told without reverence to his relationship to this great figure. Let us therefore begin at the beginning.

Life

John Cassian was born sometime in the early 360s, probably in Dobrudja in what is modern day Romania.[1] In his youth, he received a classical education which gave him linguistic flexibility in both Latin and Greek. Around 380 he and a friend, Germanus, went to Palestine and entered a monastery in Bethlehem. A few years later, after promising by vow that they would return "shortly," the two companions received permission to visit the famous monasteries of Egypt. The "visit" would last for fifteen or so years, indicating that once they had tasted the monastic life lived by the giants of the Egyptian desert, their hearts would not let them settle for anything less. Their vow, however, pricked their conscience and so after seven years they returned to Bethlehem, in order to be released from their commitment to that monastery and to settle permanently in Egypt. What neither knew was that even the desert would not be their last home.

In Egypt, Cassian and Germanus gleaned the best from the famous monks living in the Nile Delta, in Scetis and at Kellia, the communities living in "Lower Egypt" or that area not far from Alexandria. Although they intended to, they never got to the Pachomian communities of the South. Their experience was then that of the semi-anchorites among whom Evagrius was living. Although residing in the desert in the same years as our monk from Pontus, and although he pays tribute by name to almost every other great monastic athlete of this day, Cassian never mentions the name Evagrius. No one doubts that he knew him and was familiar with his teaching. So the only explanation is that Cassian's departure from Egypt coincided with the beginning of the persecution of the Origenist monks by Theophilus of Alexandria in 399. The controversy is too convoluted to detail here; suffice it to say that the monks who were advocating the kind of prayer which was supported by Origen's spiritual teaching, were branded as Origenists and forced to flee the desert. Evagrius–who certainly fell into the category of an Origenist–eluded the persecution by a peaceful death shortly before the controversy began. But his name would be associated with the condemnation of Origen both at the time and in later history. From his writings, there is no doubt that Cassian's sympathies were with the Origenists. But for the sake of circumventing the accusation of heresy, he refrains from using the name of Evagrius.

From Egypt, Cassian and Germanus made their way to John Chrysostom in Constantinople who was offering hospitality to a good number of the monks fleeing Theophilus. Cassian was ordained a deacon by John and Germanus a priest. Later Cassian will recall with joy the love he bore towards Chrysostom, his "teacher," and his "fellow-citizens" of Constantinople.[2] Cassian and Germanus seem to have spent about three years in the capital; with John's downfall in 404, they departed for Rome in order to appeal John's case before the Bishop of Rome. Cassian's movements in the next ten to fifteen years are not clear, but he probably spent until the mid 410s in Rome or at least in the service of that See. His dear friend and companion for twenty-five years, Germanus, seems to have died during this time.

We next find Cassian in Gaul: in Marseilles (Marsilia). The first of his monastic works, the *Institutes*, was written in 419 and indicate that he had by then established his monastery of St. Victor in that city. At some point he also established a monastery for women which may have been headed by his sister. St. Victor's was Cassian's last home for he lived and died there (probably in the mid 430s), in the monastic life which he loved so dearly.

The *Institutes* is a type of formation document designed to help the young monk in his initial stages of monastic life. It is concerned with the "outer person," dealing with monastic customs and with the monk's combat against the eight deadly sins, an obvious translation to the West of Evagrius' teaching on the *logismoi*. Intended as a complementary volume, Cassian's second monastic opus, the *Conferences,* is a collection of twenty-four talks dedicated to the perfection of the "inner person"[3] and put into the mouths of famous monastic personages whom Cassian and Germanus met in Egypt. The monastic topics include discretion, prayer, concupiscence, and spiritual combat. Cassian's teaching on anger appears in both works: briefly treated in *Conference* 5, and then more fully developed in a short treatise on anger in *Institutes* 8. The subject surfaces again in *Conference* 16 which is dedicated to the theme of spiritual friendship; this time anger is analyzed in relation to a specific relationship: those close ties of love with another formed in Christ. The purpose of both works is to bring to Gaul the type of monasticism which Cassian had experienced in the East.

In this section, I would like to present the highlights of Cassian's teaching on anger in two parts; first, anger as presented in the context of the eight principle vices, culled from his two earlier works, *Institutes* 8 and *Conference* 5, and then his longer presentation of anger and friendship in *Conference* 16.[4] The conclusion will attempt to bring together his complete views.

Introduction to Anger: the Eight Deadly Sins/Vices

Cassian gives a list of the eight principle vices (*octo principalia vitia*), as he calls them, at the beginning of his *Institutes* 5. The vices are the same mentioned by Evagrius, but the order has been slightly modified. The order of Evagrius' fourth and fifth *logismoi*, namely, sadness and anger (*ira*[5]), has been reversed to anger and sadness. The reason for the new arrangement has to do with Cassian's system of interrelating the vices. Each of the first six vices (except the first) has its cause in the preceding one: thus gluttony leads to fornication, fornication to avarice, avarice to anger, anger to sadness, and sadness to acedia. In order to eradicate the vices, one begins the battle with gluttony and works systematically forwards–thus sweeping down cause and effect–until one has conquered all six. Only then is one strong enough to combat the final two: vainglory and pride. Actually, the conquest of the preceding vices may subtly undermine the expulsion of these last two, since achievement or success can generate a false sense of one's ability or ego, all the more dangerous when the conquest is spiritual (5.10.4).[6]

By listing anger next to avarice, Cassian shows more clearly its dependence on the former vice, but risks implying that anger has only one source. Cassian also realizes that his neat little scheme is somewhat hypothetical. Who has ever been known to start with gluttony and work his or her way down the list until all the vices tumbled and fell in order...and then to turn to finish off the remaining two? More realistically, everyone struggles with different vices: "In one person the spirit of fornication is dominant, in another wrath.... And although it is evident that we are all attacked by all of these, yet we each suffer in different ways and manners" (*Conf.* 5.13). The solution is to discern which vice is our predominant passion and to fix our care and concern on fighting it, earnestly asking God to help us. When that one has been conquered, we turn to the next worst one and work on that (*Conf.* 5.14). The method is then: discern, focus, pray and give God the glory for each victory (*Conf.* 5.15).[7] This approach is more practical because it gives each person the flexibility needed for his or her own particular situation. Incidentally, Cassian slips in that one vice can be turned against another. The example given replicates Evagrius' exactly: vainglory can help restrain lust (*Conf.* 5.12.1).

Cassian's systematic mind also goes beyond Evagrius in the distinctions he draws up of the vices. First he distinguishes between natural and unnatural: a natural vice is one whose origin is within us; anger for example is a natural vice (*Conf.* 5.8.1), even though its *motivating cause* is external (*Conf.* 5.3). An unnatural vice, like avarice, is one whose origin is external. He then goes on to divide the group into those which depend on bodily activity (gluttony and fornication) and those which do not (e.g. pride and vainglory). A final distinction is made between the carnal and spiritual vices. Here Cassian realizes that he is departing from St. Paul who calls all vices "carnal."[8] Cassian's excuse is that he is giving a "more refined understanding of their remedies and their natures" (*Conf.* 5.4.4), but it would be more true to say that their anthropologies are dictating different approaches. For the Apostle, "carnal" is whatever is opposed to the Holy Spirit's work in the believer, while what is spiritual is the best or noblest aspect of the believer acting in accordance with His grace. What is carnal can permeate each of the tripartite dimensions of the human being as outlined by Paul: body, soul, and spirit, just as what is spiritual elevates all three levels. For Cassian, who is more dependent on Platonic philosophy, the body/soul dichotomy predominates, and vices are ascribed to different parts of the soul.[9] The carnal ones are said to "pertain especially to the enjoyment and feelings of the flesh" (*Conf.* 5.4.4) while the "spiritual [are] those that, having arisen at the promptings of the soul alone...give no pleasure to the flesh" (*Conf.* 5.4.5). The spiritual vices are cured by the medicine of a simple heart,[10] (*Conf.* 5.4.5) while the carnal vices must be checked by the mind and by bodily abstinence, specifically, fasting, vigils, and solitude (*Conf.* 5.4.3).

Turning now to Cassian's teaching on anger, we encounter more distinctions: there are, he says, three kinds of anger distinguished by three Greek terms: *thumos, orgē,* and *mēnis.*[11] *Thumos* blazes up interiorly; *orgē* breaks out in word and deed; and *mēnis* lingers, simmering for days and seasons. All three "are condemned by us with an equal horror" (*Conf.* 5.11.7).[12] Let us now turn to Book 8 of the *Institutes* which is Cassian's mini-treatise on anger.

I. ANGER: THE 4ᵀᴴ DEADLY SIN

As one reads through these pages, one begins to notice certain repetitions. As this reader continued to read and re-read chapter 8, a certain chiastic pattern began to emerge. We do not wish to say that Cassian deliberately structured Book 8 as we have imagined, for there are elements which could imply the opposite.[13] Nevertheless, there is a certain validity in presenting the following scheme, for–if nothing else–it affords us a useful tool for organizing the chapter. Our discussion then will more or less follow this pattern:

A. Anger is destructive (8.1)
    B. An Exegesis of Scripture passages quoted in defense of anger (8.2-4)
        C. Anger must be totally eradicated, beginning with the thoughts (8.5)
            D. Anger and Time (8.10-13)
                E. Anger and God, Prayer and Responsibility (8.13-14); thoughts
            D.¹ Anger and Place (8.16.19)
        C.¹ Anger must be totally eradicated, beginning with thoughts (8.20)
    B.¹ An Exegesis of a Scripture passage quoted in defense of anger (8.21)
A.¹ Anger is destructive (8.22)
        E.¹ Anger and God (8.22)

A. This books begins with a litany of the destructive elements which we have seen in all the authors reviewed: anger blinds the mind so that it cannot perceive properly and thus mars the monk's ability to judge and discern accurately;[14] it destroys as well the monk's peace and that equilibrium which goes with righteousness, even the respect which comes with good birth (8.1). As our chiasm suggests, the destructive nature of anger is again repeated in 8.22, to which is added: anger causes the monk's persevering purpose to be lost; in other words, he loses his spiritual focus.

B. Even while penning the above absolute condemnation of anger, Cassian can hear the voices of certain monastic protesters appealing to the Bible for support. These folks believe it is quite all right to be angry "with our erring brethren" (8.2) because God himself is often presented as angry against sinners. If we may for a moment enter into the minds of these protestors, it seems to us that they are trying to make their own distinctions. Anger is sometimes denounced in scripture and sometimes not, especially not when it is attributed to God himself. Since no evil can be attributed to God, it must sometimes be a virtue to be angry. When? The Bible only depicts God's wrath inflamed against the unjust, especially unrepentant sinners. Therefore the distinction must lie in the *object* of one's wrath. It is not just to be angry with good people, but it is proper and correct to be angry against "our erring brethren." Many passages in the Bible certainly seem to endorse this interpretation. But Cassian does not. He does not fall for the shift of the argument to the object, but brings the discussion back to God. The problem, he says, is that the monks do not know how to interpret these passages correctly. Anger is a *human* emotion. To attribute this human emotion to God is to blaspheme the Lord who is the "fount of all holiness" (8.2).

Cassian has particularly strong feelings on this theme, for it was the basis for his flight from the desert. We mentioned that Cassian fled with a group of monks who were being persecuted for following a type of "pure" prayer developed out of Origen's teaching on the spiritual nature of God. But if "prayer" was the occasion, the crisis was more accurately over what kind of being God is.[15] In his Conference *On Prayer*, Cassian tells his readers that many of the "simpler" (namely, those who were naive and ignorant 10.5.2) Coptic monks were accustomed to picture God as he is often portrayed in scripture, i.e. with many human attributes such as hands, a mouth, eyes, etc. They imagined God quite literally as he is described in certain texts of scripture. But alongside them were monks who had come to the desert with a good deal of classical education, as well as familiarity with the great Christian exegetes, including Origen. This background had given them a more refined notion of God as a pure spirit: "invisible, ineffable, incomprehensible, inestimable, simple and incomposite"–as Cassian echoes in 8.4.

Cassian responds by saying that the attribution of such human components as a mouth or eyes, or sleep or anything else to God must be understood as metaphors: eyes refer to God's profound perception, hands refer to his providence and activity, etc. The anger attributed to God must not be understood "anthropomorphically (that is according to base human passions) but in a manner worthy of God who is free from all emotion."[16] Anger is rather an emotion experienced in the creature, fearful of a just judgment. The meekest judge can seem wrathful to those who feel the force of law come crashing down upon them. Thus anger is not a divine attribute and no one can appeal to scripture as an excuse for one's anger, even employed against evildoers.

The other appeal to the Bible comes in 8.21 where a verse from the Sermon on the Mount is quoted: "he who is angry with his brother *without cause* will be liable to condemnation" (Mt 5:22). This certainly seems to indicate that there is such a thing as justifiable anger. But Cassian argues: who does not think that his anger is justified? But the crux of the solution comes from a bit of textual criticism: the phrase *without cause*, he says, "is an interpolation"[17] not contained in "many modern copies and in all the older ones,"[18] therefore it has no validity and no authority.

C. Total eradication: With every pretext for anger demolished, there is only one admissible way to deal with it: to drive it totally from one's life. This is St. Paul's advice: "Let all anger and indignation, violence and blasphemy be eliminated from among you along with ill-will" (Eph 4:31). Cassian notes that "when he says 'Let all anger be eliminated from among you' he makes no exception as if it could ever be needful or useful for us."[19] After such a strong statement, one would expect to conclude with "period: case is closed;" and to put Cassian into Seneca's camp of absolutism. But we soon see Cassian nuancing his position, in a way which underscores his adherence to Evagrius. The abbot of St. Victor's recalls his master's teaching that a "healthy instinct of anger" has been given us "to combat the evil passions of our own hearts."[20] When we see anger rising up in us against someone else, we should "be indignant at anger itself" (8.8), angrily driving "out its deadly urgings."[21] The proper interpretation of Ps 4:4 "Be angry and sin not" is precisely to use anger against our own feelings. To support his interpretation, he draws on a scripture text regarding David. During a campaign against the Philistines who were in possession of the city of Bethlehem, David became quite thirsty. Calling to mind the water from a well inside the walls of that city, he audibly voiced his feelings in a desire for that particular water. Three of his bravest men broke through the enemy line, procured the water and returned offering it to David. In one of those moments of great nobility, David poured the water on the ground in a kind of sacrificial offering to the Lord, declaring by the action that the satiety of his own feelings were of no consequence compared to the lives of his men. "May the Lord be good to me because I have done this, for shall I drink the blood of these men who have brought it to me at the peril of their lives?" (II Sam 23:17). Cassian sees in this verse the same great dichotomy between one's own feeling and the worth of our brothers. We must therefore turn our anger on our own feelings or passions so that they do not "come to effect"[22] (8.9) against anyone else. To do this effectively, the monk needs to expel the thought as soon as it enters his heart (8.9).

This idea is also echoed in 8.20 where Cassian encourages the monks to seek the perfection of purity of heart and its consequent reward, namely, the vision of God, by the eradication of all anger from their lives, not only in deed but in *thought* as well. The thoughts are the roots or beginnings which must be eradicated totally, for God sees into the heart and will judge it along with our deeds (8.20). Cassian, following Evagrius, underlines the need to recognize and eliminate evil thoughts as soon as they arise (cf. *Conf.* 1.17).[23] There is no mention in this parallel passage of the "exception" accorded anger in the first section, namely, that it is to be used against the passions. It seems that once the exception was made, it ceases to be an important issue, or at least not as important as it was for Evagrius. To my knowledge, Cassian never mentions it again. His focus is on denouncing that anger which is truly a vice, which is so often not dealt with properly because it is excused as "justified" or is disguised as a virtue. We now turn to some examples of anger which have not been dealt with correctly.

D. Anger's use of Time & Place. Citing the verse from Psalm 4:4 which is repeated in Ephesians, Cassian goes on to finish the second half of the New Testament text: "Let not the sun go down upon your anger and give no place to the devil" (Eph 4:26). This brings us to the important issue of conflict, namely, that anger does in fact occur from time to time and when it does there is need *to address the issue* and to do something about it *before the sun goes down*. This human understanding of the human condition is, however, not good enough for Cassian's teachers who "do not allow anger to overwhelm our hearts for an instant.... Otherwise, if we are permitted to remain angry until sunset, our ill temper would be able to vent itself in fury and vengeance before the sun could sink to its setting" (8.10). At first it seems that Cassian is misunderstanding Paul for the latter is hardly advocating a "grace period" where a person could continue to vent his "ill temper" until the cutoff point at sunset! More likely Cassian is deliberately overstating himself in order to cut off *any* pretext for the use of anger against a brother and in order to emphasize that anger is like a door which allows entrance to the devil. It is better not to give the scoundrel any footing by dealing with the incident *immediately.*

But instead of going on to tell his readers *how* to deal with the incident, Cassian himself postpones this topic for the moment in order to comment on those who use delay tactics instead of resolving their anger. Some do this through denial, others though a basic misunderstanding of the nature of this vice. Those who verbally deny that they are angry–whether they are deliberately lying or simply out of touch with their feelings (classic denial)–both groups are "shown up" by their actions which betray a hidden anger. Cassian perceptively notes the way that hidden anger is manifested in behavior: such folks a) do not address the other with their usual speech, b) nor do they converse with them in their accustomed manner (8.11). Speech and manners thus signal that something is wrong in the relationship. The worst part is that they think they are in no way to blame "as long as they do not take steps to avenge themselves" (8.11) This means that the "poison of [their] anger" which would normally be vent outwards, is turned inward and is secretly devouring the subject in its brooding state. In time, he notes, it dwindles (8.11).

Everyone knows that the avoidance of the usual friendly conversation can be just as cruel as sharp words. Whether consciously or unconsciously executed, the negative feelings need to be addressed and torn out for–regardless of whether the actions offend our neighbor–the cause, namely, anger "excludes the bright radiance of the Holy Spirit as much as if it were displayed."[24]

The other subtle way to avoid the issue is to protest that we need solitude, to go "where no one would disturb us" (Cf. 8.16). This attitude stems from believing that the *other* is the *cause* of our anger. Cassian's response has two elements. The first is to insist that blaming others for our own weakness is an indication of spiritual immaturity. We are responsible for our own vices; they stem from within our own individual nature, not from without. Situations and people, including our brothers and sisters, become occasions which may trigger off negative reactions, but the source of these is within the subject. Anger which is provoked, is no less *my* anger. Secondly, solitude is not a sinecure. The desire for solitude that comes from conflict offers an excuse not to deal with the situation appropriately. While solitude is a monastic value, it is only for those who are spiritually mature. "To those who have not amended their lives, solitude tends not just to preserve but to *aggravate* vices" (8.18).[25] The company of others keeps us somewhat civilized in our manners, while solitude throws off all constraint, unless we have first learned discipline. Cassian chooses two apt metaphors in this section to describe a person who has not dealt with his anger or other vices before entering solitude: vices are like unbridled horses, bolting from their stalls in the desire for a false kind of freedom. And poisonous snakes are just as dangerous alone as when they are with others. So hidden anger does not disappear when a person leaves the company of others. After all, even inanimate things can be the object of wrath, and Cassian humorously adds an autobiographical note about his own annoyance with a pen that wouldn't work properly. Therefore, a misuse of time or place, for example, delay tactics or solitude, is *not* an appropriate way to deal with anger (8.19).

E. Since neither procrastination nor flight offers the proper response, what is the solution? For Cassian there is only one: *immediate reconciliation*. No particular way is laid down, but an apology or some way to make amends is in order: "a ritual of forgiveness is absolutely necessary."[26] What is emphasized is that humility, forgiveness, love of our brothers and sisters must take precedence over personal hurts. Again, the relationship is more important than one's own sense of being right. So true is this that Cassian insists on *both* parties taking equal responsibility for the reconciliation process. Each person could think: "I didn't do anything wrong; he's the one who a) spoke the nasty word or b) is overly sensitive. It's his problem, not mine." But this kind of thinking is not the Christian way, and so Cassian reminds his monks that the Lord is not pleased with this kind of attitude. On the contrary, the Lord will not even hear the prayer of one who has such sentiments in his heart. "If you are offering your gift at the altar, and there remember that your brother has any complaint against you, go first to be reconciled with your brother, and then come and offer your gift" (Mt 5:23-24). And since we are enjoined to pray constantly (cf. 1 Thess 5:17 and 1 Tim 2:8), the Lord does not hear us unless we make immediate efforts to be reconciled. This means first, that no amount of prayers can substitute for reconciliation with one's brother or sister and, secondly, that the Lord takes the side of the *other* until you are reconciled with him or her. To be estranged from another is to be estranged from God. It's a matter of converting the heart (8.15), and of responding to God's grace.[27]

The core of Cassian's teaching, I believe, is at the center of the chiasm: anger disrupts a relationship and sows the seeds of hatred. Our relationship with others is the most basic element of community life. If we ignore or refuse to be reconciled, we destroy the very heart of monasticism. And very importantly: the responsibility goes both ways.

The chiastic structure has afforded us a convenient tool to organize Cassian's material, to make sense of his repetitions, and to underscore the central theme of reconciliation. But the chiasm is not air-tight. The book ends with a plea to embrace a proper attitude of heart, because anger and our life with God are diametrically opposed: "The best remedy for this disease is to begin by believing that we are never justified in being angry whether for a good or bad reason."[28] In other words, if we change our way of thinking and truly and humbly believe that anger of any sort is inappropriate behavior and unworthy of a Christian as a temple of the Holy Spirit, then anger is given no entrance into our hearts. And if we think daily of death and realize that by hoarding anger we are jeopardizing our very salvation, then again we will be inclined to dismiss quickly this vice. Cassian reminds us for the last time that our prayers are useless before God if anger–or a refusal to be reconciled–is in our hearts, and goes on to say that not only prayers, but anything and everything we do in our monastic life: fasting, going without the goods of this life, celibate chastity, and vigils are all equally useless before God and will only lead to hell, unless we banish anger and hatred from our hearts (8.22).

❖   ❖

II. ANGER AND FRIENDSHIP: CONFERENCE 16

Since anger may arise wherever human beings interact, it is profitable to study it in specific relationships. This is exactly what Cassian does in the sixteenth *Conference* which is delivered by a certain Abbot Joseph and dedicated to the subject of spiritual friendship. A good part of the treatise deals with our theme of anger. Although Cassian's intention is to speak of friendship, there is a "slight unfocusing" of the material due to the fact that "most of what Cassian says is not really specific to friendship but can apply to almost any relationship."[29] This "unfocusing" may be deliberate on Cassian's part in order to widen the topic to the various levels of closeness within a monastery. It is at least true that the rules for healthy communication and rapport apply to diverse human relationships.[30]

In his preliminary remarks, Abbot Joseph commends Cassian and Germanus on their devoted friendship; the occasion becomes the springboard for the Egyptian monk's "lecture" to the juniors on the subject of spiritual friendship. After some remarks about the different kinds of human bonds, the treatise consists of two main sections: the first gives the ideal and rules for true friendship, along with a loose commentary on the rules, ending with the virtues necessary for maintaining it. The second part deals with the right and wrong ways to react in a conflict. A conclusion summarizes Abbot Joseph's teaching on friendship. In schematic form, the chapter takes the following shape:[31]

Introduction (1-5)[32]
  1. True Friendship
      A. The Rules (6.1-2)
      B. A Commentary on the Rules (6.3-13)
          –a codicil on the distinction between love and affection (14)
  2. Conflict within Friendship
      A. The wrong ways to react (15-22)
          –some concluding remarks (23-26.1)
      B. The right ways to respond (26.2-27)
Conclusion (28)

Introduction. Of the various types of human bonds, some are enduring and some not, says Abbot Joseph. The non-enduring types begin well with shared family bonds or similar interests, but a change in interest or a different purpose slowly erodes what unites those in the relationship. The enduring type on the other hand is founded on *virtue* (3.1) which is so durable that a friendship founded on it is not disturbed even by different desires or a contentious clash (3.2). Similarity of interests is not unimportant but the real cement in friendship is what Cassian refers to as "zeal," or more specifically: "an equal zeal" (*pari studio* 16.2). What does our author mean by "zeal"? This word seems to embody a sense of eagerness or intensity for God and therefore for a life of virtue or holiness. If two friends have not this same zeal, the bond of friendship between them will be less strong. In fact, Cassian's next principle is that friendship does not work well among the spiritually weak (3.3). Those with the same zeal also have the "one heart and one soul" of Acts 4:32. This basis of unity, derived from the early Church, is closely related to the list of marks or characteristics belonging to friendship which Cassian next presents. They are: one chosen orientation (*propositum*), one desire (*voluntas*), one willing (*velle*), and one not-willing (*nolle*) (3.4). Of these, only the first–chosen orientation (*propositum*)–is somewhat vague and perhaps purposely so. It refers to a union of minds which would include the same purpose in life, for example, the same desire to seek God or more specifically the same monastic vocation. As for possessing "one desire" or "will" (*voluntas/velle*): this involves death to one's own will, for different wills destroy peace (3.4-5);[33] while the one "not-willing" (*nolle*) presumably refers to the same desire to refuse what is harmful to virtue and/or the friendship.

1. True Friendship

As one author points out, it is regrettable that Cassian says so little about what true friendship is.[34] The "little" is gleaned from the references our abbot makes about his own friendship with Germanus in the first *Conference*[35] and here in the sixteenth where he attests: "we were joined not by a fleshly but a spiritual brotherhood, and that we had always been linked by an indivisible bond from the beginning of our renunciation both in the journey which the two of us had undertaken for the sake of our spiritual soldiery and in the pursuits of the cenobium."[36]

A./B. The Rules for true Friendship (and Commentary)

Let us now turn to the text. Not surprisingly, Cassian's first step is to present the ideal of friendship as expressed in several scriptural passages.[37] These are followed by a list of rules for maintaining friendship (1-2). The rules involve:

1. contempt for worldly possessions
2. restraint of self-will
3. subordination of all things to the good of love and peace
4. never to be angered for any reason
5. desire to calm a brother if he is angry
6. daily reflection on death

What is immediately evident is that the "rules" are rather negative in their approach.[38] But–like the Ten Commandments–rules stated in the negative can lead to a positive living out of the underlying premises. What is needed then is to uncover the positive core of each injunction, which we shall attempt to do, guided by Cassian's own circuitous commentary on the rules.

1. Like his spiritual father Evagrius, the abbot of St. Victor insists that friendship flourishes where friends are not attached to possessions. Avarice–or a too greedy dependence on material things–hinders real friendship for several reasons. For one, its grasping spirit is diametrically opposed to the self-giving spirit of true friendship. And secondly, mutual concern and care for the other is greatly impaired where things take on more value than the other person. At the core of this rule, then, is the premise that people are more important than things. As expressed in Acts 4:32, this principle is the basis for Christian unity (6.4).

2. The lack of attachment to things is paralleled by a detachment to one's own will. Christ is presented as the model here for he did not come to do his own will, but the Father's (Jn 6:38, Mt 26:39). The will–being a fallen will–inclines inwardly, while friendship bends the will outward towards the friend in a truly God-like way. The love Christ spoke of in his departing speech: "By this will all men know that you are my disciples, if you have love one for another" (Jn 13:35) is that love which goes beyond the self. My will and desires take back seat to the will and desires of my brothers and sisters (cf. 6.4); my very way of thinking is subordinate to my

friends "point of view" (6.1). Two friends who already possess a common orientation, namely, a common understanding regarding the spiritual journey, are going to know that much of the spiritual road is traversed through hesitation, groping and yielding to one another. This calls for a certain flexibility in the Spirit which has nothing to do with the rigidity associated with self-will. The latter is one of those pitfalls in the journey of spiritual growth which both friends know at the outset needs to be restrained.[39]

3. The third rule "is that he should realize that all things, even those which he considers useful and necessary, must b e subordinated to the good of love and peace."[40] We may state it in this way: relationship is more important than even what is useful and necessary to the individual. Friendship always involves some sacrifices in order to allow the other to take precedence over oneself. In modern colloquial speech we would say: it's not about "me" but about "us." It might be apropos to mention here that even such a term as "relationship" betrays a certain modern approach to the subject of friendship, but without doing an injustice to Cassian's thought. Cassian's phrase "the good of peace" (6.5) or "the good of love and peace" (6.2) between friends expresses the same reality in fifth-century vocabulary.

4. In the fourth rule, we come to our main theme: anger. The rule states that one is never for any reason—just or unjust—permitted to become angry.[41] This at first seems rather unreal or too severe since flare-ups can and do happen among friends without necessarily damaging the relationship permanently. Cassian says as much at the beginning of this treatise: "Once the relationship has begun, neither a difference in desires nor a contentious clash can do it damage."[42] Is he then simply giving an ideal towards which he hopes his readers will aspire? I think not. Cassian has such a high regard for friendship that he sees every conscious moment of annoyance or anger as a deliberate distancing of oneself from a friend. Put in a positive light: if you are fortunate enough to have a friend who never gets angry with you, even when you have been angry or annoyed with him or her, then you are truly blessed. Such a friend is not a weakling who is afraid of you or who does not want to rock the boat of your friendship, rather he (or she) loves you truly as the person you are. Such persons can distinguish between the friend they love and the immediate behavior which they do not endorse. They accept, love and have an attitude of forgiveness before you have even done anything.[43] This level of love is truly God-like, and supremely manifests something of God's own love for us: God is never affronted by our actions; he looks beyond them to the person whom he loves. He knows our less attractive sides, even our dark sides, but he continues to love us and deeply desires that we change from our non-God-like ways. So too, friends who refuse to be angered by our unkindness, possess the kind of divine virtue which Cassian insists is the basis of true friendship. And if two friends have the same mutual regard and level of virtue there is nothing that can come between them.

5. The fifth rule follows upon this loving attitude. If one of the friends has become annoyed, the other immediately desires to calm him. True friends want harmony to reign in their relationship. If one is annoyed with the other, the other

wants to do something about it. If on the contrary, a person has an attitude of "I don't care if he's annoyed," then surely these two are not real friends. There is even an obligation to go to him and put him at peace with "your own graciousness" (*tua mansuetudine* 6.7). As we've seen in Book 8 of the *Institutes*, a refusal to set things right leads to what could be called: "dysfunctional prayer." At the same time, there is in friendship a need simply to tolerate with patience another's inadvertent annoying behavior. When we feel annoyed by some action which is not intended to annoy us, the proper response may be to tolerate the situation, especially if it is something that cannot be changed or might upset the person to be told this (e.g. some quirk of character). To tolerate such, says Cassian, maintains "the tranquility of love and peace" (7). The root of patience is *passio*: suffering and reminds us that being patient with another's anger is a way of redeeming our brothers and sisters.[44]

6. The sixth and final rule is to think of death. This indeed seems rather negative! But it is a very sobering solution and we all know that those who have a terminal illness take life in far greater stride than their brethren who are caught up in minor details which have only this-world significance. Taking a back seat and looking at the "bigger picture" can assuage hurt feelings and allow us to accept things that cease to matter in the light of eternity. Judgment day also looms large when death is contemplated; a look at ourselves from the perspective of the "other world" puts things in perspective and can convict us of our own pettiness.

In summary, Cassian points out that a great dichotomy exists between love and wrath (7)–which is incidentally how the Scriptures depict judgment day. On which side do we want to be? Our author is deadly serious here: love puts us on the side of God who wants the salvation of all while wrath puts us on the side of the devil, the "enemy," who delights in sowing division among those living in harmony (6.7-8).

Returning to the beginning of the rules–as if he were on a spiral staircase, covering the same ground while advancing higher–Cassian underscores the notion of detachment once again. But this time he is less concerned with material things than with an attachment to spiritual reality as perceived by our "spiritual thoughts." The weaker or carnal-minded are separated through attachment to "some paltry and earthly thing" (8), the more advanced are divided over "a difference of perception" (8). Anyone who has lived in a religious community knows what Cassian is addressing. Many are deceived by the temptation that their personal "spiritual" views are not only superior to their brothers' but a reason for keeping them at a certain distance. Cassian suggests an antidote drawn from the desert: *detachment from one's own ideas.*[45] How? The monk *humbly* reveals his thoughts to a mature senior who helps him to avoid the pitfalls of pride (12) and the deception of Satan who disguises himself as an angel of light (11.1). Accepting advice from another is the monastic plumb line which protects the monk from self-deception. Along with humility goes love, specifically God's love poured out in our hearts by the Holy Spirit (13), by which we can love everyone, even our enemies.

At this point, Cassian makes a slight digression. We are commanded to love everyone and yet friendship is something distinct, for it is particular and given only to a few. Love (*agapē*) is different from affection (*diathesis*). He insists that affection is built on virtue and similarity of behavior (14.1), so the division is not between divine love and human affection; rather the difference is at first seen to be a universal love versus a particular love. But the distinction breaks down when he says that even in particular love, there are differences for children love their parents one way, spouses love each other in another, etc. (even apart from the question of virtue). To support his thesis that one can have a greater love or affection for one person than for others, he cites two biblical figures: Jacob who had a preferential love for Joseph (disregarding the fact that his father's preferential love drove his brothers to try and kill him) because Joseph was "a type of the Lord" (14.2); and Jesus who loved John "more" even though by so doing he did not love the other disciples less. Jesus was justified in loving John more because "of the privilege of his virginity" (14.3).[46]

Of all that Cassian says about love and friendship, this part seems to be the most problematic. There is a lack of clarity in his thought for one. For example, he bases his premise that one person can be loved more than another on the fact that the person loved is more virtuous. But the example he then gives does not support this, namely that parents love their children unequally–as if parental preference was normally based on virtue. The premise is also not supported by a closer look at the scripture texts he cites: Jacob is hardly being commended for showering gifts and a special affection upon only one of his sons; and the inspired text never says that Jesus loved John *more than* the others. Cassian may be confusing a natural *attraction* (or a *feeling of closeness* due to an understanding of one person more than another), with love for that person. Parents may understand or even feel closer to one child more than to another, but what virtuous parent doesn't love all of his or her children equally?

Furthermore, the idea that love is legitimately given unequally has theological consequences. Presenting both Jesus and parents as legitimately loving one or some more than others, could easily give rise to the idea that God loves some more than others. A god who holds back his love from some of his children does not seem like the Christian God. Most spiritual writers today would probably agree with me that God loves all his children equally, even if some are closer to him on account of their virtue. Closeness brings with it an experiential knowledge that one is loved, as John realized. But this is not the same as saying that Jesus loved him *more* than the others, or that God loves some more than others.[47] I suspect that Cassian is trying to express the reality of levels of human closeness as something which legitimately belongs to the Christian's search for God. But his attempt to justify and ground a diversity of human love in Christ's own actions needs to be thought out more carefully than is done in this section.

2. Conflict within Friendship

E contra! The second half of the treatise makes an abrupt transition from love to its contrary. The first section presents five examples of the wrong way for a monk to react to a brother's anger. The examples pulsate with real life situations as Cassian allows some of his own irritation to surface at the behavior he describes. Several of the situations are rather bizarre, tempting one to smile at the stupidity portrayed, except for the fact that the existential element provokes more sadness than glee.

A. Wrong ways to react

1. The first example might be labeled: "false spiritual demeanor." When a conflict occurs, instead of humbly saying a soothing word, the monk withdraws and begins "to sing some verses of the psalms in order to conceal the mental annoyance that has arisen from the anger caused by whatever the disturbance may have been."[48] These brothers display stubbornness, pride and spiritual self-righteousness. They deny responsibility for their brother's annoyance, disdain Christ's command to be reconciled, and are ashamed to be humbled. The remedy is for them to humble themselves and be considerate to the other. Again, Cassian's oft-repeated warning reappears: God will not accept your prayer if you disdain your brother and hide behind the false security of thinking that: the conflict is his problem and no concern of mine (16.1-2).

2. Refusal to accept apologies. The next case describes a brother who, overly sensitive to a remark, refuses to accept the apologies and even the pleading for forgiveness of the one who offended him. He thinks he has the right to be so wounded because a *brother* who should have known better has done this. If a pagan had done it, he would forgive him, but a *brother*... it's impossible! Cassian points out though that the scriptures condemn such a person for Christ does not say that we should be reconciled with *strangers*, but with our *brothers* (cf. Mt 5:23). The abbot of St. Victor lashes out at the stubbornness of such and "their dull and brutish minds" (17.3).

3. The contemptuous silence. Another false response is to act thus: "when we are aroused, we disdain to respond but mock our irritated brothers with a bitter silence or by a derisory movement or gesture in such a way that we provoke them to anger more by our taciturn behavior than we would have been able to incite them by passionate abuse."[49] Such a person considers himself utterly blameless before God for he has done nothing which would condemn him according to the judgment of human beings. Cassian is particularly irritated with this monastic scoundrel. His spiteful attitude is a mockery of real virtue. Instead of calming the annoyance in his brother's heart, his silence provokes it, revealing his own lack of peace and giving the lie to his own calm demeanor. The remedy is to understand that behavior is linked to intention. Our actions might seem virtuous, but the disdainful attitude towards our brother connotes a hidden vice. Cassian is particularly strong in declaring that such a person deserves to be cursed for his duplicity.

4. The fourth example, Cassian says, would not be worth mentioning–presumably because it seems rather far-fetched–except that he knows it exists and therefore needs to warn against it. There are monks who when they are aroused to

anger, simply stop eating. It is as if their wrath gives them extra energy to do what they ordinarily cannot do, namely: fast. Again, a false facade hides the root of this vice, which is pride. Since the fast is not done with the right intention, Cassian calls it a sacrilege which only increases their sin (19.1-2).

5. The last example has some of the same elements demonstrated in the other cases, but in a unique form. In this case, the monk actually provokes someone to anger and then plays the victim feigning a counterfeit patience. His actions after the provocation seem holy, even to the point of offering the other cheek if he is struck. But his underlying intention is anything but virtuous. The fruit of his actions reveal the real intention. Is he spreading mildness and patience or stirring up rage and impatience? (20-22.1) Jesus is our model of patience and mildness (22.2), since he possessed an outer *and* an inner attitude of humility and submission. Furthermore, real mildness conquers rage and does not provoke others (22.3).

Cassian concludes this section with several remarks. First, these wrong ways of reacting to anger reveal a person's spiritual weakness. Since "one weak person never puts up with another weak person," [50] it takes a spiritually strong person to submit to another. It is the weak who sow discord, the strong sow peace. We are now closer to understanding Cassian's central theme that friendship requires a strong and stable love and cannot exist except among men of the same virtue and chosen orientation (24). And what about the weak? asks Germanus. Abbot Joseph responds in a straightforward way: They should change or depart: someone else's magnanimity is no excuse for the continuance of their behavior (26.1).

B. Right ways for friends to respond

As our abbot lays out five appropriate ways to help maintain friendship in a moment of conflict, one is reminded of the "skills to learn" in the various self-help books, at least in the sense that they offer "tools" for staying in relationship. [51] The earlier rules dealt with a certain mentality one should have in the friendship, while these suggestions guide a person through a moment of conflict. The skills listed below are not well delineated in the text and another reader might very well come up with a different number; we have discerned five which stand out as needing to be mentioned. The number five also offers a positive parallel to the five erroneous ways to react. In the hypothetical scenario which the skills presume, a friend has just hurled an insulting remark or in some way has mistreated you. What is the proper response?

1. *Do not react; be silent; stay calm* (26.2). The first point is to do the opposite of what one is tempted to do. Agitation and more excitement will only make the situation worse. Staying calm and silent will help to reduce the tension, or at least not add to it. Cassian insists that the external tranquility must be met with an interior one as well. One does not put on an act while either seething underneath or killing the feelings in a "I don't care attitude" (cf. above: Wrong ways to react #1). Total peace inside and out is the proper response to your friend.

2. *Think of your friendship*. Cassian knows that such calm is not easy and so adds some ways to achieve the calm. One way is to take yourself out of the present moment and "recall the joy of past love" and "look forward to the restoration of peace"[52] speedily taking place, foreseeing the "sweetness of a soon-to-be amity."[53] In other words, let the joy of friendship replace the momentary bitterness caused by your friend's words. *Wanting* a reconciliation is important for moving towards one as soon as possible.

3. *Restrain yourself with discretion.* Although this suggestion sounds like a repeat of the first, the introduction of discretion adds an important note: "contain every moment of wrath and temper it with discretion" (27.1). Now the mind takes control like a helmsman fortified with the memory of past and future harmony and the desire for reconciliation as soon as possible. With some rational governance, the emotional side of human nature experiences a sobering sense of restraint, or so at least thought the ancients. Discretion–the queen of virtues in monastic literature–brings to the particular situation the sense of knowing how best to respond here and now.

4. *Be a broad harbor of love.* But with all the restraint and wisdom in the world, there is still the need to deal with the bitterness caused by our friend's anger. It hurts. How is one to swallow that? Cassian conjures up a picture of a harbor receiving into itself the tension of storm-tossed waves. In the same way, we should enlarge our hearts "receiving the adverse waves of wrath in the broad harbor of love" (27.2). Real love–which is an ingredient in every friendship–"suffers all things, endures all things" (1 Cor 13:7); love is by nature compassionate which gives it the "breath of forbearance and patience" (27.2). In such a harbor, anger disappears, like embraced waves.

5. *Yield and submit.* Cassian is now at the center of the issue, having taken his reader from external restraint to internal calm, then from the mind to the heart. Now he is at the core of the person: his identity and sense of worth. This moment in the conflict might be paraphrased thus: how does one respond spiritually in this situation in order to profit the most from it? The abbot of Marseilles directs us to yield to our friend's upsetting behavior with a "humble and tranquil mind" recognizing that "we deserve (*dignos*) mistreatment,"[54] in whatever form it takes (*qualibet*). A person is now being asked to rethink out who he or she is, around the key word: *dignos*. Cassian is insinuating that the human *dignity*–hurt by the insult– is really governed by an element of pride hidden in the depths of the soul. He knows well that if this pride is squelched, anger will disappear entirely even from the deepest recesses of the human person. It is true that another's anger has an incredibly subtle way of getting to this false center of self: our pride, which when aroused cries out "who do you think you are, talking to me like that?" "Do you think you can treat *me* like that?" Cassian is suggesting that we substitute that demon of untruth with the salutary truth of our own real worth (*dignos*). What might that be? He does not elaborate; he only reminds us that as sinners we deserve such mistreatment *qualibet*. Since we were created out of nothing, at base we are nothing, so why are we grasping after the "nothing" of our being and insisting that another

acknowledge it as if it were something? If Christ did not grasp after his own divinity or humanity (Phil 2), should I grasp after my own "nothingness"? And if that is not sobering enough, I have merely to think of my own sins and realize that enduring another's wrath is really minuscule compared to what I deserve. Yielding and submitting may do much, not only in maintaining the friendship, but in purifying a false sense of dignity.

The Conference ends with the central theme repeated at various points throughout: "true harmony and an indivisible fellowship exist among men of faultless behavior, who share the same virtue and chosen orientation."[55] Thus mutual vision and virtue are the two pillars on which Cassian sets the bridge of spiritual friendship. If either are missing or weak, the bridge will collapse; if they are strong, it will endure...and bring both friends to God.

Conclusion

Cassian's purpose throughout is spiritual growth in perfection, i.e. in "purity of heart" which brings the monk to the threshold of the kingdom of heaven. Initially, the monk familiarizes himself with certain monastic practices and then begins seriously to work on his vices. This is the road map on which we locate Cassian's discussion of anger: it is presented as one of the eight deadly sins which the monk must rid himself of if he is to be pleasing to God and make spiritual progress. It is a particularly fierce and deep rooted sin which calls for radical surgery and a high degree of personal honesty in dealing with it.

In choosing to continue his treatment of anger in the context of spiritual friendship in *Conference* 16, the abbot of Marseilles is doing something very particular. The author of the *Conferences* has often been criticized for his frugal remarks on the positive merits of spiritual friendship versus his rather lengthy exposition on the dangers of anger in friendship–all seemingly rather negative to the whole discussion of friendship. But in defense of Cassian, his purpose is less on friendship in itself than on its impact on community life.[56] We shall return to this in a moment. First let us give due credit to his presentation of friendship. Although there are some restrictions on friendship noted especially in the *Institutes*,[57] Cassian opens the door to friendship in a way which goes beyond such legislators as Pachomius and Basil.[58] By dedicating a *Conference* to the topic, a strong horizontal note on relationships in monasteries has been introduced into the fabric of monastic literature which is otherwise heavily vertical in its approach. The two references to his deep friendship with Germanus indicate that he was no less capable of valuing friendship than were Augustine or Sulpicius Severus, but he lacks the same ability to express his feelings as do the latter. Nevertheless, this *Conference* establishes the value of friendship within the cloister and even implies that life in the monastery among the brethren is one of various degrees of friendship. His concern is that friendships are integrated into the monastic discipline; with that caveat: "Carefully disciplined friendship that does not threaten community is seen as an acceptable part of the discipline of the cloister in the West."[59]

As regards anger, the decision to align it with friendship could not have been a haphazard one. In the arena of spiritual growth, the moments of real advancement are often intimate ones involving other human beings. Certainly the loving support of a senior, to whom a junior discloses his thoughts, is a welcome bridge which conducts the junior to higher grounds. So too, the element of love, already present in every friendship, is another bridge beckoning the quarreling monks to look beyond themselves. The solitude that a person might feel at a moment of crisis involving anger–always involving a choice between himself and the other–is thus made less absolute by the presence of the friend. Spiritual friendship is therefore a blessing which means that every effort should be made to die to oneself so that the relationship lives and thrives. Another reason for the alignment of anger with friendship may be to underscore the impact of anger on community life. Cassian's concern is not only on anger's effect on one or two individuals, but also its *impact on the whole community*. Disharmony between two individuals has repercussions on the larger group. If, as St Benedict says, we go all together to God, then both horizontal and vertical harmony are vital to that journey.

Therefore, in approaching *Conference* 16, we should view it from Cassian's wider purpose. It is not to be read as if spiritual friendship were one of the goals of monastic life. And although monastic brochures abound with smiling monks on the cover, no monastery solicits newcomers with captions that read: if you are in need of friends, come to us! Rather, one enters a monastery to grow closer to Christ which inevitably means hard work on the vices. Nevertheless, in the spiritual arena of the monastery, one's friends play a very important and sometimes decisive role in a person's struggle for virtue. In this context, the ability to deal honestly and effectively with one's anger is greatly enhanced by caring friends. By situating his fuller treatment of anger within the context of spiritual friendship, Cassian is saying that this vice–perhaps more than any other–calls for the help of friends.

Notes: Chapter 3

1. For the details and the difficulty in pinning down much of Cassian's history, including his birthplace, see Columba Stewart's Introduction to his *Cassian the Monk,* Oxford University Press, Oxford (1998): 4ff. I am indebted to his work for this historical introduction.

2. From his *On the Incarnation* 7.31. Post-Nicene Father, (series 2) vol. 11. Hendrickson Publishers, Peabody, MA (1994 reprint): 620-621.

3. For this distinction between the "outer person" and the "inner person" see C. Stewart, 30.

4. This approach accords with the chronology of the texts. Cassian wrote the *Institutes* in 419 or shortly thereafter, followed by the first set of *Conferences* (1-10) in the early to mid 420s. See C. Stewart, 16. The second set (11-17) were composed before 426. Cf. George

68   Cassian: Anger & Friendship

Lawless, book review in *Augustinian Studies* 31/1 (2000) 126. Translations from the *Institutes* have been taken from *The Monastic Institutes*, translated by Jerome Bertram, The Saint Austin Press, London, 1999; those from the *Conferences* are by Boniface Ramsey, O.P. *The Conferences*, Paulist Press, Mahwah NJ, 1997.

5. *Ira* (and its cognates: *iracundia*, *iratus*, and *irasci*) as well as *furor* (and *furere*) are used throughout the text. The more violent form of anger: *rabies* is not used, as far as I could determine.

6. Evagrius had also shown the interrelatedness of the vices, but in a less systematic way. The reader will recall that our desert sage had made anger the fruit of avarice and vainglory, while anger in turn brought about depression (*Prak.* 10). The fact that anger could also be caused by another's sadness or depression (*Skem.* 43) is irrelevant to the discussion, for both Cassian and Evagrius are concerned with what vices a person possesses and how that may lead to another vice within the same person.

7. The theme of needing God is constant throughout Cassian's works, often being presumed because the idea is underlined elsewhere. Let us note at the beginning that, in the Christian context, "it is grace which enables us to turn away from anger." Mary Margaret Funk, *A Mind at Peace: The lessons of John Cassian and the Desert Fathers*. Lion Publishing plc. Oxford (1999): 66.

8. See Rom 8:1-17 and 1 Cor 3:1-4.

9. The Platonists divided the human person into body and soul and then the soul into the three faculties designated as "rational," "irascible," and "desiring." Cassian follows this system which he learned from Evagrius. See C. Stewart, 64-65. *Conf.* 4.10-11 shows that Cassian is aware of the different meanings of the word "flesh" but he seems deliberately to interpret it as "fleshly desires" rather than of sinful desires in general. See also Boniface Ramsey, O.P. "John Cassian: Student of Augustine." *CSQ* 28 (1998): 12.

10. *Simplex cordis* or Cassian's preferred term: *puritas cordis* (cf: *Conf.* 1.4.3 [CSEL 13 (10:7), i.e. volume 13, page 10, line 7]) is central to his monastic theology, as the proximate goal which the monk strives for in this life. It is a phrase rich in meanings which include: love, monastic perfection, spiritual integrity, freedom from sin, and the possession of a deep peace. See C. Stewart, 38-45.

11. The reader will recall that these are the three nouns found also in Evagrius.

12. [Q]uae omnia aequali sunt a nobis horrore damnanda. CSEL 13 (134:8-9).

13. For example, the exegesis of Eph. 4:26: "Be angry and sin not" in 8.8 has no obvious counterpart and yet is an important part of the chapter.

14. "Blindness disqualifies me from spiritual work, since I am out of relationship with myself, with others and with God." And: "Anger is the most devastating of the thoughts because it leads so quickly and absolutely to blindness. I lose my power to judge rightly." Funk, 66 and 75.

15. This is at least the view of the Origenists who (like Cassian) tended to present the Anthropomorphites "as simple native Copts who came from pagan backgrounds." According to Mark DelCogliano, the real issue seems rather to have revolved around the image of God in man: whether it still exists there after the Fall, and if so, whether it is only in the spiritual soul or in the composite human nature. Those who favored the latter interpretation of Gen. 1:26 (the Anthropomorphites) logically moved to the assumption that it was therefore permissible to "image" God in the mind by a physical representation, since that image is totally consistent with his image stamped in creatures. DelCogliano, "Situating Sarapion's Sorrow: The Anthropomorphite Controversy as the Historical and Theological Context of Cassian's Tenth Conference on Pure Prayer," *CSQ* 38.4 (2003): 416, n.204.

16. [I]ta igitur et de ira dei uel furore cum legimus, non ἀνθρωποπαθῶς, id est secundum humilitatem humanae perturbationis, sed digne deo, qui omni perturbatione alienus est [.] 8.4.3. CSEL 17 (153:27-154:2). In this section, all references beginning with the number 8, refer to *Institutes* 8.

17. Cf.: ...superfluum esse *sine causa* et adiectum esse [.] 8.21. CSEL 17 (164:21-22).

18. Cf.: [M]elius tamen est ita tenere, ut et nouella exemplaria multa et antiqua omnia inueniuntur esse perscripta [that is, without the phrase *sine causa*]. 8.21. CSEL 17 (165:5-6).

19. [C]um dicit : omnis ira tollatur a uobis, nullam penitus uelut necessariam et utilem nobis excepit [.] 8.5. CSEL 17 (154:27-155:2).

20. Cf.: Habemus sane irae ministerium satis commode nobis insertum, ad quod solum eam recipere utile nobis est ac salubre, cum contra lasciuientes cordis nostri motus indignantes infremimus [.] 8.7. CSEL 17 (155:18-21).

21. Cf.: uel certe cum contra hanc ipsam iram, cur nobis aduersus fratrem inrepserit, commouemur et irati letales instigationes eius extrudimus.... 8.8. CSEL 17 (155:26-156:1).

22. Betram's translation of: *ad effectum* scilicet eas noxium *perducentes*. 8.9. CSEL 17 (157:4-5).

23. Although Cassian translates Evagrius' *logismoi* as *vitiae* instead of *cogitationes*, the idea is substantially the same. The term, *vitium*, already had a place in the ascetic tradition of Latin literature (cf. Seneca)–which Cassian is continuing. Nevertheless, in passages such as noted above, he underscores the need to recognize that vice originates in thoughts. For the importance of eliminating the thought of anger according to Cassian, see Funk, 69-82.

24. [F]uror.....spiritus sancti splendidissimum iubar ac si prolatus excludit. 8.12. CSEL 17 (159:16-17).

25 . Repeated as: "flight inflames [wrath] rather than diminishes it" in *Conf.* 16.27.4.

26 . Funk, 71.

27. "Grace anticipates the opportunity and provides the moment that makes reconciliation genuine, heartfelt and lasting." Funk, 82.

28. [C]uius morbi haec erit medicina perfecta, ut primitus credamus nullo modo siue iniustis seu iustis ex causis licere nobis irasci[.] 8.22. CSEL 17 (165:8-10).

29. Boniface Ramsey, O.P. tr. *The Conferences*. Paulist Press, Mahway, NJ (1997): 553. As mentioned earlier (n.4), his translation of the *Conferences* is used throughout.

30. It is also true that the Christian concept of love–which embraces all persons–makes the defining barriers between friends and others less exact. This would be all the more true in a monastery where the monks live as "brothers." Thus the classical tradition of friendship overlaps in Cassian with the Christian ideal of brotherly love. See David Konstan, "The History of Christian Friendship," *Journal of Early Christian Studies* 4.1 (1996): 87-113.

31. For greater detail, see Appendix VII.

32. In this section, the references to *Conference* 16 will presume the number 16 before the chapter and section. Thus 1-5 refers to *Conference* 16, sections 1-5. However in citing the Latin in the endnote, the complete reference will be given.

33. "The union of will required for spiritual friendship, therefore, demands mature self-control and selflessness." Mother A. Fiske, R.C.S.J. "Cassian and Monastic Friendship," *American Benedictine Review* 12 (1961): 201.

34. Ramsey, 553.

35. "...with [Abba Germanus] I was so closely befriended from the very time of our basic training and the beginnings of our spiritual soldiery, both in the cenobium and in the desert, that everyone used to say, by way of pointing out the identity of our companionship and our chosen orientation, that we were one mind and soul inhabiting two bodies": ...cum quo [abbate Germano] mihi ab ipso tirocinio ac rudimentis militiae spiritalis ita indiuiduum

deinceps contubernium tam in coenobio quam in heremo fuit, ut cuncti ad significandam sodalitatis ac propositi nostri parilitatem pronuntiarent unam mentem atque animam duobus inesse corporibus.... *Conf.* 1.1. CSEL 13 (7:17-22).

36. [N]on carnali, sed spiritali essemus fraternitate deuincti, nosque ab exordio renuntiationis nostrae tam in peregrinatione, quae ab utroque nostrum fuerat obtentu militiae spiritalis arrepta, quam in coenobii studio indiuidua semper coniunctione sociatos[.] 16.1. CSEL 13 (439:10-14).

37. For example: "The Lord makes those of one mind to dwell in the house" (Ps 68:6), and: "Behold how good and how pleasant it is for brothers to dwell in unity" (Ps 133:1). This last is cited earlier in the *Conferences* (12.11) to refer to the harmony ("brothers in unity") achieved once the flesh and the spirit have united in the mutual pursuit of chastity. The same verse thus does double duty spiritually symbolizing both the unity and harmony of the interior life as well external spiritual relationships. In regard to Cassian's use of Ps 133:1, see Conrad Leyser, *Authority and Asceticism from Augustine to Gregory the Great.* Clarendon Press, Oxford (2000): 47, n.53.

38. "It is interesting to see that these rules treat the subject more from the negative than from the positive side; that is, they aim more at preserving a friendship from collapse than at promoting it, although of course the former implies that latter." Ramsey, 551-552.

39. "[M]any of [Cassian's] provisions about 'renunciation of self-will' are eminently practical insights into how to make a community function." Brian Patrick McGuire, *Friendship & Community: the Monastic Experience.* Cistercian Publications, Inc. Kalamazoo, MI (1988): 80.

40. [T]ertium est ut sciat omnia, etiam quae utilia ac necessaria aestimat, postponenda bono caritatis ac pacis. 16.6.2. CSEL 13 (443:1-3).

41. We saw the same absolute condemnation of anger when it is expressed towards another human being in the *Institutes,* Book 8.

42. [S]emel initum foedus nec desideriorum uarietas nec contentiosa disrumpet contrarietas uoluntatum. 16.3.2. CSEL 13 (440:26-27).

43. Cf: "I am willing to reconcile even before the other is, this helps to not escalate (*sic*) the situation, becoming a sound basis for a harmonious community." Funk, 71.

44. Funk, 84.

45. The two detachments mentioned in relation to friendship are part of a three-step detachment which Cassian teaches is necessary in order to develop a significant relationship with God: detachment from things, from our own ideas, and from our particular notion of God. See Funk, 21-24.

46. This is the opinion of Jerome (*Adv. Iovinianum* I.26; PL 23 col. 246D-247A), who echoes the apocryphal *Acts of John.* See David Hunter, "The Resistance to the Virginal Ideal in Late-Fourth-Century Rome; the Case of Jovinian," *Theological Studies* 48 (1987): 59. Augustine relates four ideas: Christ's greater love for John, the Lord's words that "he remain until I come" (Jn 21:22) and the Apostle's virginity and contemplative nature (he leaned on the Lord's breast at the Last Supper). Christ's greater love for John stems from the fact that John in his virginal and contemplative nature is a symbol of the life in heaven, "where there will be no marriages," and where a soul will remain in contemplation and love without end (*Tract.*124.7).

47. Cf.: God shows no partiality (Acts 10:34).

48. ...ad dissimulandam mentis suae tristitiam, quae ex indignatione alterutrae conmotionis exorta est...aliquos psalmorum incipiant decantare uersiculos.16.15. CSEL 13 (450:13-14,16).

49. [Q]uia respondere contemnimus lacessiti, sed ita conmotos fratres amara taciturnitate uel motu gestuque inrisorio subsannamus, ut eos magis ad iracundiam uultu tacito prouocemus quam tumida potuissent incitare conuicia[.] 16.18.1. CSEL 13 (452:22-25).

50. [N]umquam enim infirmus sustentat infirmum. 16.23. CSEL 13 (458:15-16).

51. Cf. Funk, 82.

52. ...uel recolat gratiam praeteritae caritatis uel reformandae pacis redintegrationem mente prospiciat[.] 16.26.2. CSEL 13 (459:26-27).

53. Cf:...se ad dulcedinem reseruat concordiae mox futurae[.] 16.26.3. CSEL 13 (459:29).

54. Commenting on St. Paul's injunction to "yield to the wrath [of God]: date locum irae (Rom 12:19), Cassian says: damus locum irae, quotiens conmotioni alterius humili atque tranquilla mente subcumbimus et quodammodo dignos nos qualibet iniuria profitentes inpatientiae saeuientis obsequimur. 27.3. CSEL 13 (460:25-27).

55. ...concordiam ueram et indiuiduam societatem nisi inter emendatos mores eiusdemque uirtutis ac propositi uiros stare non posse. 16.28. CSEL 13 (462.13-15).

56. "Cassian was not concerned with how one monk can love another with affection but with how a community of monks can manage to live together in peace." McGuire, 80.

57. The young monks are forbidden to go off by themselves or to hold hands. The concern is that the monks do not form a clique or any kind of special relationships which could potentially separate them from the larger group. *Institutes* 2.15.

58. McGuire, 81-82.

59. McGuire, 82.

CHAPTER 4

AUGUSTINE: ANGER IN COMMUNITY

A comprehensive study of anger in Augustine would fill a book in its own right. A more modest goal, however, is possible without doing an injustice to this great father's thought because of his general consistency on the subject. We have therefore limited ourselves to three areas which we believe will present a synthesis of his views on anger. In the first we will draw on Augustine's own spiritual journey[1] since it is the source from which he draws out lessons offered to his fellow "travelers;" the journey includes several moments or "signposts" which bear personal witness to Augustine's own struggle with anger. This will be followed by an analysis of anger in the context of his monastic *Rule*. Finally we shall look at the great bishop's pastoral concern regarding anger which surfaces in his *Sermons*, notably those delivered during Lent.

1. AN OVERVIEW OF AUGUSTINE'S JOURNEY[2]

Signposts along the way

- 386   While residing at a rented house in Milan, Augustine hears again the story of Antony of Egypt which leads to his conversion and his decision to live a celibate life in the Church.
- 387   At Easter, Augustine is baptized along with his friend Alypius and his son Adeodatus.
- 388   Returning to North Africa, Augustine turns his family property in Tagaste into a house where he and about 5 companions (Alypius, Severus, Evodius, Honoratus, and Adeodatus) live an ascetic life. The immediate alienation of his own property brings Augustine into closer contact with the Gospel ideal as well as that of Antony of Egypt (who did just that, "Go, sell what you possess..."Mt 19:21).[3] There is no reason to think that this early period is anything but the monastic life. No

doubt they learn through their mistakes, since none of them has had
any previous experience. Possidius, his biographer, says of this period:
"He lived there for God with those who were united with him in fasting, prayers and good works; he meditated on his law day and night."[4]
To these ascetical practices are added chastity and poverty, and they
have an emphasis on studies which is peculiar to them.[5] Augustine is
carefree in this period as we hear from a letter he wrote to a friend
saying that "to be free from business and so be made more like God–
was that for which they now had time."[6] During these three years, he
writes seven treatises.[7]

- 391   Augustine goes to Hippo to recruit a man who is interested in the
monastic life; while there, he is apprehended by the people and almost
forcibly ordained. At Augustine's request, Bishop Valerius gives him
a garden near the church where he establishes a monastery. The men
who join him in this endeavor are laymen who remain lay monks at this
stage. Augustine is the only priest among them.[8]

- 395   Augustine is ordained co-adjutor bishop to Valerius, but not without
the opposition of the Primate of Numidia, Megalius. At this time he
moves out of the garden monastery into the bishop's house, where he
establishes another monastery made up of clerics who live with him in
the episcopal residence.[9]

- 396   Bishop Valerius dies and Augustine succeeds him as Bishop of Hippo.

- 397   Death of Megalius, bishop of Calama. A letter to a friend discloses
Augustine's feelings at the news of the death of his former slanderer.

- ±397   The proposed date for the writing of the *Rule*, known as the *Praeceptum*.[10]

- c.420   Death of Augustine's sister, the superior of the monastery of nuns in
the vicinity of Hippo. Under her successor, Felicitas, a contingent of
angry nuns appeal to their bishop for her removal.

- 422   Date of *Ep*. 20* which recounts the case of Antony, a young monk
whom Augustine appointed some years earlier as bishop of Fussala. He
turns out to be such an ecclesial fiasco that the townsfolk are outraged
by the scoundrel. To a lesser, but real, degree they vent their anger
against Augustine for appointing the inexperienced youth.

- 430   Augustine dies with the Vandals at the gates of Hippo. The Vandal
incursions are responsible for the exodus from that region of many
monks who very likely carried the *Rule* of Augustine to Italy, Gaul and
Spain.[11]

Before turning to Augustine's objective advice to others on the vice of anger
contained in his *Rule* and *Sermons*, we shall revisit several of the incidents mentioned above. The first is the scene at Milan and the impact of Rom 13:13-14 on
Augustine's conversion and pastoral vision; we shall then turn to show Augustine's
response to anger experienced firsthand in two incidents concerning fellow bishops:

namely Megalius of Calama and Antony of Fussala. The case involving the nuns of Hippo will reappear in the section on the *Rule*.

1. *non in contentione et aemulatione.*

This phrase from St. Paul is the middle injunction of Rom 13:13 which effected the famous watershed moment of grace on Augustine in the garden at Milan. Augustine had minutes before heard the story of Antony in the desert: how he had left home, family and all that the world offers, to follow Christ in a spirit of complete abandon. Seized with a positive spirit of jealous zeal, he sees in Antony's resolute action both the epitome of all his aspirations and the glaring truth of his own bondage in the quagmire of fleshly desires. In the struggle which ensues the grace of the inspired words of St. Paul in Rom 13:13 enables Augustine to break out of the darkness of his enslavement into the light of that "day" (cf. Rom 13:11), which is Jesus Christ. These words, then, imprint themselves in his soul in a powerful way. Yet, for all that, Augustine comments on them in relatively few passages of his corpus. Given their link to his own journey in the Lord and related as contention or strife are to anger, our topic can only gain from an examination of a few of these texts.

The earliest and most important text is that of *Letter* 22. Augustine, ordained a priest only a short time before, writes to his friend Aurelius who has himself only recently been made bishop of Carthage.[12] The two men had met in 388 when Augustine, Alypius and Adeodatus disembarked at Carthage on their way to Tagaste. It was fitting for the new band to pay their respects to the ecclesial authorities of the city and to inform them of their allegiance to the Catholic Church. Perhaps they also expressed a desire to be at the disposal of the Church. If Aurelius' "fire for holiness and love of Christ's Church"[13] which Augustine mentions three years later were evident in this Carthaginian deacon from their first meeting, then we can surmise Augustine's joy in finding on his own soil a man of inspiration and support not unlike one whom he had left behind in Milan. At some point, either brought up during this stay or in subsequent letters exchanged after the little band had departed the city and settled into their life of prayer and study at Tagaste, the two great men discussed the need for reform in the Church of North Africa along the lines of Rom 13:13-14.

Now, as a newly ordained priest, catching his breath after the unexpected turn of events his ordination imposed upon him, Augustine takes advantage of the time granted him by his bishop, Valerius, to study the scriptures in preparation for his role of preaching. From *Letter* 22, it is obvious that Augustine has been reflecting on the needs of the Church as the starting point for the direction his preaching will take. His firsthand experience of the Catholic Christian communities of Tagaste and Hippo, and what reaches him about the other cities, incites the priest to write to his friend and lay his soul bare. In doing so, he reverts to Rom 13:13-14 looking into the text as into a mirror: "not in rioting or drunkenness, not in chambering and impurities, not in contention and envy; but put ye on the Lord Jesus Christ, and make no provision for the flesh in its concupiscences." What is immediately apparent to the young priest is that–although the second injunction is taken seriously with transgressors being punished by the Church–the other two vices: namely drunkenness on the one hand and the hostility between persons indicated by the terms: contention/strife and jealousy/envy are so tolerated that they are not even seen as vices (*Ep.* 22.2).

We shall mention briefly the issue of drunkenness, which actually receives most of Augustine's attention in this letter since it is often sacrilegiously associated with honoring the martyrs at their tombs. It seems that the festivities of the saints became an excuse for excessive drinking akin to the celebration of the feast of St. Patrick in worldly circles today. Augustine asks Aurelius to call a council so that the bishops might make a concerted effort to stamp out this practice in North Africa.

The third injunction dealing with strife and jealousy are sins which Augustine finds particular to the clergy (as drunkenness is to the laity). They are rooted in that pride which arises when the honor bestowed on the clergy goes to their head and causes them to believe that they are more than they are before God. Baring his soul, Augustine explains to Aurelius that he himself suffers from the delight which accompanies the praise he receives from others. His remedies are the holy scriptures, and the fear and love of the Lord. He is, therefore, still measuring himself against the initial grace received in his reading of Rom 13:13 at Milan. We usually look only at the second injunction as that which propelled Augustine out of his miry stronghold, but Augustine's conversion did not come to a standstill with amending that one vice...he continued to see in Rom 13:13-14 "a most fitting expression of Christian life"[14] for himself and others. Drunkenness and pride (and its offsprings of contention and envy) are equally dangerous vices which need to be extirpated as well.

The clergy are, presumably, especially susceptible to temptations of envy and pride because their office is inherently honorable. The steps i) from legitimately receiving the honor due one's office to presuming that the honors are personally due one, ii) to envying and opposing those who are perceived as having more, or other, honors, iii) to being at odds with one's brother (or sister) because of these honors.... are all subtle transitions that plague persons of position. Having formerly held an honorable public position himself and now forced into the priesthood, Augustine knew the dangers from the inside: "only one who had declared war on this enemy feels its strength, because, even if it is easy for someone to do without praise when it is denied, it is difficult not to take delight in it when it is offered."[15] The remedy he offers is one which he first used on himself: Go to the scriptures. There particular texts (testimonies) will inculcate into the reader the fear and love of God. The patience and humility which arises from these two virtues will then allow a person to respond to honors in a balanced way: "taking less for himself than is offered, but in any case accepting from those who honor him neither everything nor nothing."[16] The scriptures also teach that whatever is truly praiseworthy in us is a gift from God to whom the honor is to be directed. These salutary injunctions, Augustine informs Aurelius, he repeats to himself daily. Therefore, in this early letter Augustine is targeting hostility between human beings as a major obstacle to living an authentic Christian life. As we will see, whatever the cause of the hostility, the accompanying emotion of anger rears its head and tends to continue and increase the nascent opposition. At the core, strife (*contentione*)–which is singled out with precision in this letter–should be a frame of mind avoided by anyone who aspires to put on the mind of Christ.

Turning now to the other passages where the Pauline "treble injunction"[17] is again cited, our first citation chronologically, appears in the treatise *Contra Epistolam Manichaei* written in 396 A.D. As a one-time Manichee himself, Augustine felt a certain concern for his former co-religionists and a responsibility to awaken them from their errors, as he himself had been awakened. Perhaps also meant as a defense of his Catholic identity, the letter set out to refute the sect's doctrinal tenants, including dualism and their false claims on Christ and the Holy Spirit. But Augustine's method of refutation is not intent on directing bitter rebukes at the enemy with the intention of winning a victory of words. He tells us in the first chapter that God wishes erring men's recovery rather than their discomfiture, their amended ways rather than their destruction. Augustine's aim therefore is "to attain our end in your correction, not by contention and strife and persecutions, but by kindly consolation, by friendly exhortation, by quiet discussion."[18] In order to accomplish this, the cultivation of gentleness, patience and meekness will be virtues that must accompany his teaching.[19] Here then is laid down the proper principles for religious debate, i.e. one cannot be intent on winning arguments but on winning souls. Therefore, *contentione* (Rom 13:13) is not allowed even when the opposition is between truth and error, faith and heresy. The proximate object of debate and apologetics might be truth, but the ultimate object is brotherhood in the one faith. For a man who will be debating issues throughout his life, Augustine recognized early on that truth mingled with love and gentleness does more to win souls than truth delivered with false zeal.[20]

The next two occurrences are found in sermons, one delivered at the beginning of Lent, the other during the Easter octave. They both deal with the transformation in Christ that the Christian should be conscious of during these two holy seasons. Augustine offers Rom 13:13 as a salutary approach to the season of Lent which is a time "to crucify the old-self" (*Sermon* 205.1) by purging out lingering vices. The list of vices mentioned this particular year[21] are the three disorders which St. Paul excoriates in the Romans' passage, namely disorders in the area of 1) food and drink, 2) sexual activities, 3) personal relationships, specifically where animosity has set one person against another. Although he does encourage his people in many of the Lenten sermons to fast, and to fast correctly (not merely substituting one dainty for another), he does not need to convince them that fasting is spiritually advantageous; it seems quite the norm to expect them to fast. The second injunction generally receives passing mention, and reminds Augustine to encourage married couples to abstain from legitimate conjugal pleasure during Lent for the sake of penance, a practice which again seems to be firmly in place. The third injunction brings up a topic which Augustine often lingers over since the area of personal relationships is one which calls for ongoing conversion. In this sermon, Augustine warns his congregation against envy and quarrels. They should not envy a natural gift which one of their brothers or sisters possesses because to do so is tantamount to mocking God who has in his providence bestowed this gift as he pleases. Rather, at least in regard to spiritual goods, one should "regard as your own what you love and admire in your brother and sister"[22] because belonging to the same Body, what one possesses, all possess. Of even more import (*prae caeteris*), the community should cease quarreling and forgive their offenders (205.3). As the local civil magistrate, called upon to make secular as well as ecclesiastical judgments, Augustine was well aware of the North African tendency to react at the "slightest provocation."[23] Since the need to cease from quarreling was as continual as it was basic, Augustine returns to the topic periodically displaying his pastoral care.

In our discussion of anger, it will be good to keep this pivotal verse in mind (Rom 13:13) as one which at the beginning of his journey taught Augustine the inherent incompatibility between following Christ and living at odds with others. Even when Rom 13:13 is not quoted, it still can be seen as the basis for his condemnation of anger or of any feeling of animosity between persons, along with other passages in the New Testament which castigate vices that put brothers or sisters at odds with each other.

The transformation into Christ the Light is the theme of the Easter *Sermon* 230. This sermon dovetails nicely with the previous Lenten exhortation, since one is a commentary on the first half of Romans 13:13-14 and the other continues Paul's thought that the spiritual movement is out of the darkness of destructive behavior into the glorious light of Christ: "Let us walk honorably as in the day, not in revelry and drunkenness... not in wrangling and rivalry (*non in contentione et aemulatione*); but put on the Lord Jesus." The decision to deny oneself for the sake of the kingdom leads, then, to Christ assuming our lives into his own, so that "walking in the day" becomes walking *in Christ*. And if Christ is the day, then we too become that day: "If you follow that advice, you can sing with your whole heart: *This is the day which the Lord has made.* What you are singing, you see, is what you are, if you are living good lives."[24] The season of Lent carries the sinner out of the darkness of his or her degenerate habits into the Easter light of Christ's resurrected life, a life which pulsates within the believer in a way which enables this person to live drastically differently, as different as light is from darkness. The believer becomes as transparent and good as the "day."

2. Episcopal altercations
a. Megalius: A lesson in forgiveness

Our next two incidents in Augustine's life concern fellow bishops. The first brings us back to Augustine's early life as a cleric: the aging Valerius knows his days are limited. Desiring to keep his gifted priest in Hippo and fearing that Augustine would be snatched from his grasp before his own death, Valerius secretly plots to secure Augustine's episcopal ordination together with the right to succeed him as Bishop of Hippo. With at least the tacit approval of Aurelius, the Primate of Carthage–but without informing the Primate of Numidia, Megalius of Calama– Valerius calls together some neighboring bishops, including Megalius.[25] With prelates and people assembled in the Great Basilica, Valerius surprises everyone with his plan, to the consternation of Augustine, but to the joy of the citizens of Hippo. The Primate Megalius, however, not the least bit pleased, flies into a rage.[26] For one, he is surely miffed at Valerius for going over his head;[27] but the intensity of the reaction points to more, that is to an unresolved reservoir of animosity perhaps due to jealousy,[28] or perhaps to Augustine's former association with the now-imperially-condemned Manichaenism.[29] Besides, Augustine's pre-baptismal days gives Megalius reason to believe a vicious rumor that the young priest had sent a love token to a married woman. Whatever lay behind the anger, the senior prelate of Numidia vehemently opposes the consecration. The accused priest is quite naturally disturbed by the whole affair. A commission set up to investigate the case finds him innocent: the "love token" was a harmless *eulogia,* a kind of blest keepsake commonly exchanged and no cause for scandal. And in regards to his Manichaean past, we can imagine Augustine employing his greatest rhetorical skills in conveying the sincerity of his conversion for it convinces Megalius that he has over-reacted.[30] To his credit, the aged prelate asks Augustine's pardon and acquiesces to the proposed episcopal consecration, over which he himself now presides. Nevertheless, the incident teaches Augustine a lesson both in the dangers of slander and in forgiving. When Megalius dies a few years later, the pain and anger associated with the memory of the incident surfaces again, as is evidenced in this letter to his friend, Profuturus:

> I have no doubt that you have already heard that the primate Megalius has died.... There are scandals, but there is also a refuge. There are sorrows, but there are also consolations. And you very well know, best of brothers, how amid these trials we must be on guard for fear that hatred for anyone should take hold of the depths of our heart and not allow us to *pray to God in our room with the door shut* (Mt 6:6), but should rather close the door on God himself. But it sneaks up on us since no one who is angry thinks that this anger is unjust. For, when it takes root in that way, anger becomes hatred while the sweetness added as if from righteousness holds it longer in the cask until the whole becomes sour and spoils the cask.... You certainly know the care and concern with which I write these words if you recall what you spoke about with me recently on a certain journey.[31]

Augustine's "care and concern" is great indeed, but enough is said to indicate his struggle to conquer the natural feelings of anger against Megalius for his slanderous accusation. He is, even in these early years, subtly aware of the temptingly sweet but destructive dangers of anger which can so easily turn into hatred. There is also the hint of anger's power to nullify prayer, a theme which will become central to his thoughts on anger and will be explored more fully further on. Note that his careful attention to root out of his heart any ill will towards Megalius which might suggest itself–even justly–is reflected in the discreet avoidance of any uncomplimentary remark aimed against the recently deceased primate.

b. *Fussala: Antony and his victims: compounded rage*

The story of Antony is colorful, but sad. It begins with a desperate need for a bishop in a rural area which was previously Donatist but has recently been reunited to the Catholic Church. Under pressure, Augustine chooses a young monk from his lay monastery who could speak Punic, a necessary qualification for this peripheral diocese. The choice is an unhappy one, however, for the lad (merely twenty years old) lacks maturity and ecclesiastical experience. With little or no supervision on a daily basis, the honors of the episcopal office go to the young man's head and turn him into an obnoxious, grasping thief of his own congregation. Dictating orders, making useless promises and monetary transactions which are never respected, Antony victimizes his parishioners until they refuse *en bloc* to accept his authority. The bishops of Numidia attempt to discipline the rascal and to pacify the populace during some unhappy years leading up to 422 A.D. Augustine's *Letters* 209 and 20* leave the issue at the doors of Rome where the guilty prelate has gone to appeal his case to Pope Boniface. The details given in *Ep.* 20* indicate what a thorn in the side this young man is to Augustine. The latter feels particularly responsible for the chaotic situation because it was he who had suggested Antony. Augustine admits in the letter that he had not known the lad well, but on the advice of the Prior of the monastery, he had decided under pressure of time to risk imposing a raw and unknown recruit on the poor people of Fussala. It is these latter whose justified anger would reveal a side to Augustine not normally evident. As combative as the Bishop of Hippo can be, he dares not on this occasion enter the town of Fussala and look the citizens in the eye.[32] Is he afraid of being lynched? The inhabitants of Fussala are certainly at their wits end with Antony and intensely angry at the Bishop of Hippo for his part, but Augustine never hints that his life was in danger. It seems rather that the emotionally charged situation unnerves him. He is intrinsically a man of peace. He can fight when the good of the Church demands that he defend its doctrine and rights, but he does not go looking for a fight. As we have seen, even in debate he prefers to achieve his end by "quiet discussion" rather than by "contention and strife."[33] It does not surprise us then that he is choosing to avoid open conflict. Since, in the present case, his presence would serve only to stir up the angry Fussalians further, a bit of discretionary distance is judged the prudent course of action.

Conclusion

What Augustine legislates in his *Rule* and preaches in his *Sermons* about anger derives from his own experience. Besides the fact that he himself had felt the emotion of deep resentment against a detractor and had to deal with justified anger aimed at himself, there are instances in his life which bear out the truth that the

"Africans frequently manifested a litigious temperament."[34] More instances will be encountered in the next section. The importance of the experiences is seen in Augustine's integration of a new experiential knowledge of himself empowered by the grace of God. The same power which broke the bonds of carnal habit is also present in situations where a human being finds himself (or herself) tempted to such vices as drunkenness, jealousy or anger. Let us now turn to Augustine's advice on anger contained in the very specific context of his monastic communities.

❖   ❖

II: ANGER IN THE CONTEXT OF THE RULE

General Introduction: Augustine's Model of Monasticism

Augustine's preferred word for "monk" is "servant of God" or "one who serves God."[35] The expression would apply to either of the two male communities which Augustine established in the ecclesial complex.[36] As for the origin of the second monastery, Augustine himself tells us that he could have chosen to stay in the garden monastery even as bishop, but he knew that the bishop is expected to be constantly giving hospitality and mingling with all kinds of people. Since all this coming and going is not proper for a monastery of monks, he moved into the episcopal residence, leaving–no doubt–a trustworthy "senior" in charge of the lay monks.[37] His own desire to continue to live the monastic life in community with others, led him to make a unique proposal: he called the priests together and asked them if they were willing to live a celibate life in common and to dispossess themselves of all their property and goods, boldly promising them that they would in turn possess God.[38] To a man, they declared themselves ready.[39]

Garden Monastery: Most monks came from the class of laborers (*Op. Mon.* 33)[40] and would therefore have been accustomed to working.[41] Augustine felt strongly that all monks should use their spare time not in just sitting still but rather in ascetical exercises and works of mercy. Besides the allotted times for work, the monks also chanted the divine office, and spent time in private prayer[42] and *lectio divina*, i.e. a kind of spiritual reading for which the librarian would supply them with books from the library. They also listened silently to spiritual reading in the refectory during meals. Their lives were simple in food and dress, where self-denial was the norm but without "painful want."[43] Augustine's asceticism lacked the fanaticism that sometimes accompanied the more Eastern types of monasticism.[44] For the most part, the lay monks stayed in their monastery, but they could be called on to be priests and so serve the community. Instead of the monastery being a stepping stone to more solitude–as with Cassian's–Augustine's was often a venue to more active ministry, not unlike the monasticism of St. Martin (+397) who died saying: "Lord, if your people need me, I will not refuse the labor."[45]

Once he entered the lay monastery, the choice to be a priest or not did not lie with the monk. This was due to the difference in the early Church between the vocation to be a monk and a priest. A monk felt an interior call to leave the world and follow the Gospel in a more radical way. A priest was, instead, chosen by the church for ministry, often by the people in conjunction with the bishop. Just as today no one would say: I think I have a vocation to be a bishop; so in the early Church, it was considered unseemly to put oneself forward to be a priest. (This is not to say that there was no politicking: the wealthy sometimes pressed to have the honor bestowed on one of their sons, and bishops would sometimes choose their relatives regardless of the candidate's suitability.) Monasteries thus became an asset in the process of selection of bishops. The candidates were at least educated, with some degree of piety and usually willing to serve. Also, having been under the eye of a superior or a bishop for sometime, their character would, generally speaking, be better known, though even here mistakes were made. In this sense, monasteries were a kind of fish pond, from which to hook perspective priests and bishops.[46] This was true of Augustine's monastery–although he was careful, he says, to choose only the best.

Clerical monastery: We actually know more about life among the clerics than about Augustine's lay community. The clerics' life was more specifically marked by service to the Church. Although they would have had more contact with the laity than the monks had, Augustine nevertheless took care to shelter them from the continual traffic which beat a path to his office. While his door remained open as a sign of welcome and service, the doors of his clergy remained closed.[47] As regards women visitors, he made a policy of not meeting any of them in the house–including his sister and his nieces, all of whom were nuns; these were greeted outside his reception room and always in the presence of another person.[48]

In the refectory, Augustine and his clergy ate vegetables and cereals, while meat was allowed the visitors. Wine was also served daily in the bishop's house,[49] while it seems to have been allowed to the lay monks only on Saturday and Sunday. The vessels were made from earthenware, wood and marble. Only the spoons were silver. There were also restrictions in speech at table. Some reading as well as talking was the norm,[50] while cursing and gossiping were unacceptable: anyone who swore at table ("by God," "God knows it," etc.) lost one glassful of wine (*Vita* 25). To deter gossipers, Augustine had carved into the table the saying:

> *"Whoever thinks that he is able,*
> *To nibble at the life of absent friends*
> *Must know that he's unworthy of this table."*

Once, when some intimate friends of his, fellow bishops, were forgetful enough of his verses as to gossip, he upbraided them so sternly that he lost his temper, and said that either they should rub these verses off the table, or [if they were to persist in their gossip] that he would get up and go to his room in the middle of the meal.[51]

Augustine demanded that he be given nothing personally that he couldn't share with his brothers, including clothing–wanting nothing that would make him less poor than they. He once declared that the income of his bishopric was more than twenty times the amount of the little legacy which he had given away in Tagaste, but all went into the hands of others and ultimately found its way to the deacons for distribution. Actually, he left all the administration and management of temporal things entirely to others. When the yearly statements of income and expenditure were read over, he scarcely troubled to listen to them,[52] having no interest; yet he could raise money when needed. But his concept of poverty was not fanatical; it depended rather on a person's needs–as we will see–and for Augustine, one of these needs was always a good library.[53]

Creating this clerical monastery, perhaps the first seminary, was to be a great service to the Church, for it came to be an elite group, educated under Augustine's supervision, in his own house and largely by his own efforts. There was quite obviously a shortage of priests with adequate intellectual training.

The lay monastery became then a fount from which to draw out the potential deacons and priests for ministry in his churches. Eventually, other dioceses began to ask for bishops from among Augustine's priests. Possidius says that about ten future bishops came out of Augustine's monastery and when they took possession of their own see, some of these set up similar monasteries there. Possidius himself was one of Augustine's former monks and later bishop of Calama. After his own ordination Augustine spent the next thirty years and more of his life writing, preaching, judging court cases as was normal for a bishop of his day, and generally living a very busy life. He often complains in his writings that he lacks the leisure that he once had to read and to study. In a letter to Abbot Eudoxius, at the island monastery of Capraria, Augustine exhorts the abbot and his monks to pray for him, to keep their resolution to be monks and to persevere to the end. But then he adds: "if Mother Church has need of your help, do not accede to her request with eager pride, nor refuse it with slothful complacence.... Do not prefer your peaceful retirement to the needs of the Church as she gives birth to children; otherwise, you would find no way to be born, if no good men were willing to minister to her."[54]

Introduction to the Rule and Anger

Of the eight brief chapters which make up the *Rule* of Augustine, one entire chapter is dedicated to dealing with anger. This is enough to indicate its importance to its monastic legislator and a reason to probe further into his mind on the matter. Embedded within the *Rule*, chapter six is meant to be read, analyzed and plumbed as an integral part of the text. Therefore, after beginning broadly with Augustine's theology of community, this study will undertake an analysis of the *Rule*, with special emphasis on chapter six. We will also be drawing on his other monastic writings in order to fill out his monastic theology as presented in the *Rule*. Although throwing our net into the waters of the other monastic writings will somewhat delay our arrival at the shore of anger, the final picture will be a more complete appreciation for how Augustine understands the way that this vice undermines the essence of what a Christian community is.

Augustine's theology of community flows from his ecclesiology.[55] The same love which binds the members of the Church into the one body of Christ is operative in the monasteries, forming the brothers or sisters into a single entity. The foundation for the monastic community is the primitive Church in the Acts of the Apostles, described as having "one heart and one soul"[56] and "possessing all things in common" (Acts 4:32). This unity, founded on love and dispossession, provides Augustine with nearly all of his monastic theology. The link between the monasteries and the primitive Church is first of all an historical one: fundamentally, the monasteries owe their very existence to the larger Church. Comparing the ointment which descended upon the beard of Aaron (cf. Ps 132:2) to the Holy Spirit's descent upon the Apostles at Pentecost, Augustine comments: "If the ointment had not descended [upon the Apostles], we would have had no monasteries...the Church followed and begat the monasteries."[57] As we shall see, the first community in the Acts is also an inspiration and model for Augustine's own monastic communities. There is a third connection as well: in Hippo the link between the monastery and the Church is united in the very person of Augustine, the monastic bishop, caught up in the affairs of the world and the Church, yet ever the monk at heart. This is borne out in the same letter cited above to Abbot Eudoxius in which Augustine expresses his consolation in living the monastic life in the heart of others. "We are one body under one Head, so that you are care-worn in us and we are care-free in you" (*Ep.* 48.1).[58]

In speaking of monastic life, Augustine goes from depicting the idyllic community to describing the epitome of hard core reality, with all its warts and wrinkles. The first is a model to strive for, the second addresses the problems encountered along the way. The *Rule* is in fact a mixture of the two, the ideal and the real. Our study will follow Augustine from his vision of the ideal to the more practical considerations which govern community life, including his treatment of anger. There is an inherent wholeness and organization in the work which is centered around the concept of unity in community, specifically: what makes community, what breaks it down, and what repairs it.[59]

I. What "makes" Community

The two basic elements of community life which Augustine garnered from Acts 4:32 are unity as an effect of love and harmony, and spiritual poverty as a consequence of a voluntary dispossession and sharing of goods. These two factors furnish the foundation for building a Christian community. Let us look at how each of these are theoretically and practically proposed in the *Rule* as a guide for monastic living.

1. Love and Harmony

The first words of the *Rule* make abundantly clear Augustine's vision of common life:

The chief motivation for your sharing life together
is to live harmoniously in the house
and to have one heart and one soul seeking God.[60]

The life of the first Christian community in Jerusalem provides the inspiration for those who "share life together in a house" (*congregati in domo*), i.e. in a particular time and place. All precepts in the *Rule* are intended to support this harmonious life. Our first element of investigation is therefore to ask: what is the nature of this harmony, this living with "one mind and one heart" which the *Rule* enjoins on its members?

As early as 388, only a year after his baptism, Augustine describes the life of the "perfect Christians" who live an ascetic life of fasting and prayer "in perfect harmony," and poverty: "no one possesses anything of his own." But what strikes him above all is the love which is the guiding principle in all they do.[61] Thus early in his Christian life Augustine grasped the essential nature of the double principle of Acts 4:32 for living the fulness of the Christian communal life.[62]

Augustine's addition of *in deum*[63] to the verse from the Acts: "one heart and one soul" finds an echo in the last chapter of the *Rule* where the monks are exhorted to observe the precepts "with love as lovers of spiritual beauty" (8.1). The two references can be seen as a literary inclusion with God as the beginning and the end of the monastic life. But the Lord is also the means, i.e. the one who makes the community able to live in harmony with one mind and one soul. Through the gift of his *grace* he supplies what is lacking to human nature: "the more generous grace of God....enables you not only to renounce marriage, but also to choose living together in harmony under the same roof, so as to have one heart and one soul seeking God."[64] And it is through grace that the monks can observe the *Rule* in freedom, as opposed to the spirit of servitude which characterized the Old Testament stance towards rules and regulations.[65]

"One heart and one soul" is Augustine's preferred phrase for monastic unity, "heart" resonating with the message that unity is the effect of *charity* (*Serm.* 356.8). We find this echoed and expanded in his commentary on Ps 132:1 *Behold how good and pleasant it is for brethren to live together in unity*, where he speaks of that "sweet charity which causes brethren to dwell together in unity."[66] This psalm, says the Bishop of Hippo, begat monasteries, for the idea of living together in this way was an inspiring "trumpet blast" which gathered together those who had been divided. Christian love, however, differs from ordinary human love, having at its core the love of Christ: "None, therefore, grow together as one except those in whom the love of Christ is perfected."[67] Shed abroad in our hearts by the Holy Spirit (Rom 5:5), this love is the unifying force which unites the Father and the Son as well as all Christians in the Church and in monastic life. He is the very love by which they love each other.[68]

The Trinitarian aspect of monastic unity is thus present in Augustine's thought: the monks are "one heart and one mind *in deum*"; they grow together as one in the love of Christ; and it is the very love of the Holy Spirit which is the unifying bond between them.[69] This puts the whole discussion of unity in the supernatural realm, and shows that Augustine is not equating it with mere human friendship. It is true that even in the monastery, we are attracted "to some more eagerly and to others more reluctantly,"[70] but under the grace of God, the frontiers of friendship are expanded to include even our enemies–all the more those with whom one shares a common life and purpose.

Thus at the outset is stated the ideal: community is a life of love and harmony in God. But how is this achieved? Augustine singles out four practices or areas which build up Christian unity in the monastery: mutual respect, harmony of voice and heart, service, and the role of superiors.

a) *Honor God Mutually in Each Other*

> Live then, all of you, in harmony and concord;
> honor God mutually in each other;
> you have become his temples.[71]

In communities such as Augustine's at Hippo, the first requisite for harmony is to establish some degree of equality in an environment where the rich and poor mingle side by side. Augustine tells us that the equalizing element is God himself who calls each to the life and allows them all to live as true *brothers* on an equal footing before him and before each other. This is because he lives and is honored in each one.

b) *Harmony of Voice and Heart*

Common prayer is an essential element in building up a monastic community. Augustine has left two precepts which will help the community prayer to have a unifying effect: first, the monk himself should exhibit a personal alignment between what his voice is singing and what his mind or heart is thinking:

> When you pray to God in psalms, and hymns,
> the words you speak should be alive in your hearts.[72]

The first meaning is that the heart should be attentive to what is being sung so as to avoid distractions. At a deeper level one is to be really receptive to the revelation contained in the inspired verses being sung, so that the life contained in the word of God flows over into the life of those chanting the text and forms them in the same divine source.

The other norm:

> Keep to the prescribed text when you sing:
> avoid texts which are not suited for singing,[73]

seems at the bare minimum to be practical advice on the need to avoid cacophony and confusion during the liturgy. The reference to "prescribed texts" is a reminder that diverse translations of the psalter into Latin existed in Augustine's time. The great monk-bishop himself touched up the translation from time to time. The psalms were, furthermore, popular prayers–used extensively in the liturgy and in private prayer; consequently some of the psalms would have been recited or sung from memory. It would have been quite easy–in an unattentive moment–for a person used to a different translation to sing from memory rather than from the text in front of him (a text chosen in part for its poetic or musical character). Augustine would then be saying in this passage: be attentive to the text and sing what everyone else is singing![74]

Another factor may also be at play. As someone who wrote a treatise *On Music,* Augustine would have been aesthetically sensitive to the liturgical chant to want it done well, or at least not carelessly.[75] Anyone who has had some experience in singing the psalms in a monastic choir knows that the dynamics of community life overflow into the choir. If there is tension in community, the tension is obvious in the way the monks or nuns are singing; or if someone has an independent streak and is not concerned with doing what everyone else is doing, then he or she may very well be singing at a different pace or in a different style than everyone else in choir. That is, a person out of sync with the community generally speaking, is also not in sync when singing with the group.[76] So, aesthetically speaking, these lines of the *Rule* may be concerned with both the quality of the liturgical office as well as its value as symbolically reflecting and creating harmony among the brethren.[77]

c) *Service to the Community*

Every well-functioning community shares the responsibility of the house among its members. This gives each a chance to serve the others and the common good above themselves. Although all the work in the monastery is a service to the community, there are specific assignments which are singled out in the *Rule* for special attention, most especially: those officials who are responsible for the food, the clothing, the books and the sick. Their task is primarily one of service.... "let them serve"(*serviant*: 5.9.296). It is also stipulated that the monk in charge of the clothes and the shoes should honor a request as soon as it is made (5.11); like Benedict,[78] Augustine realizes that if needs are met without delay, they eliminate legitimate reasons for complaints.

Care of the sick is one of the most important services rendered to a member of the community. A special person is assigned to the care of the sick (5.8), who is instructed to take the complaints of the sick seriously (5.6), and to allow them a special diet when necessary (3.5). Physicians should be consulted when the matter is beyond the competence of the infirmarian (5.6). On their side, the sick should co-operate by following the advice of the physician (5.5) and should return to normal life willingly when they have recovered (3.5).

One can easily see that special care of the sick is a mark of love and concern, just as–on the part of the sick person–willingness to accept and cooperate with the care, and when cured to return to the normal life of the community is equally a loving communitarian gesture, advantageous for living harmoniously in community.

d) *Role of Superiors*

What is strikingly different about Augustine's *Rule* in contrast to other early monastic rules is that the role of the superior is not center stage.[79] Most of the regulations regarding the superior are actually found near the end of the *Rule*. This is not accidental, for Augustine's emphasis is on community and the role of the superior is presented as one who preserves the essential values of community life. If all the members are called to serve one another, the superior is par excellence "the one who serves you in love,"[80] like Christ who asked his disciples to imitate him as he washed their feet at the Last Supper. But if the superior should be the first to prostrate himself before the community, they on their side are to show the superior the respect and honor due to his office (7.1). For those who need more than inspiring models!–the superior must also use discipline, as well as encouraging, supporting, and restraining them according to their different temperaments and spiritual growth (cf. 7.3).

It is the superior's task to "pilot" the group, being ultimately responsible for their needs (cf. 1.3 in conjunction with 5.9), and such things as how often the clothes are to be laundered (5.4). He also assigns the monk who accompanies a brother outside the monastery (5.7) and makes sure that the sick brother follows the advice of the doctor. In all this, he is not to dominate those under him (7.3); on the contrary: he is to strive to be loved rather than feared (7.3). The picture is definitely one of service, with the superior setting the tone which should inspire the others to do the same: serving one another in love.

Augustine tells us a few details about superiors some of whom he knew personally, either in Milan, Rome or his native North Africa, and some of whom he had only heard.[81] Of the former he writes:

> I saw at Milan a lodging-house of saints, in number not a few, presided over by one presbyter and a man of great excellence and learning. At Rome I knew several places where there was in each, one eminent for weight of character and prudence and divine knowledge, presiding over all the rest who lived with him, in Christian charity and sanctity and liberty.... And this among not men only, but women, who also live together in great numbers as widows or virgins, gaining a livelihood by spinning and weaving and presided over in each case by a woman of the greatest judgment and experience, skilled and accomplished not only in directing and forming moral conduct but also in instructing the understanding.[82]

The best depiction of a superior, however, is that which Augustine unwittingly paints of himself. As bishop–and we can presume the same was true of him as superior–Augustine knew his position was primarily one of service. He also had a high level of trust for his brethren which comes out in a lecture on some "house matters":

> I have a good opinion of my brothers, and believing the best of them, I have always refrained from making any inquiries because to make such inquiries would–so it seemed to me–indicate I had a low opinion of them. I knew, you see, and I still know, that all who were living with me knew about our purpose, knew about the law governing our life together.[83]

His service, trust and a love which made him "reluctant to discover faults it must punish,"[84] must have gone far to create a true Christian community "of one mind and one heart."[85]

2. *Everything in common*

The full quotation from the Acts of the Apostles puts loving harmony together with common ownership of property: "No one said that any of the things which he possessed was his own, but they had everything in common" (Acts 4:32). The harmony of being "one heart and one soul" is forged in the fire of personal poverty or dispossession, because having "all things in common" establishes a base of interpersonal dependence. One heart and one pocketbook are intimately entwined. The injunction is not, however, primarily practical or psychological, but theological. That is, the primary possession which the monks have in common is God himself. He is their source of unity and their most precious possession. This was Augustine's dream and purpose even from the very beginning of his monastic life:

> Just as I had sold my slender poor man's property and distributed the proceeds to the poor, those who wished to stay with me did the same, so that we might live on what we had in common. But what would be our really great and profitable common estate was God himself.[86]

Some thirty-five years later, he is still giving his clerics the same challenge: they could live in the bishop's house with him only if they agreed to live in poverty: *for whom God and the Church are enough* (cf. *Serm.* 355.6).

Prayer too is one of the monks' most powerful common possessions, especially those choral "prayers, psalms, readings and the Word of God"[87] in which the monks participate every day. But besides its important communal element, prayer also has a place in Augustine's theology of dispossession. In his letter to the rich widow Proba, Augustine tells her that her state in life is well suited to prayer, for prayer arises more spontaneously from a heart which is poor and desolate, like that of a widow who is totally dependent on God. If dispossession of things makes one more dependent on the community, then the poverty of the heart makes one experience a need for and dependence on him who made us: "All those who understand that every heart is desolate in this world....commit their widowhood to God their protector in unceasing, whole-hearted prayer."[88]

While God and prayer are the monks' common spiritual possession, there is also much in the *Rule* which regulates the common possession of *things*. The monk has no private property, no estates, no money, no things which he can call his own. He has the use of some things but the ownership remains in the hands of the community. Augustine's inspiration comes from the Lord himself who says to the rich young man in Mt 19:21: "If you would be perfect, go, sell what you possess and give to the poor, and you will have a treasure in heaven; and come, follow me." One who did just that and had an incredible impact on thousands who followed him into the desert, was the great Antony of Egypt. Having heard this Gospel passage read in church one day, he felt an interior call to follow it and immediately sold his property and went out to live the solitary life, totally given to the Lord. As we have already seen, the story of Antony had the same tell-tale effect on Augustine; he felt the call to follow Christ in poverty and chastity, dispossessing himself of any desire for a career, a wife, or material possessions.

In the *Rule*, the superior is to make sure that the monks are provided with what they need (1.3). Food comes from a single storeroom and a single wardrobe stores the clothes (5.1). As regards clothing, a certain detachment is in order as regards both ostentation (4.1) and personal use. It seems Augustine was not able, however, to convince all his brothers to be content with whatever clothes they were given, regardless of who had worn it previously. But–here in his wisdom the bishop makes a concession–even if someone's complaints result in receiving what he wants, the monk should at least turn in the clothes that he is not wearing[89] to be kept in the common closet.

There is also the question of gifts. Poverty is not only the state of affairs at the moment one enters the monastery, but it governs the whole of life, and thus refers even to future gifts that might be received. Gifts are "not to be pocketed on the sly but given to the superior as common property, so that [they] can be given to whoever needs it."[90] Naturally, any gifts or letters received secretly from a woman are strictly taboo (4.11). The same poverty lived by the monks in the garden monastery was expected of the clerics. Anyone who wanted to give gifts to the clergy was told to give it to the common store and distribution would be made as there was need. In his personal life, Augustine insisted that he, even as the bishop, live the same poverty that he expected of his monks and clerics. He wanted no one to offer him anything that he alone could make use of personally, as for a bishop. He was poor and would wear the same things as his fellow priests and deacons. If he received something better, he would sell it (Cf. *Serm.* 356.13).[91]

The sermon which occasioned this personal remark was the consequence of a scandal in the house of clerics regarding poverty. One of the clerics died leaving a will. Since the clerics were committed to living without anything of their own, the will was a direct contradiction to the way of life this particular cleric, Januarius, had promised. The will came to light only with the man's death. Augustine is shocked and furious, and since the matter had became known in town, he feels obliged to dedicate two sermons to clearing up the scandal. Frankly confessing what happened and why and declaring his own ignorance of the will, he goes on to challenge all his clerics to do some immediate "house cleaning." They are to make sure that they have truly relinquished all their possessions and if anything is still pending—such as the sale of property or money in trust for a minor—they should inform him immediately. Everyone does so and Augustine publicly makes known all the details in the second sermon, thus placating the town and avoiding any future scandal or misunderstanding.

Manual Labor

One final area regarding poverty has to do with the monks' work. The *Rule* lays down:

> Let no one work for himself alone, but all your work shall be for
> a common purpose,
> done with greater zeal and more concentrated effort than if each
> one worked for his private purpose. The Scriptures tell us: "love is
> not self-seeking" (1 Cor 13:5).
> We understand this to mean:
> the common good takes precedence over the individual good,
> the individual good yields to the common good. Here again,
> you will know the extent of your progress
> as you enlarge your concern for the common interest
> instead of your own private interest;
> enduring love will govern all matters pertaining to the fleeting
> necessities of life.[92]

Augustine's point hardly needs elaborating. He is very clear that work belongs to the realm of the common dispossession of all things, because it too pulls us out of our own self-sufficiency and makes us look outward to what benefits all. If one is guided by love rather than self-interest, one will make correct practical decisions regarding the community.

The Bishop of Hippo was also once called on to settle a problem of work which his colleague, Bishop Aurelius of Carthage, was having with some monks of his diocese. The monks thought they were following Christ more radically by refusing to work, since the Master himself had said: "Be not solicitous for tomorrow" (Mt 6:34). Augustine responds by countering the monks' position with several arguments. First, Christ did not intend these words to be taken literally, since he himself had a purse in common (*Op. Mon.* 31). Secondly, Paul, who is also inspired, says "he who does not work shall not eat" (2 Thess 3:10). Paul himself did manual labor, although as a minister of the Gospel he could have received compensation for his preaching. He chose to work, so as not to be a burden to anyone, not to scandalize the weak (*Op. Mon.* 8) and to give an example. Bishops and the clergy are accorded the same privilege of being able to be provided for by the Church, since they too are ministers of the Gospel. The monks, however, are not ordained ministers, even if they at times are ministering to the spiritual needs of others (*Op. Mon.* 2, 24). They can also work. If they refuse to do so, they give scandal to the weak who interpret their behavior as an excuse for laziness. Besides, work is not incompatible with prayer: one can easily pray and work at the same time (*Op. Mon.* 20).

Augustine wants to make sure that the monks are not a financial burden on the Church. Since they can work, they do not fall under the category of those who receive an income from the Church's revenue, as do bishops, widows, the sick, etc. To expect a handout is to take away from those who really need it. Theologically speaking, all Christians form one commonwealth; while helping each other, it is Christ in one who bestows goods upon another more needy Christ (*Op. Mon.* 33).

Perhaps to chagrin them, Augustine adds that he would gladly do "manual labor every day at certain hours, as much as is appointed by the rule in well-governed monasteries...and have the remaining hours free for reading and praying," rather than to have to deal with the annoying business of seculars which as a bishop he is required to do.[93] He agrees that labor might be burdensome, but Christ makes it easy: his life is an example, since it had griefs in it too (*Op. Mon.* 37).

II. What Breaks Down Community

The ideal community living in love and harmony sketched above is not a myth just because it is an ideal. It becomes a reality by God's grace to the extent that one earnestly strives for it and aims to make love a real part of one's life. Love does not just happen, it is willed. When it is not willed another type of community or lack of community results. Life lived in this world is always a mixture as some strive for goodness and virtue and others do not. Even within an individual, a person is sometimes virtuous sometimes not. As articulated above, the monastic community for Augustine is similar to the Church: just as the Church is made up of good and bad members, the wheat and tares of the parable (Mt 13:24-30), so the monasteries have their good and bad or their good and their not-so-good. The outright "bad" or false monks become an object of sarcasm in ancient literature.[94] The attractive elements of monasticism no doubt drew some aspirants for the wrong reasons. It gave scope to their vices instead of developing their virtues! Augustine too mentions them and, in some cases, he is clearly speaking from experience. Not wanting the monks of Carthage to follow in the footsteps of the false monks, he challenges them with what can happen when the "holy purpose" of monastic life is blasphemed because of:

> the many hypocrites under the garb of monks, strolling about the provinces, nowhere sent, nowhere fixed, nowhere standing, nowhere sitting. Some hawking limbs of martyrs, if indeed martyrs; others magnifying their fringes and phylacteries, others with a lying story, how they have heard say that their parents or kinsmen are alive in this or that country and therefore are on their

way to them: and all asking, all exacting, either the costs of their
lucrative want, or the price of their pretended sanctity.[95]

Circumcellions were a distinct problem. They were fanatic Donatists who were
a disgrace even to their own sect. They outdid the false monks of the Catholic
Church in their evil ways in that, taking up the "cause" of the Donatists with vengeance, they added violence to their misdeeds, by wounding, murdering, pillaging
and burning the houses of their Catholic enemies. They were a terror which sometimes made travel difficult.[96] Augustine prefers to remain laconic in describing
them: "For they are wont to go hither and thither having no abiding place and to do
things of which you know well."[97] There are false monks, whether Catholic or
Donatist, but Augustine adds: "the pious brotherhood is not annulled because of
those who profess to be what they are not."[98]

In normal life, one should expect to find saints and sinners living side by side.
One finds false monks in monasteries just as there are false men among the clergy
and among the faithful. All three categories of Christians have their good and their
bad (*En. in ps.* 132.4). This was prefigured in the pericope about the end times.
"Two shall be in the field, one shall be taken, one shall be left..." (Mt 24:40 and Lk
17:34). The three places mentioned by the Evangelists: the field, the bed and the
mill, are for Augustine representations of the three categories of the faithful: the
field refers to the clergy, since they are laboring for a spiritual harvest, the bed
refers to those in the consecrated life, i.e. "those who love quiet," and the mill–the
center of activity in a town–represents the life of the laity (*En. in ps.* 99.13). In each
profession, one finds the good and the wicked. But this should neither surprise nor
alarm us: "Fear not because the wicked are found there, for some men are hidden
and their true state is not discovered until the end."[99]

In a homily which is both humorous and perceptive, Augustine jokingly makes
fun of anyone who thinks he can avoid the company of evil people. If one thinks
that solitude is the answer, he must ask himself why he is separating himself from
them? If it's because he cannot endure them, then his very refusal to put up with
others convicts him of not being virtuous! (*En. in ps.* 99.9) Besides, is there nothing
in this person which others have to endure? Or perhaps instead of solitude, this
person will choose to live apart with a few good men. To live a quiet life far from
the hustle and bustle of the noisy crowds is actually laudable. Others have done and
are doing this...they live in monasteries. But is there enduring joy in these places?
In one sense, the monastery is like a quiet harbor, secluded from the waves and tem-
pests of the open sea. But unfortunately, even harbors have an entrance which both
allow in the boats and give access to the wind which at times rushes in and in the
swelling waves, causes the boats tied together to bump into each other. Even so, the
boats in harbor have greater security and are better off than those afloat on the main.
"Let them love one another, as ships in a harbor, let them be bound together hap-
pily, let them not dash against each other."[100]

Augustine extends his humor: Perhaps the individual who wants to live undisturbed by the wicked is the abbot who says: "I will be careful to admit no wicked

man....with a few good men I will be happy."[101] Augustine rhetorically asks: how are you going to recognize the person whom you wish to exclude? "That he may be known to be wicked, he must be tested within."[102] How then can one keep out a person on the verge of entering, who must be tested and proved and cannot be either unless he be admitted?

> You say you know how to inspect them, [but] do all come with their hearts bare? Those who are about to enter, do not know themselves, how much less do you know them? Many promised to live the holy life....[but when] put into the furnace, they cracked. How do you know him who is unknown even to himself?[103]

And as if that isn't enough, he concludes magnificently: Can you really keep out the wicked brethren from the company of the good?

> Whoever you are who speaks like this, keep out—if you can—all evil thoughts from your heart; let not even an evil suggestion enter into your heart. "I consent not" you say, "yet it entered, so as to suggest itself to you. For we all wish to have our hearts strengthened, so that no evil suggestion may enter. But who knows how it enters?[104]

But the presence of false or evil monks in monasteries is not the total picture. As we have seen, great and holy people also live there. Perhaps someone joins the monastery because of the holy ones and then finds within those with vices as well. This can shock the newcomer. He may even become irritated and impatient: "Who asked me here? I thought that love was here."[105] Leaving the monastery and breaking his vows, he becomes worse than those cracked pots who stay... (Cf. *En. in. ps.* 99.12).

Augustine is refreshingly realistic. No matter how saintly one strives to be, there are always the storms that make the ships in the harbor bump against each other. The monk must put up with his brothers and his brothers must put up with him. "There is so much unknown and undependable about the human heart that the Apostle was surely right to counsel us not to judge anything prematurely 'before the Lord comes, who will bring to light the hidden things of darkness and reveal the intentions of the heart' (1 Cor 4:5)."[106] True in regard to others, it is equally true for the monk himself: one who has advanced in the love of God and neighbor, should never imagine himself to be without sin. "We do not know ourselves well enough to feel secure about what tomorrow will bring."[107]

What is the difference between the good and the wicked? What makes some become virtuous under the same circumstances in which others fall into vice? For the virtuous, it is the love of Christ which moves and motivates them. Those perfected in the love of Christ are "quiet, peaceable, humble, submissive, pouring forth prayers instead of murmuring."[108] On the contrary, "those in whom the love of God is not perfected, even when they are together [in community], are full of hatred, troublesome, turbulent, disturb others by their *anxietate*, and seek what they may say of others; just as a restive horse on team refuses to pull its weight and damages the rig with its hoofs."[109]

To summarize: First, love is the aim and the motive for all the good we do in community. But we are pilgrims on the way in whom the love of Christ is not yet perfected. To the extent that we lack the fulness of love, we battle with temptations and tendencies to selfishness, and therefore are a source of trials to our brothers and sisters who must endure us and we them. There are some even in the holy profession in whom the love of Christ–if it exists at all–is not evident. These are the false monks who give a bad name to the monastic enterprise, but who cannot by that fact nullify it. Most of humanity and even most monks, however, fall neither into the camp of the very wicked nor the very good. We live with a mixture of both, even within ourselves.

In the *Rule*, Augustine warns against certain vices which we might even call "monastic vices" not because they do not exist elsewhere, but because they are the particular imperfections which the fire of the fraternal furnace tends to bring to the surface. Augustine probably chose these four because they are particularly detrimental to community life. He does not (like Evagrius and Cassian) give an exhaustive list of the vices the monk should avoid, but is content to concentrate on what we might call the "the fearsome foursome."

The Fearsome Foursome:
1. Seeking Affection/Love outside the Community
A rather large section of the *Rule* is concerned with prohibiting and putting the monks on guard against flirtatious behavior, especially as regards amorous glances exchanged with a woman. Any cursory reading of the *Rule* cannot but strike the reader with its importance for the North African legislator. Some may dismiss it as Augustine's own problem projected onto the community, or consider it culturally conditioned and therefore irrelevant. Even those who might admit the general lines of precaution may believe Augustine has overstated his case. It is not my purpose here to psychoanalyze Augustine's intention or to discuss the chapter's cultural dependence. What remains valid is his insight into the relation between a celibate commitment and its impact on community life.

The section is introduced by the notion of integrity: "In all your external comportment....act in a manner worthy of your holy profession."[110] Just as Christ said that the evil which comes forth from the heart defiles a person, even before external actions take place (Mt 15:19), so here Augustine–in conjunction with the monastic tradition–wishes to cut off the beginnings of temptation before they have a chance to take root in the heart. To the monk who has promised his heart to God, Augustine is saying: don't sully it or compromise the gift of self by desiring to give or receive even the beginnings of an amorous exchange. He is careful to say that the monks are not forbidden to see (or look at) a woman. If he were using our words he might say: Listen, brothers, you know that there are looks and there are looks. The first are harmless and are not forbidden; I hardly want you to be unnatural and to keep your eyes on the ground if a woman chances to pass by or stops to speak to you. However, be careful and do not turn the freedom you have in the Spirit into an excuse to exchange forbidden glances.

The danger is twofold. First, the one who does indulge in an illicit exchange has personally compromised his vows and "purpose." Secondly, it also weakens and is potentially destructive of community life. This is our area of concern. Let us recall that what binds the community together is love. It is not just a casual friendship, but deep dependent love for each other. Once a person *is not* dependent on the community for its most basic component, community rapidly dissolves into a shell. The monks or the nuns might be living side by side and might even have a kind of care for each other, but if they do not need the love of each other, both to give and to receive, then there is no community in the Augustinian sense or–for that matter– in the true Christian sense. And Augustine seems to ask if the love of the community no longer draws one, what about God? Has the person totally lost the desire to please God? And if so, can he at least fear to displease him? (Cf. 4.5).

2. Murmuring

Murmuring is a vice which shows up in nearly all ancient monastic rules. Monastic legislators were therefore well aware of its destructive character. Augustine is no exception. He warns against this vice three times in the *Rule*, twice addressing those being served and once the officials. The first instance regards those receiving clothes from the wardrobe. They should be content with whatever they receive, and not murmur if the clothes they receive have previously been worn by someone else. To complain about clothes shows a certain weakness (*infirmitas*) and a lack of spiritual clothing (5.1).[111]

In this proscription against complaining, Augustine chooses no less than four terms in depicting the scene, showing that he is concerned with more than a mere spontaneous gesture of disappointment:

> If arguments (*contentiones*) and grumbling (*murmura*) occur among you and someone complains (*queritur*) that he has received worse clothing than previously and that it is beneath his dignity to be dressed in clothes which another was wearing, you thereby demonstrate to ourselves how deficient you are in the holy and interior clothing of the heart, arguing (*litigatis*) as you do about clothes for the body.[112]

The second occurrence has to do with the sick. They should accept the advice of the doctor without complaint (*sine murmure*). The physician may well order things contrary to a person's desires and perhaps unpleasant things as well, but since he is the expert, his advice should be followed. Augustine is obviously not unsympathetic to the sick, but wishes the best for the infirm brother or sister which includes recovery and a peaceful state of mind. Being more receptive to medicinal counsel can help the whole ambience of the infirmary (5.5).

The third case deals with those responsible for the food, clothing and books. They "are to serve their brothers without grumbling."[113] Things which individuals need on a daily basis can be taxing on those in charge, but it is a service and sacrifice necessary for a smooth running of the house. If everyone has what he or she needs, there will be less worry and fuss and therefore fewer complaints. Peace reigns where there is tranquility of order.[114] It may not yet be that deep spiritual peace which comes from accepting the existing situation in line with St. Paul's learning to be content "with abundance or want" (Phil 4:12), but it is a first step in creating an atmosphere of care and respect. Complaints and murmuring turn the service into a mere job and an unpleasant one at that. It does not build community.

The subject of murmuring also surfaces in the other monastic treatises. We find in *En. in ps.* 132.12 that the murmurers are those in whom the love of Christ is not perfected. The perfect *serve the Lord with gladness* (Ps 99:2) just the opposite of the bitterness which comes from murmuring (99.14). The term bitterness (*in amaritudine*) is a good word to describe the taste left in the air after a murmurer has voiced his negativity. Appealing to another sense, Augustine compares murmurers to the creaking wagon wheels passing by his window in Hippo (Cf. *En. in ps.* 132.12). A very apt and vivid metaphor,[115] for what is more annoying than squeaky wheels or tiresome complainers? In another remark, Augustine facetiously chides the "work-less" monks of Carthage with the wish that their tongues were as idle as their hands! (*Op. Mon.* 26). These *obiter dicta* remarks confirm what Augustine proscribes in the *Rule*: murmuring does not come from a heart full of love and disinterestedness, but reinforces a negative element of self-pity and spreads the lack of peace to others in a destructive way. It is at root self-centered and breaks down the bonds of community.

Murmuring is often, unfortunately, only the beginning of other disruptive behaviors. Perhaps that is the reason Augustine and other monastic legislators want to cut if off before it grows and does even more damage. Its close allies are annoyance (*molestum*), contention (*contentiones*), and disturbance (*tumultus*). The expression of annoyance or agitation is disruptive by nature, and even more so when these become stronger and take on the character of strife or commotion.[116] As a site where everyone meets, the refectory seems to be a place where unpleasant disagreements could easily arise: "Listen to the customary reading from the beginning to the end of the meal without commotion or arguments."[117] One is left wondering if the problem is over food or the reading, but perhaps the wording is purposefully vague to cover both. The next injunction however is clearly concerned with food, i.e. whether in the refectory or outside of it, there should be no complaints about who gets what. The principle that distribution is to be made according to need means that not everyone receives the same thing: "No one is to be annoyed, nor should it seem unjust, when a special diet is provided for brothers whose health has been adversely affected by their former status in life."[118]

3. Anger

We have come at last to our main topic: *ira*.[119] It is the third of the vices which break down community life as presented by the *Rule*, after murmuring and the more serious arguments and petty strifes which are the daily trials concomitant with communal life. Since anger is the underlying element which is the cause of many types of quarrels and disturbances, Augustine speaks of it more directly. In doing so, he is less concerned about its minor manifestations than with that anger which grows in intensity and places brother against brother. As usual, he begins with the ideal:

> Either have no quarrels (*lites*)
> or put an end to them as soon as possible.[120]

If life were only thus! The North African doctor is aware that even in good relationships and healthy communities, misunderstandings arise which can cause a moment of anger. One must face the difficulty, clear it up and put the conflagration out immediately before the fire gets out of hand. Such immediate action prevents unresolved quarrels/conflicts from smoldering and posing a potential threat.[121] Using a scriptural metaphor, Augustine likens anger to a splinter which should not be allowed to turn into timber. "Timber" is a particularly apt translation for it not only implies a larger piece of wood compared to a splinter but it captures its inflammable nature as well. Also implicit in the metaphor is the link between anger and condemnation: being angry with a brother brings down divine judgment on oneself (Mt 7:1-5).[122]

The second metaphor is even stronger: "lest anger....turn the soul into the soul of a murderer."[123] Since *the* murderer in scripture is Satan whom Christ calls "a murderer from the beginning" (Jn 8:44), these words are meant to strike the heart of the brothers with terrible fear, as if Augustine were saying: "Realize under whose influence you are acting and the consequences of your action: no murderer inherits the kingdom of heaven." This kind of shock therapy is employed in scripture by Christ himself, and Augustine does not hesitate to use it from time to time when the consequences are dire: anger can separate one person from another, and a person from God for all eternity. If monastic life should lead to greater and greater harmony, anger is diametrically opposed to it. Anger is a "great danger" (*Ep.* 210.2), a poison whose malicious power breaks down the normal functioning of the body and can cause its death. Thus Augustine's strong censure.

Anger aimed at another person has the intent to hurt (*alterum laesit*) and may take the verbal form of insults (*conuicio*), harmful words (*maledicto*), and serious accusations (*criminis obiectu*), or the more general: harsher words (*uerbis durioribus*).[124] All negative words have a wounding power. The way to deal with them is to look directly into the ugly face of their cause: anger. From whence does it arise? Who is responsible? What is to be done?

Since the rest of chapter six deals with reconciliation, we will put this aside for a moment and turn to some specific instances of anger which Augustine had to deal with in the monastic communities of North Africa. First, there are two letters addressed to the abbess of the women's monastery in Hippo. It is difficult to know whether both letters are concerned with the same situation or two different ones. Regardless, for our purpose they both deal with the question of quarrels and their consequences in community and thus provide more ample teaching on anger and its effects.

As he does in the *Rule*, Augustine begins *Letter* 210 to Mother Felicitas with the positive appreciation for the value of mutual love and unity in the Spirit. He then goes on to discuss correction in community. It is not clear whether a quarrel has already occurred between Mother Felicitas and one or more of her nuns due to a rebuke by the abbess, or whether Augustine is advising the superior to exercise her role as corrector in order to heal an existing division. Whatever the case, the bishop goes on to outline the two classic scriptural reactions to a legitimate rebuke: the wise man will be grateful, the fool or scorner will harbor resentment and may respond with hatred. If the latter occurs, the love of the one reproving is put to the test. She (i.e. Mother Felicitas) must not return hatred for hatred; instead the same love which prompted her to reprove in the first place, must "endure unmoved." If she were to react in kind, by returning evil for evil, or hatred for hatred, she would be most unworthy to reprove another but would rather deserve to be reproved herself. The motive in all this must be an earnest desire to live in concord and peace–never to win an argument.[125] At the end of the letter, Augustine leaves his readers with another of his "shock phrases" this time employing his most telling image of anger in his whole monastic corpus:

> As vinegar corrodes a vessel if it remain long in it,
> so anger corrodes the heart if it is cherished till the morrow.[126]

The second letter,[127] directed to the same monastery, deals with the issue of a serious schism which has broken out in the monastery. From what can be gathered from the letter, the majority of the nuns have petitioned for the removal of the abbess (211.4). However, as Augustine reminds them, the convent increased in numbers considerably under her guidance and all seemed to be going well until a new priest was appointed as the priest-superior.[128] There may have been a difference of opinion between the priest and the abbess and the majority of the nuns felt that the priest–being a cleric–had the greater authority. This is pure conjecture since Augustine does not give us details, seemingly because he is not particularly concerned about them. What does concern him is the resultant split in the community. Wisely, he refuses to visit the community to settle the issue....precisely because this would result in their airing the detailed accusations which have already reached his ears. He has no stomach (or heart) to hear more of it; it would only cause him more pain, not to mention the pain he would cause them by his unsympathetic stance to anything leading to disunity and a lack of charity.[129]

The whole thrust of the letter is an exhortation to end the division within the community and the resultant "quarreling and jealousy, angry tempers and personal rivalries, backbiting, general disorder, and hushed comments about one another."[130] The very list shows the magnitude of the problem. As in the *Rule*, Augustine does not mince words. Where is this leading? ....*in mortem* (211.4). He is again utterly serious.

Augustine appeals to the nuns' sense of unity by comparing their schism to that of the Donatists, which ended not many years earlier. The larger division within North African Christianity which set brother against brother offers an apt comparison of the divisions within monastic communities which set brother against brother and sister against sister. Whether large or small, in essence, separation caused by anger or hatred results in the same deadly reality wherever it occurs. It destroys that spiritual unity which gives life, freedom and peace.

Another case of anger involved a member of Augustine's clerical community who was mentioned earlier. Although not a monk, he was a priest and had promised as did all the others to live in poverty with the bishop. Augustine is hurt and shocked to discover Januarius' testament and the dissimulation of his promise. Besides causing a scandal in the city, the will occasioned a quarrel between his two children, both of whom were minors and were living in the monasteries of men and women. Januarius had not left the money to either of them, but to the Church. Actually, he had previously given the money in trust to the Church until his children were of legal age to decide their own future. Going back on his promise, he disposed of the money as if it were his own. Augustine, however, will have none of the money for the Church: to take money that rightly belonged to the children would be to take dirty money. Besides, the father died angry and unreconciled with his son, which again has tarnished the gift. If the Church were to receive the money, it would be endorsing such actions among its parishioners. Augustine's stance underscores the biblical message that parents have no right to disinherit a child (cf. 1 Tim 5:8) and that God's will is for angry fathers to be reconciled to their sons before their death. As for the money, only that which is untainted will be accepted by him in the name of the Church. As for the quarrel between the two young people: the daughter wanted the money for herself, since the father had always said it was hers, while the son wanted it to go to the Church. Like a father, the bishop promised to sit the children down and listen to them, enlisting as well several lay members of his congregation to advise him in settling the matter amicably for all (*Serm.* 355.3).

The repercussions of Januarius' anger reinforces the advice which the bishop gives in his first letter to Mother Felicitas: do not let anger carry over till the next day, or it will eat away at the heart. If the priest had not allowed the anger towards his son to simmer, both the quarrel between his children and scandal to the town would have been avoided.

Till now, we have considered those texts which refer to the vice of anger, i.e. to that wrath which effects a negative and destructive reaction to a situation and has another person as its object. On occasion, the bishop of Hippo speaks of another kind of anger, a righteous anger. First, God himself is sometimes presented in scripture as angry. Since no evil can be ascribed to God, this anger has no vice attached to it. What is the divine anger? Augustine adopts the Old Testament way of speaking: God gave the Israelites a king, even when it was not to their best interest. Since they obstinately insisted on one, he allowed them to have what they impatiently asked for, knowing it would backfire on them and become a source of purification. What God granted, he granted *in anger*, annoyed at their obstinacy and lack of trust in himself as their king. This is anger against their evil hearts which would not be converted until they experienced firsthand the consequences of their choice. God's wrath is therefore not a passion in God, but a sign of the dichotomy between holiness and sinfulness, expressed in biblical language (Cf. *Ep*.130.14).[131]

Anger as an intense emotional reaction to a negative situation is also dealt with at the end of chapter six, although the term anger is not used. Instead, Augustine speaks of the use of *verba dura* in the case of a someone who, in correcting a *minor*, feels as if he or she has exceeded the limits of emotional restraint. It is thus not a matter of simply using strong words, but excessively harsh words that have probably arisen from some degree of anger. Who exactly the *minoribus* are is not clear. It may refer to boys growing up in the monastery, since the practice of receiving young boys was not uncommon and we know that Augustine's monastery had several; or the term may refer to anyone "younger" in age or in rank than the person issuing the correction.[132] Regardless, Augustine feels that one should not in this situation ask for pardon, since the abasement could undermine the person's authority, nullifying the correction. If the advice is culturally conditioned, then Augustine's reluctance to upset the social order of things has to be seen as preferring a lesser evil (not requesting forgiveness) to a greater one (encouraging pride or lack of respect in another). Besides, the lesser evil can be amended by the corrector repenting interiorly before God.[133] However, as in the case of God, the anger is not directed against the persons themselves, but against the evil that is done. Both are classical cases of that famous Augustinian dictum: hate the sin, but love the sinner.[134] In each case, the conversion of the sinner is desired, not his or her downfall.

Another example of this type of anger is seen in Saint Stephen. He raged (*saeviebat*) against his audience which was unreceptive to his message. His words were like stones hurled at them, harsh words aimed at convicting and converting them. While ignoring his reproach, they responded instead with anger and hatred and stoned Stephen to death. And what was Stephen's response to their stones? In imitation of Christ and anointed with the Holy Spirit, he did not return evil for evil. He responded to their anger with *gentleness* (*mitis*) and forgave them. Like God and like the "superior" in the Rule, Stephen's anger was not incompatible with his love.[135]

A final example is Augustine's own behavior against the bishops who, ignoring the words carved into his dining room table, continued to gossip even when reminded to desist. To underscore the seriousness of their detracting behavior, Augustine raised his voice in anger showing thereby that he would not compromise when fraternal charity was at stake.[136]

4. Contumacy

The fourth deterrent to community life in the *Rule* is contumacy. It is that aspect of sin which has hardened into a refusal to amend. In biblical language it is called "hardness of heart" (e.g. Mt 19:8). It is the final stage in the breakdown of community relations since it is the refusal to take any step towards conversion or reconciliation. Augustine refers to it in the *Rule* in the context of refusing to do penance for a fault (4.9). As long as there is communication and a willingness to do what is right, there is hope for a person's conversion. But outright refusal to obey in matters of personal amendment, is contrary to the purpose of monastic life. What is to be done with such a person? Augustine is once again strong and clear: he is to be shown the door. "If he refuses to submit to punishment, even if he is determined not to leave, expel him from your society."[137]

The reason for the extreme measure is that such a person becomes a "toxic agent" (*contagio pestifera*) in the community where he or she has promised to live in love and harmony. A will determined against unity is a contradiction in such a group. To continue like this or even to allow such a one to continue constitutes a lie and a compromise of what the community is all about. Again, the motive is charity, not for the expelled person (although one would hope that the radicality of the act would serve as a kind of shock treatment even here), but for the community as the *Rule* says: "Even this is not an act of cruelty, but of mercy: to prevent the contagion of his life from infecting more people."[138]

Although the immediate context in the *Rule* regards one who has been reported exchanging glances with a woman–the first of our fearsome foursome– nevertheless, the procedure for detection and punishment applies to any of the serious matters dealt with in the *Rule*. That is, for whatever the cause, if a person refuses to do penance–a sign that he is willing to change and amend his behavior– after a series of corrections, then he must be cut off from the rest of the body. Nothing could be further from fraternal love than the building of an impenetrable wall around the self.

This too is Augustine's fear in the *De Opere Monachorum*, where he refers to those who refuse to work as *homines contumaces* (38.14). His fear is that their contagion will spread to other monasteries which will be corrupted by them in a two-fold way: by refusing to work and by thinking this is the holier way to God!

Summary: Anger has been shown to be one of the four ways presented in the *Rule* to break down that unity which is the very purpose of community. It is first of all destructive of the individual like vinegar in an ancient vessel, the longer it remains there, the more it corrodes the very thing/one in whom it exists. It is also destructive of a person's relation with others, by transforming them into an enemy and an object of hatred. Such a posture is equivalent to that of a murderer, harboring anger and hatred by secretly wishing the death of the other–or if that seems too strong, then at least one's removal from life. Whether such removal involves geographical distance or the temporal ontological separation caused by death, the wish amounts to the same thing: total rejection of the person as a brother or sister. This is contrary to the Gospel, specifically contrary to Christ's words "love your enemies," and ultimately to the life of the Triune God whose very nature is communitarian. Thus Augustine sees the implications of destructive anger only too well and will have none of it.

III. Repairing the Damage

Although anger is the focus of this thesis, it is not Augustine's focus in chapter six of the *Rule*. If the first seven verses expose it as a serious threat to community life, the next twenty-one verses present how the monk is to undo the harm done once a rupture in a relationship has occurred. The principal theme of the chapter is, then, *reconciliation*, i.e. a return to the "one heart and one soul" from which anger has drawn one away.

In the broader context of the *Rule*, reconciliation–or a return to harmonious relationships with others in community–is achieved in three ways: by forgiveness, patient endurance and correction.

1. *Forgiveness*

Forgiveness is presented in the *Rule* as the immediate corrective to anger. Anger is so damaging that it demands a suitable counterpart by which the wounds it causes can be healed. Since peace has been broken by a deliberate act, some equally deliberate reconciliation needs to take place. Notwithstanding its length and density, the following text requires full citation:

Whoever has offended another with insults or abusive language or even a head-on attack, must remember to right the wrong he has done at the earliest opportunity.

The injured must remember to forgive without further bickering.
If they have offended each other,
they shall mutually forgive their offences
for the sake of your prayers.
The more frequent your prayers are,
the sounder they ought to be.

An individual who is prone to anger,
yet hastens to beg forgiveness from someone he has consciously harmed, is better
than another who is less inclined to anger
and less likely to ask pardon.

An individual who absolutely refuses to
ask pardon, or does so without meaning it,
is entirely out of place in the monastery,
even if he is not dismissed.

Quicumque conuicio, uel maledicto, vel etiam criminis obiectu, alterum laesit, meminerit satisfactione quantocius curare quod fecit,

et ille qui laesus est, sine disceptatione dimittere. Si autem inuicem se laeserunt, inuicem sibi debita relaxare debebunt, propter orationes uestras, quas utique, quanto crebriores habetis, tanto saniores habere debetis.

Melior est autem qui, quamuis ira sae-
pe temptatur, tamen inpetrare festinat,
ut sibi dimittat, cui se fecisse agnoscit
iniuriam, quam qui tardius irascitur et
ad ueniam petendam difficilius
inclinatur.

Qui autem numquam uult petere
ueniam, aut non ex animo petit,
sine causa est in monasterio,
etiam si inde non proiciatur.

Spare yourselves the use of words too harsh. If they have escaped your lips, those same lips should promptly heal the wounds they have caused.	Proinde uobis a uerbis durioribus parcite; quae si emissa fuerint ex ore uestro, non pigeat ex ipso ore proferre medicamenta, unde facta sunt uulnera.

(*Rule* 6.2 lines 310-331)

We shall draw attention to four major elements in the reconciliation process which lie are at the heart of Augustine's teaching on anger. The reconciliation should be:

a) "as soon as possible." There are several terms expressing the idea that the disruption should be repaired swiftly: *quam celerrime*[139] (line 304), *quantocius* (line 312), *festinat* (line 320); *non pigeat ex ipso ore* (line 330). A swift course of action is called for since the heart itself suffers corrosion until peace is reestablished (cf. *Ep.* 210.2).

b) The one who has caused the injury is to take the first step "to right the wrong" by asking for forgiveness (*satisfactione curare*). It may be a single occurrence or the person may ask for pardon rather frequently. Augustine is aware that some people are more prone to anger or at least more prone to expressing their anger. In either case, what matters is that they hasten to ask forgiveness. This is the attitude which is pleasing to God, more pleasing than one who gets angry rarely, but is less inclined to ask pardon (lines 319-323). Asking for pardon develops humility, since it is an acknowledgment of one's faults. Furthermore, a person who refuses to do so is out of place in a monastery where continual conversion and spiritual growth constitute the essence of common life.[140]

c) The injured party must also forgive readily without further bickering (*sine discreptatione dimittere*) (line 313). The injured can equally well hold grudges and keep his or her heart from harmony. The human psyche reveals a tendency to want to strike back, to wound in return which can be even more calculating than the original hurt. If the wounder fears to approach the wounded lest he receive a retaliation, then the art of reconciliation is doubly difficult and may be nearly impossible. Augustine sagely stipulates for an easy restoration of relationship: if someone asks pardon, give it to him or her immediately without in any way making it difficult or worsening the situation. This is not the time or place to justify oneself. Furthermore, the daily recitation of the Lord's prayer puts the petitioner into a fragile position, in as much as he asks that his offences be forgiven to the same extent that he has forgiven others.[141] It therefore binds a person to forgive an offender who asks for pardon. If pardon is not given, one's prayer is not sincere and the person runs the risk of not receiving pardon for his own sins (cf. *Ep.* 189.8).[142]

Awareness of our own debt before God nourishes our fount of mercy towards others: "forgiving injuries even as God has forgiven you,"[143] through the grace of the Holy Spirit (cf. *En. in ps.* 132.7-8). Secondly, it is a matter of a vital openness towards one's neighbor. "We learn too, how willingly and with what gentle peace God fulfills the good desires of those he knows have forgiven others their trespasses."[144] This willingness to forgive must be absolute extending even to our enemies, as Christ commanded (Mt 8:44) and Stephen practiced (*En. in ps.* 132.8). The reason is not so much for the good of our enemy (though he too profits from our forgiveness), as the benefit it bestows in our own hearts. If anyone is excluded from our love we are divided individuals and "you do not bless God in division of heart."[145] Our hearts, therefore, must be open to and at peace with every one if we want to enjoy harmony with God.

d) If the fault is mutual, mutual forgiveness is in order: "If they have offended each other, they shall mutually forgive their offences for the sake of your prayers" (lines 314-316). Forgiving and being forgiven is the very heart of our Christian life;[146] thus they should not be seen as rare, isolated acts but as common as the daily recitation of the Lord's prayer. The meaningful addition of "your prayers" is a salutary reminder that what happens between two members effects the whole body. A loving community observes acrimony between any of its members with heartfelt anguish and earnestly prays for a speedy reconciliation...for the sake of the hostile parties as well as for the sake of the whole body.[147]

2. Patient Endurance

To endure the minor faults and foibles of others which one encounters in the midst of the myriad rubbings of daily life are part and parcel of communal living. So much is this virtue at the core of cenobitic life that the bishop often defines those who live in community as "those who bear with one another."[148] In the famous sermon on *how good and beautiful it is to dwell together in unity* (Ps 132:1), Augustine speaks of perfection in terms of knowing how to live together. What brings a person to the perfection of love is nothing else than having one's love purified in community life, which is precisely the divine injunction *bear one another's burdens and thus you will fulfill the law of Christ* (Gal 6:2). We recall Augustine's sarcasm in his homily on Psalm 99, when he pokes fun of the would-be monk who wants to live only with good men, since he cannot endure anyone else. His refusal to live with those whom he considers less virtuous than himself is, as Augustine notes, a judgment on his own lack of virtue (cf. *En. in ps.* 99.9). And it is certainly not in conformity with that other scripture verse which challenges us with the injunction to live *forbearing one another in love, endeavoring to keep the unity of the Spirit in the bond of peace* (Eph 4:2-3).[149] How could one say more clearly that the acceptance of each other in love leads to that unity which is so precious in community, formed by the Spirit and in peace?

Our primary model is Christ himself who in the self-emptying of his incarnation and passion (cf. Phil 2 and *Div. quaes.* 71.3) bore all things in obedience to the Father (cf. *Ep.* 130.XIV.26) out of love for us. "By loving Christ we easily bear the weakness of another, even him whom we do not yet love for the sake of his own good qualities, for we realize that the one whom we love is someone for whom the Lord has died."[150] It is therefore a Trinitarian phenomenon to endure like Christ and so be filled with his same love, in the Spirit, for the Father.

A secondary but important model is the superior him/herself, who as a "model of good deeds for everyone" is commanded to exercise "patience towards all."[151] In the superior, this means toggling between restraining the overzealous, compassionating with the weak and prodding the lazy. It is an especially discerning superior who neither discourages those truly trying their best nor indulges the indolent who use weakness as an excuse. Everyone knows that a superior who expects constant perfection causes more unrest than peace in the house, and one who refuses to challenge the status quo out of fear of retaliation or moodiness in those corrected is simply shirking his or her responsibility. Patience is therefore an immensely necessary trait in every superior. Whether the patience is shown us by God (4.5), by the superior or by our brothers and sisters, its purpose is to provide the loving temporal and spatial ambience within which spiritual growth takes place.

Even though the *Rule* expects this virtue to be shown above all by the superior, the context shows that each member of the community must learn as well how to endure both an imperfect situation and imperfect souls. Therefore, when an individual is tempted to separate himself from others in the community due to a lack of virtue or character in the other, an exercise which keeps him united to his brothers is to accept them lovingly with patient endurance, knowing that they are also accepting him in the same enduring love. In fact, as Augustine says, "the stronger you are in forbearing others, the less there is in you which others have to endure."[152] And if some days we have to bear them and other days, they us, it is good if the mutual "bearing" occurs when neither is weak at the same moment: "Different times and different sorts of weakness enable us to bear one another's burdens. For example, you will bear the anger of your brother at a time when you yourself are not angry at him, so that he in turn may support you by his own gentleness and calm at a time when anger will have seized hold of you."[153]

3. *Correction*

If the superior's role is primarily to protect and cultivate love and harmony within the community, then it belongs to him or her to be the first to ensure that nothing is done contrary to the rules which protect that harmony and if a rule is disregarded, to correct the person involved as soon as possible so that harmony is restored promptly:

> The superior has the principal task of seeing to it that all these precepts are observed.
> He should further provide that infractions are not carelessly overlooked but punished and corrected.[154]

There is a procedure laid down for correcting which is drawn from the New Testament. First a person is reproved privately; if no change occurs in his behavior, he is accused before the superior and if need be, before two or three witnesses. The process is actually very humane, going from simple detection through a series of steps to punishment if necessary (4.10).[155] Obviously not every fault will need such elaborate process for its amendment! Augustine deals here with a fault which at first is denied and then requires proof and punishment to eradicate it. We presume that most faults are acknowledged and dealt with at the first reprimand(s). But realistically, even with good intent, some faults are harder to overcome immediately and thus require stronger community pressure to help the person reform.

As a protocol, it presents an external framework to follow. What is lacking is an internal element of love without which the process risks coming to fruition. For this reason, Augustine sagely concludes the process: "with love for the person and hatred for sin."[156] This places an enormous responsibility on the superior to correct in love, i.e. from a desire to help the person grow in virtue. The correction targets the vice, not the individual. Augustine knows that correction is seldom easy: "it is difficult to find someone willing to be reproved,"[157] and the sting of correction can–as we have seen–cause an angry reaction. Administered with love, correction is far easier to accept. Conversely, it is difficult to see any fruit (barring God's grace) coming from a reprimand made in anger against another person.

As is clear from chapters four and six of the *Rule*, fraternal correction is expected to be a normal element in an Augustinian community.[158] This does not mean that Augustine wants his monks to be mutual policemen, on the outlook for infractions against the *Rule* and eager to run and tattle-tale to the superior. Such behavior would be contrary to that mutual trust which naturally thinks well of each other and presumes the best, as we saw in the bishop's own trust of his clerics in *Sermon* 355.2, and his reluctance to discover the faults of his nuns in *Ep.* 211.1. But once something has become evident, charity requires a certain discreet disclosure. The exposure chagrins the offender and prevents its repetition. The ancients were aware that social pressure prevents further lapses. If greater charity were practiced at the initial stage, bad habits would not have a chance to develop and more serious problems could be prevented. Whether the word of correction comes from a superior or a brother, the correct response is conversion, aided by grace.[159] Perhaps the loveliest description outside of the *Confessions* of how grace works is found in *Ep.* 210.2:

> It is a common and frequent experience, that when a brother is found fault with he is mortified at the time, and resists and contradicts his friend, but afterwards reconsiders the matter in silence alone with God, where he is not afraid of giving offence to people by submitting to correction, but is afraid of offending God by refusing to be reformed and thenceforward refrains from doing that for which he has been justly reproved; and in proportion as he hates his sin, he loves the brother whom he feels to have been the enemy of his sin.[160]

Conclusion

Our study began where Augustine begins, namely, with the ideal; but this does not imply that either the individual or a community starts out perfect and must try to maintain this perfection. Perfection consists in continually striving for the ideal, of falling and rising like the sun, if need be on a daily basis. Thus it is our lot to alternate between pain and reconciliation: "Why is it that our part of creation oscillates between decay and growth, pain and reconciliation? Perhaps because this is the proper mode of being for these things...."[161] but the sorrow need not discourage anyone for the greater the pain, the greater the joy of reconciliation: "greater sorrow issues in greater joy."[162] This helps to explain the reason why restored friendship after a rupture is even stronger, because the effort at restoring love increases and strengthens the bond ever more. The same is true for a community seeking love and harmony in God. The diverse parts of the *Rule* are orchestrated towards building community *in the bond of peace*, through the process of caring, enduring, serving, forgiving, honoring, and correcting. And peace is not an unbroken reality in this life, but one achieved through constant effort at putting others first. Neither is it about winning arguments (cf. *Ep.* 210.2), but–as Augustine tells the quarreling nuns of Hippo–about ever renewed reconciliations: "If you do all these things, *the God of peace will be with you.*"[163]

Postscript

Unfortunately we do not know the outcome of his advice to the nuns. Did they end their schism and accept the guidance of Mother Felicitas? And did the monks of Carthage peacefully agree to work? The fact that we hear no more of either group may indicate that things settled down all around. One happy resolution is recorded: the children of Januarius reached real concord in an equal and amicable settlement of the money (*Serm.* 356.11).

❖   ❖

III: THE SERMONS

Whether as a monastic legislator or as a bishop, Augustine exhibits the same pastoral concern for those for whom he is spiritually responsible. We now turn to his *Sermons*, and especially to those given annually at the beginning of Lent, which afford his audience an opportunity to refocus on their spiritual journey, and to look carefully at any behaviors which have alienated them from a brother or a sister. No attempt will be made to present a comprehensive treatment of anger in the *Sermons*; nevertheless, the general consistency of the great pastor on the subject assures the reader that the essentials of his thought are reflected in a less ambitious presentation.

1. Lenten Exhortations

The Lenten milieu which provides the backdrop for many of these sermons adds poignancy to our subject. Augustine reminds his people that since all of life has its trials and tribulations, there is never a time when the cross is not present in some way or another.[164] Therefore, all of life has a certain Lenten character about it. Even so, the days of Lent are an especially fruitful time for them to take stock of their lives and increase in prayer, fasting and almsgiving, while decreasing in those behaviors which are destructive to their lives as followers of Christ.[165] They are asked at the beginning of Lent to examine their consciences regarding unresolved animosities, and to determine to use this holy season to ask for forgiveness.

Augustine appeals to what is now a familiar scripture text to make his point that one's prayer is not pleasing to God if there is any animosity toward anyone left in one's heart: "if you are offering your prayer at the altar and there recall that your brother has something against you, leave your gift at the altar and first be reconciled with your brother, and then come and offer your gift" (Mt 5:23). The reason, of course, is that "God wants you much more than your gift.... Christ wants one he has redeemed with his blood much more than he wants what you have found in your storehouse."[166] God will be satisfied with nothing less than all, the total gift of self in which we exclude no one from our heart in our act of worshiping God.

Another text is the verse from the Our Father: "forgive us as we forgive." If a person says this prayer with anger in the heart, anger blocks the prayer, putting up a kind of barricade (315.10). Since most of the sermons were preached in the context on the Eucharistic celebration, the bishop took the occasion once to remind his flock that they would soon be reciting that same prayer in the liturgy: Let anger now beat a retreat from your breasts, "so that your prayer may proceed without any anxiety or worry, and not stumble or stammer or grow dumb under the pricking of conscience when it comes to the place where it has to say 'forgive us our debts, as we forgive our debtors'" (Mt 6:12).[167]

And if the soon-to-be-recited Our Father is not enough of an incentive to lay aside any animosities, Augustine challenges them to settle the matter before sunset that day,[168] since they have already allowed too many suns to rise and set without taking positive action to "set" their anger forever (209.1; cf. 58.8). And for those who need both a greater incentive and a bit more time, Augustine begs them to recall and imitate the Lord himself: "if anger has remained locked up in the breasts of any of you, at least let the approaching day of the Lord's passion thrust it out, because he, after all, was not angry with his killers, but as he hung on the cross poured out for them both his prayers and his blood."[169]

The sermons are peppered with the usual Lenten exhortations to give alms, to increase one's prayer to God, and to curb the desires of the flesh through fasting and through abstaining from delights of taste.[170] But he also suggests that his "brothers and sisters" should "above everything else, fast from quarrels and discord." [171] If they are tempted to raise their voice, they should raise it to express their love for God in praise, not in angry shouts against another.

Before proceeding further, let us keep in mind that Augustine's often strong invectives against anger are tempered by compassion. First of all, Augustine readily acknowledges that anger is part and parcel of our very humanness,[172] and when it is a reaction against evil, it is not to be lightly dismissed.[173] Is not a lack of reaction to evil an implicit approval? An indifference which lacks sensitivity towards evil surely implies more apathy than disciplined self-control. Augustine leans towards the idea that some emotional response is called for, albeit a controlled one. This may be the reason he does not categorically condemn the phenomenon of anger. In a sermon delivered in his maturity, he says: "You can't destroy her, you can restrain her."[174] The fact that anger is a human emotion is merely the starting point in learning to control it: "In our discipline (Christianity), the question is not whether the devout soul is angry, but why."[175] The Christian learns not to be swept away by the emotion but to reflect on what it does to oneself. Mature and deliberate inquiry into its origin and effects and one's proper response to its arousal are the way forward.

And what does anger do to its subject? Augustine reminds his people that while an angry man is fuming about an external enemy, the real enemy is in his heart. Whatever anyone does to his neighbors cannot really hurt them; his anger against them might inconvenience them or ruin them financially, or even physically cause them pain, but he cannot truly hurt another person. Only individual sin truly harms a person, and the cause is always one's own will. For this reason, the one who is angry and hates his neighbor is the one who is inflicting evil on him- or herself:

> Internally, you see, you are your own enemy, if you hate someone else. But because you don't feel the bad damage you are doing to yourself, you rage against the other guy, and put your life in all the greater danger precisely to the extent that you don't realize how badly you are treating yourself; because in fact by raging like that you have lost your senses.[176]

Thus, stored up anger is the true enemy, not the person with whom you are angry. "What could be sillier than to avoid your enemy outwardly and retain a much worse one in the depths of your heart?"[177] The transposition of the "enemy" from outside to inside is poignantly presented in a homily where Augustine says:

> Let's not expect to be avenged, brothers and sisters. [178] What is being avenged but feeding on somebody else's misfortune? I know that people come every day, kneel down, bang their foreheads on the ground, sometimes wash their faces with tears, and in all this humility and distress of soul, say: "Lord avenge me, kill my enemy." By all means pray that he may kill your enemy, and save your brother; let him kill enmity, animosity, and save nature. ...[M]ay the one who was persecuting you perish, but the one who can be restored to you remain.[179]

Anger, then, inflicts far worse tribulations on its subject than ever it does on the object of its wrath. Its meaner cousin, hate, likewise inflicts punishment on its own subject; it shackles a person to a virtual prison, where he is "bound hand and foot by guilt. Don't imagine he's without a dungeon; his dungeon is his own heart." [180]

2. Responses to Anger

We shall now take up Augustine's teaching on the various responses to anger: three are spiritually inappropriate and harmful; five are proper and beneficial. A person may react or respond to anger by:

Negative: a) denial
  b) nurturing resentment
  c) seeking revenge

Positive: a) turning anger on itself
  b) taking personal responsibility in admission
  c) asking for forgiveness/pardon
  d) forgiving
  e) refraining from taking sides in others' quarrels

A. Negative reactions

a) *denial.* Speaking to his congregation, Augustine bemoans the fact that some of them think that their sins, including anger, are too trivial or insignificant to mention to God for pardon (17.6 and 82.5). We might label this as a state of "denial" today– when repeated sin has made someone blind to the real state of affairs. A first step out of the darkness is to reflect honestly on one's behavior.

On a number of occasions, Augustine pokes fun of those who, blinded by their own (greater) sin of hatred, have the audacity to complain about those who get angry![181] We have here another kind of denial, again due to a lack of sincere, personal reflection. These later lead us directly into our next type.

b) *nurturing resentment.* This is an area of special concern to the bishop. If anger is allowed a foothold in the heart, it increases and turns into hatred. In this context, Augustine once again compares anger and hatred to the speck and beam of

Matthew's parable (cf. Mt 7:3-5): "Anger grown chronic becomes hatred, the speck that is nursed becomes a beam." [182] The transition from anger to hatred is often described as growing over time, while the sun rises and sets (58.7, and 209.1), or while a person sleeps (49.7), highlighting both the temporal conditions which are necessary for change as well as the increase in strength which occurs with growth (114A.6). In a sermon where the newness of anger is compared to the oldness of hatred, a translator has rendered *vetustatem* as "old and musty."[183] The idea conjures up another more modern image of a virus in a culture dish growing in a dark and damp cellar. Whatever the image, what is at the heart of Augustine's message is the importance of checking small beginnings while they are still relatively easy to squelch. "Simple," not-attended-to, anger has the lethal potential of hardening the heart (*inveterata*) which is at the core of hatred. [184] Anger is also fueled by self-righteous indignation. Who, after all, doesn't believe that his anger is justified? But this very righteousness is a subtle temptation not to dismiss it and so it grows.[185] Besides "heedlessness" or "neglect" (*negligentia* 209.1) (i.e. doing nothing to purge the anger) and a self-righteous mentality, other factors which feed the fire of wrath are: stubbornness (*pertinancia* 209.1), evil words (*mala verba* 49.7), and evil suspicions (*malae suspiciones* 58.8, 82.1 and 114A.6). The thrice-mentioned "suspicions" makes one pause to reflect how quickly unverified rumors are maliciously believed.

In the context of going from anger to hatred, Augustine cleverly explains that the inspired text "Be angry and sin not" (Ps 4:4/Eph 4:26) is an injunction not to let the first half "be angry"– which arises because we are human–turn into sin ("sin not") by nursing the anger in the heart (58.8). Thus it is not the emotional reaction which is sinful, but the decision to allow wrath to remain in the heart. Note that the very fact of choosing not to do something is doing something.

Let us also note that the factors mentioned above actually change the quality of anger turning it into hatred. Therefore, the vast difference between the two vices involves more than mere magnitude...as if anger were only a lesser degree of hatred. The radical difference is caught in the comparison between a sore eye and one that has been poked out. The two vices might be related, as both types of eyes are, but the qualitative effect on the personal subject is radical: anger causes an inner disturbance, while hatred kills (cf. 82.2). A further illustration drawn from family life highlights their distinction: a father may feel anger while disciplining his son, but he certainly does not hate his son; he disciplines him rather out of love (211.1 and cf. 82.2). The context shows that anger and love are compatible, while hate and love can never be (387.2).[186]

The difference between anger and hatred is reinforced in the example of one, for instance a woman, who loses her temper. If she takes steps to undo the effect of her anger by apologizing or in some way making amends, she is very different from the person who perhaps has not blown up but harbors resentment, ready to settle the score at the first opportunity. In fact, "not being angry can sometimes be proof of hatred."[187]

These examples illustrate that what is lacking in anger which is always present in hatred is the deliberate and vicious desire to maintain the animosity; furthermore, with hatred often goes an intensity of vengeance which far outstrips that of simple anger. Thus our next topic:

c) *seeking revenge*. Resentment can easily turn into a desire for revenge (*libido vindictae* 58.8). In fact, it is common-place to want to repay an insult with some sort of retaliation (63.2). However, as we've seen, the "feeding on somebody else's misfortune" (211.6) is not a sentiment which God endorses. One who professes to be a Christian must instead imitate the Master who did not seek revenge (58.8, 123.1) against his enemies. We must ask ourselves:

> Who am I, brandishing menaces against another human being? I may well die before I get my own back. And when I depart from the body in a rage, breathing out fire and slaughter, thirsting for revenge, that one who did not wish to be avenged won't receive me. No, he won't receive me, the one who said, *Give, and it will be given you, forgive, and you will be forgiven* (Lk 6:38.37). So I will restrain my anger, and return to calmness of heart.[188]

B. Positive responses

a) *turning anger on itself* (or yourself! And not upon your enemy!) Because the real enemy is within, Augustine advises his people to take up the quarrel with their own hearts (49.8). And what does it mean to turn anger upon oneself? It means to repent: "Everyone, after all, who repents is being angry with himself; being sorry for what he has done, he works off his anger on himself."[189] An example of one who did so is the prodigal son; he "returned to his heart," was angry with himself and was ready to do penance. The parable leads Augustine to relate the general manifestations of penance to a kind of anger turned against oneself: "Repentance, you see always means being angry with yourself, seeing that because you are angry, you punish yourself... Surely, [the gestures of a penitent] are all indications of being savage with oneself, being angry with oneself."[190] One can almost hear the bishop pleading with his congregation to turn their gaze away from the personal object of their anger and to make their very anger the moral object of their attention. He realizes that anger can be a struggle, but God is there with us and wants to help us gain this victory more than he wants to give us external things:

> See to it, my children.... Put your heart into the fight, as much as ever you can. And if you see your anger standing up to challenge you, plead to God to help you against it; may God make you the conqueror of yourself; may God make you the conqueror, not of some enemy outside, but of your own temper inside. He will be there, and he'll do it, you know. He would much rather we asked him for this than for rain.[191]

Redirecting angry feelings back on oneself leads to a more conscious personal realization of the evil of one's angry thoughts and actions. This leads directly to our next section:

b) *taking personal responsibility by admission*. A major step out of the darkness of anger is to reflect honestly on one's behavior and to take responsibility for
it by acknowledging one's guilt: Admit your sinfulness: "Say 'I've done wrong;' say
'I've sinned.' You won't die when you say this; you certainly will die if you don't
say it."[192] But the admittance must go further than a mere interior acknowledgment
of it before oneself and God. Anger usually–and animosities always– affect another
human being. Often the humility needed to "own" our own sinfulness needs to extend to humbling ourselves before another person. Augustine humorously describes
both states as being "flat on your face"...with a twist:

> But of course, people find it easy to give offense, and difficult to restore
> harmony. Ask pardon, he says, of the person you have offended, the
> person you have harmed. He replies, "I won't humble myself." At least
> listen to your God, if you insist on ignoring your brother: *Whoever hum-*
> *bles himself shall be exalted.* You are unwilling to humble yourself, you
> that have fallen flat on your face anyway? There's a world of difference
> between someone humbling himself, and someone flat on his face.
> You're already flat on your face and you refuse to humble yourself?
> You would have every right to say, "I refuse to lower myself," if you
> had refused to come hurtling down in the first place.[193]

One therefore needs to acknowledge and accept responsibility for one's anger
before another. Again, this leads directly into the next response:

c) *asking for forgiveness*. Augustine is aware that it is difficult to undo the
damage we have done, especially when it requires humbling ourselves. He nevertheless confronts the "many" who are "ashamed to beg pardon," or won't say "Forgive
me," telling them that such refusals are "weeds" which he wishes that God would
uproot from his field, "that is from your hearts"! (211.4). In a Lenten sermon delivered when Augustine may still have been a mere presbyter, the young preacher
challenges his people to attend courageously to any animosities that might still be
lingering in their lives: "If you recall that you have neglected to make up with
someone, then wake up and shake off your torpor.... If you are ashamed to ask your
brother or sister to forgive you, overcome this bad sort of shame with a good sort
of fear."[194]

Not every attempt to be reconciled ends favorably, however. The other party
may not want harmony and may therefore refuse to lay down his or her own anger.
What should a person do in that case?

> If you said ["forgive me the wrong I did you"] from the bottom of your
> heart, if with genuine humility, not with a pretense of love, as God can
> see in your heart how you said it, but the other fellow refused to forgive
> you, don't be anxious....appeal to the Lord of both of you."[195]

As long as you are willing to make up, even if the other party is not, you've
done your duty, you've paid your debt (211.2).

Augustine deals also with the case when an actual apology could cause other problems, such as insubordination or pride. For example, if a master has gone too far in his discipline of a slave and wishes to ask pardon of him, the slave could react to the master's act of humility with a feeling of superiority. Since no master would want to offer such an occasion to a slave, Augustine says, it is better to ask God silently in the heart for mercy, and to make amends to the slave by speaking to him in a friendly way. "A friendly approach is a way of asking pardon."[196]

d) *forgiving*. The other side of the reconciliation process is forgiving–a recurring theme in the Sermons: "Forgive absolutely.... Forgive, forgive from the bottom of your hearts.... So if you are angry, don't let [today's] sun go down upon your anger."[197] In one sermon Augustine says that he has given the person who is withholding pardon from someone asking for it, a good talking to (211.4). To refuse to forgive is not an option; we must "Lavish pardon on those who are sorry."[198] But what about those who have not asked for it? Are we obliged to grant pardon to one who shows no remorse for his or her offense? Augustine makes no distinction: even if a person is not asking for pardon–forgive him (or her)![199]

As in the case of one asking for forgiveness, if a person is careful to do his or her part in the process, even if the other party does not respond with the same desire for harmony, the first individual is exonerated before God. As for the uncooperative person, he or she should take note that the name of Christian should not be applied to someone who is unwilling to put an end to animosities.[200]

Sometimes a third party may be necessary in the reconciliation process. You may be willing to forgive another person, but perhaps the offender refuses to ask for forgiveness. The third person could "scold the offender into first asking pardon from you." On your part, "all you must do is to be ready to forgive, totally ready to forgive him from the heart."[201] If the offender delays in asking, then occasion should be taken to pray for this person to receive a spirit of forgiveness.

What is more important is one's own willingness to forgive: "If you are ready to forgive, you have already forgiven."[202]

A final consideration concerns the role which forgiveness plays in binding and loosening a person from sin. Although it fell to the bishop to forgive major sins in the public arena, nevertheless every Christian was and is expected to play a non-sacramental, but vital, role in loosening a fellow Christian through forgiveness. Forgiveness *frees* (*relaxare*) the other from his or her sin, as the following text shows: "How is what you say [viz. 'forgive us...as we forgive] going to be true, if you *fratri tuo noluisti relaxare peccatum*?[203] Although this should not be taken in a strictly legalistic sense, nevertheless there is an important element here which points to un-forgiveness as an obstacle fettering the unforgiven person: to be forgiven is truly to be set free.[204]

e) *refraining from being party to others' enmities*. And what should you do when you find yourself between two friends who are at odds with each other? Each "friend" would like you to take sides with him or her against the other. Augustine nobly advises a person during this time of trial and testing: "Remain the friend of both of them.... If you hear nasty things about each of them from the other, don't betray them to the other.... You have heard a word from an angry man, from someone who's been deeply hurt, who has flared up in a temper. Let it die in you.... After all, if it stays in you, it won't burst you."[205]

Conclusion

The same teaching on anger is evident in both the *Rule* and the *Sermons*, namely that although "human," it is a dangerous passion of the human heart. Unless it is eradicated promptly, it grows (sometimes almost imperceptibly) into many different strains of animosities. Once anger has developed into whatever stage–from a quick angry outburst to years of hard-hearted hatred–Augustine offers the consoling truth that, with the help of Christ, all enmity can be put aside in a definitive manner (63.3). Humbly asking for pardon and forgiving from the heart restores a person to communion with God and with one's neighbor. Anger need not have the last word. By taking control of their lives with the tools that the word of God offers them, all Christians can live in true Christian harmony and freedom.

Notes: Chapter 4

1. For the concept of journey as central to Augustine's idea of spiritual progress, see Thomas Martin, *Our Restless Heart: The Augustinian Tradition*, Orbis Books, Maryknoll NY, 2003: 25ff.

2. For a portrait of Augustine, see Appendix I.

3. George Lawless, *Augustine of Hippo and his Monastic Rule*, Clarendon Press, Oxford, (1987): 57. Henceforth, *Monastic Rule*.

4. [C]um iis qui eidem adhaerebant, Deo vivebat, jejuniis, orationibus, bonisque operibus, in lege Domini meditans die ac nocte. *Vita Augustini* 3:1-2. PL 32 col. 36.

5. Frederick van der Meer, *Augustine the Bishop*, translated by Brian Battershaw and G.R. Lamb, Sheed and Ward, London and New York (1961): 208.

6. *Ep.*10.2 to Nebridius. The above is the translation of : *in otio deificari* in the translation of van der Meer's work by Battershaw and Lamb. See previous note.

7. Namely, *Di quantitate animae, De libero arbitrio* (Bk 1), *De moribus ecclesiae catholicae et de moribus Manichaeorum, De Genesi contra Manichaeos, De diversis quaestionibus, De Magistro, De vera religione.* Cf. *Augustine of Hippo: A Biography* by Peter Brown, Dorset Press, New York (1967): 74.

8. Although not specified by Possidius, these first monks may have been his fellow companions of Tagaste, now relocated to Hippo. Jason David Beduhn, "Augustine Accused: Megalius, Manichaeism, and the Inception of the *Confessions.*" *Journal of Early Christian Studies* 17.1 (2009): 94.

9. *Sermon* 355.2.

10. Proposed by Luc Verheijen, van Bavel and others, this date has met with general acceptance. See Lawless, *Monastic Rule*, 148-152. The author gives a brief summary of the history of the manuscripts in "Regula," *Augustine Through the Ages: an Encyclopedia*, 708.

11. For an afterlife of the *Rule*, see Appendix VI.

12. Felix Asiedu places *Ep.* 22 in the context of Augustine's conversion and in his particular pastoral situation as a new cleric, emphasizing the importance of Rom 13:13 as an important link between the two moments in Augustine's journey. What follows relies heavily on his article: "Paul and Augustine's Retrospective Self: The Relevance of *Epistula* XXII." *Revue des Études Augustiniennes*, 47 (2000): 145-164.

13. Cf.: "Zeal in the Lord and in our care for the Church (*nostrum studio in domino et cura ecclesiastica*)." *Ep.* 22.1.1. CSEL 34[1] (54): 13-14.

14. Asiedu, 157.

15. [N]on enim huius hostis uires sentit, nisi qui ei bellum indixerit, quia, etsi cuiquam facile est laude carere, dum denegatur, dificile est ea non delectari, cum offertur. *Ep.* 22.2.8. CSEL 34[1] (60): 16-18.

16. ...minus sibi adsumendo, quam offertur, sed tamen ab eis, qui se honorant, nec totum nec nihil accipiendo. *Ep.* 22.2.7. CSEL 34[1] (59): 18-20.

17. Asiedu, 158.

18. Cf: Nostrum igitur fuit eligere et optare meliora, ut ad vestram correctionem aditum haberemus, *non in contentione et aemulatione* et persecutionibus; sed mansuete consolando, benevole cohortando, leniter disputando. *C. Ep. Mani.* 1.1. PL 42 col. 173. Italics added.

19. Ibid.

20. An allusion to Rom 13:13 and the manner of debating is also found in *De agone Christiano* 10.11, a work composed in the same period (396-397 A.D.) with references to the Manicheans. Augustine believes that the ignorance of those who do not comprehend

God's nature as absolutely unchangeable is due in part to their contentious attitude. Cf.: quoniam omni modo incommutabilis intelligitur Deus, sed ab eis qui *non in contentione et aemulatione* et vanae gloriae cupiditate amant loqui quod nesciunt, sed humilitate christiana sentiunt de Domino in bonitate, et in simplicitate cordis quaerunt eum. PL 40 col. 297. Italics added.

21. Every year Augustine would give a Lenten sermon at the beginning of the season to encourage his people to take advantage of the holy season by applying themselves seriously to the disciplines of Lent for the sake of inner conversion. No particular date has been assigned to this sermon, but Edmund Hill believes it was probably delivered after 415. Hill, *Sermons*, vol. 6, p.105, n.1.

22. Cf: Donum Dei, quod ipse non habet, nullus in altero invideat, nullus irrideat. In spiritualibus bonis, tuum deputa, quod amas in fratre: suum deputet, quod amat in te. *Sermon* 205.2 PL 38 col. 1040.

23. Van der Meer, 141.

24. Hoc si facitis, toto corde cantatis, *Hic est dies quem fecit Dominus.* Quod enim cantatis, vos estis, si bene vivatis. *Sermon* 230. PL 34, col. 1104.

25. Megalius and the local bishops may have been returning from the Council of Carthage in 394 or to some other gathering the following year. Beduhn, 89, n.13.

26. Cf. Serge Lancel, *St Augustine*, Librairie Arthème Fayard, 1999. English translation by Antonia Nevill, SCM Press (2002): 184. His source, *Contra Litt. Pet.* Book III. XVI.19, mentions Megalius' anger (*iratus*) which may very well have expressed itself in a heated outburst. It is very interesting that Possidius, does not mention Megalius' initial refusal to ordain Augustine.

27. Lancel, *ibid.*

28. *Ibid.* While it seems likely that Augustine would have stirred up jealous reactions among the lesser gifted clerics, there might be other explanations for Megalius' outburst as well, e.g. a longstanding opposition between Megalius and Valerius.

29. Beduhn believes that Megalius' chief accusation was Augustine's former life as a staunch supporter of Manichaenism. Since Megalius put his accusations in writing, Augustine would have had to make a formal, written response to them as well. Since such an accusation would have called into question the very sincerity of Augustine's conversion, Beduhn argues that Augustine's response is embedded in *Confessions* 5-9 (or an early version of it) which specifically deals with that period of his life when doubts about Manichaenism eventually led to his conversion to and baptism in the Catholic Church (383-388 A.D.). Megalius' accusation may thus be the occasion which lies behind Augustine's composition of the *Confessions*. Beduhn, 112.

30. Beduhn, 109. To change Megalius' mind–given his earlier rage–was no easy achievement. This lends weight to Beduhn's argument that some form of *Confessions* 5-9 lies behind Augustine's defense since it is nearly impossible to doubt the authenticity of Augustine's conversion after reading the *Confessions*.

31. Quod senex Megalius defunctus sit, iam uos audisse quis dubitet?... non desunt scandala sed neque refugium; non desunt maerores sed neque consolationes. atque inter haec quam uigilandum sit, ne cuiusquam odium cordis intima teneat neque sinat, ut *oremus deum in cubili nostro clauso ostio*, sed aduersus ipsum deum claudat ostium, nosti optime, optime frater; subrepit autem, dum nulli irascenti ira sua uidetur iniusta. ita enim inueterescens ira fit odium, dum quasi iusti doloris admixta dulcedo diutius eam in uase detinet, donec totum acescat uasque corrumpat.... recolis certe, qua cura et quanta sollicitudine ista scripserim, si recolis, quid mecum nuper in itinere quodam locutus sis. *Ep.* 38.2. CSEL 34^2 (65: 11-12, 15-23, 66:11-13).

32. Cf: "I did not go because I did not dare look the people of Fussala in the eye. After they had accepted my choice of a bishop in silence and then were upset by concern about him, I became hateful to them." [E]go aberam, quia nec Fussalenses uidere audeo quibus post nostrum iudicium accepto episcopo iam quietis et per huius inquietudinem denuo sollicitatis etiam ipse odiosus effectus sum. *Ep.* 20*15.2 CSEL 88 (103:2-5).

33. See n. 18 above.

34. Lawless, *Monastic Rule*, 21.

35. Besides expressing a spirit of service which Augustine sees as inherent in the vocation to be a monk, it also avoids the term "monk," which the Donatists argued was not scriptural. Lawless, *Monastic Rule,* 50. Note also that the members of the bishop's clerical monastery were called *conservi (Vita* 15.1). See Terrence G. Kardong, O.S.B. "Monastic Issues in Possidius' *Life of Augustine,* ABR 38:2-June 1987: 169.

36. For the topography of Hippo and what is known of this ecclesiastical property, see Appendices II and III.

37. This may have been his monk, Urban, who was a priest and Prior of the monastery before his consecration as Bishop of Sicca around 415. See *Ep.* 20*.2

38. *Serm.* 355.6.

39. Van der Meer, 200 and cf. the clergy's willingness to acquiesce in *Serm.* 355.2,6.

40. For a list of the majority of Augustine's monastic writings, see Appendix IV.

41. Even if a few of these monks may have followed Augustine from Tagaste to Hippo, and therefore have been decidedly more intellectual than the general breed of monks, nevertheless, some degree of manual labor was expected of everyone.

42. Besides a reference in the *Rule* to the oratory which should be available for private prayer outside the times for the divine office (chap. 2.2), Augustine refers to that kind of prayer which demands solitude and silence: "We seek unity, the simplest thing of all. Therefore let us seek it in simplicity of heart. 'Be still *(agite otium)* and know that I am God' (Ps 46:10). This is not the stillness of idleness *(otium desidiae)* but of thought *(otium cogitationis)*...." *Vera Rel.* 35.65. Cf. Lawless, *Monastic Rule,* 51.

43. Van der Meer, 216.

44. See George Lawless, "Augustine's Decentring of Asceticism." *Augustine and his Critics,* 142-163.

45. Sulpicius Severus, *Ep.* 3. PNF 11, p. 22.

46. If van der Meer (pp.10-11) is correct, the number of bishops in North Africa was extraordinary, ranging from between 500-700 around the year 400 AD. This number does not include the Donatist bishops. The towns were small, but larger than villages. After 445 A.D., Pope Leo took over the two provinces of the Mauritanias–to the west of Hippo. Since he considered it degrading for bishops to be living on small estates in the country, Leo ordered that henceforth bishops should not be appointed to such places which a priest could adequately serve.

47. Van der Meer, 199.

48. *Vita* 26.1.

49. Possidius (*Vita* 22.2) places the serving wine at table in an Anti-Manichaean setting, citing the I Tim 4:4: "all that God has created is good." Timothy himself was exhorted to: "drink no longer only water, but use a little wine for your stomach's sake" (5:23). However, the number of cups was strictly allocated for each person (*Vita* 25.2).

50. *Vita* 22.6.

51. *Vita* 22.6-7. Translation of Peter Brown, *Augustine of Hippo,* 200; I have added the brackets and contents for clarity. Did the painful experience of Megalius' slanderous gossip,

prompt Augustine to carve these words into the table? If so, his charity is sparing others what he himself had suffered.

52. *Vita*, 24.

53. Van der Meer, 216.

54. [S]i qua opera uestra mater ecclesia desiderauerit, nec elatione auida suscipiatis nec blandiente desidia respuatis.... [N]ec uestrum otium necessitatibus ecclesiae praeponatis, cui parturienti si nulli boni ministrare uellent, quo modo nasceremini, non inueniretis. *Ep.* 48.2 CSEL 34²(138:2-4, 7-9).

55. Cf. George Lawless, "Psalm 132 and Augustine's Monastic Ideal," *Angelicum* 59 (1982): 526.

56. *Cor unum et anima una* from the Greek: kardía kaí psuchē mía.

57. Sed si neque a barba descendisset unguentum, modo monasteria non haberemus.... secuta est ecclesia, de ueste Domini peperit monasteria. *En. in ps.*132.9.2-3,5-6. CCL 40 (1932).

58. [U]num enim corpus sub uno capite sumus, ut et uos in nobis negotiosi et nos in uobis otiosi simus. *Ep.* 48.1. CSEL 34² (137:7-9).

59. For an outline of our treatment of anger in the *Rule*, see Appendix V.

60. Primum, propter quod in unum estis congregati, ut unianimes habitetis in domo et sit uobis anima una et cor unum in deum (1.2.3-5). The citations from the *Rule* of Augustine will include the chapter, section and lines of the Latin text found in George Lawless' *Augustine of Hippo and his Monastic Rule*, Clarendon Press, Oxford, 1987. Citations in this chapter without further reference refers to the *Rule*. Citations from *Ep.* 211:1-4, known as the *Obiurgatio (Obj.)*, will also be from Lawless' work, pp. 104-108.

61. Cf. *De moribus ecclesiae* 31.65-67 and 33.71.

62. By the time Augustine comments on Psalm 99 (the sermon cannot be dated precisely, however the scholarly consensus places it between 399 and 413) the twin principle has become standard and forms almost a definition of monastic life: "for many [live]...the holy life, which has all things in common, where no man calls anything his own, who have one soul and one heart in God." *En. in ps.* 99.11. Other descriptions of the monastic life can be gathered from the same *Sermon* 99.12 and from *De Opere Monachorum* 2.

63. The importance of this addition is seen in the number of times Augustine uses it: namely, out of forty-two instances he adds *in deum* twenty-eight times. The ensemble of vv. 32a-35b occurs eighty-two times, in whole or in part, twelve of which occur in a specific monastic or clerical context. George Lawless, "Enduring Values of the Rule of Saint Augustine," *Angelicum* 59 (1982): 60. The article which first brought Augustine's addition of *in deum* to the notice of the public was T.J. Bavel's "'Ante omnia' et 'in Deum' dans 'Regula Sancti Augustini'." *Vigiliae Christianae* 12 (1958): 157-165. For Augustine's use of Acts 4:32-35 see Luc Verheijen, *La règle de saint Augustin II. Recherches historiques.* Paris: Études augustiniennes (1967): 90-91.

64. [L]argiorem gratiam dei quae data est uobis, ut non solum nuptias carnales contemneretis, uerum etiam eligeretis societatem in domo unanimes habitandi, ut sit uobis anima una et cor unum in deum. *Obj.* 2.

65. "The Lord grant you the grace to observe these precepts with love....you are no longer slaves under the law, but a people living in freedom under grace." Donet dominus, ut obseruetis haec omnia cum dilectione....non sicut serui sub lege, sed sicut liberi sub gratia constituti. 8.1.372-3, 376-7. The comparison is borrowed from St. Paul: cf. Rom 6:14-22.

66. Cf: Tam dulcis est, quam dulcis est caritas quae facit fratres habitare in unum. *En. in ps.* 132.1.4-5. CCL 40 (1926).

67. Non ergo habitant in unum, nisi in quibus perfecta fuerit caritas Christi. *En. in ps.*132.12.4-5. CCL 40 (1934).

68. Cf. *Tract. in Joan.* 27.6.1 and note: Dilige ergo proximum: et intuere in te unde diligis proximum; ibi videbis, ut poteris, Deum. *Tract. in Joan.* 17.8. PL 35, col. 1532.

69. The Trinitarian dimension of Augustine's monasticism is expressed by George Lawless thus: "For Augustine, *monos* means...'a sole individual' who is linked with others in fraternal love and forgiveness. Exemplifying the ideal of Acts 4,32, sanctified and strengthened by the Holy Spirit, the monk possesses solidarity with Christ and his Church on their way to the Father." Lawless, "Psalm 132...": 539.

70. [I]n alios propensius in alios suspensius inclinetur. *Ep.* 130.VI.13. CSEL 44 (54:17).

71. Omnes ergo unianimiter et concorditer uiuite, et honorate in uobis inuicem deum cuius templa facti estis.1.8.58-60.

72. Psalmis et hymnis cum oratis deum, hoc uersetur in corde quod profertur in uoce. 2.3.70-71.

73. Et nolite cantare, nisi quod legitis esse cantandum: quod autem non ita scriptum est ut cantetur, non cantetur. 2.4.72-73.

74. Luc Verheijen, *Nouvelle Approche de la Règle de Saint Augustin,* I: 385.

75. The *Confessions* relate the joy Augustine experienced in singing the psalms in the early days of his conversion. "[Is it not good] to enjoy the serenity of a psalm?" (Conf. 8.10.24) and "How copiously I wept at your hymns and canticles, how intensely was I moved by the lovely harmonies of your singing Church!" (9.6.14).

76. I owe this insight to Sr. Aquinata Böckmann, O.S.B. communicated to her class on the *Rule of Benedict,* Collegio Sant'Anselmo, Fall 2001.

77. They may also contain a warning, or better, an imperative against the use of Donatist texts.

78. Cf. *Rule of Benedict* 31.16 and 35.12-13.

79. As for example, the *Rule of Benedict*, which deals with superiors straightaway in chapter 2.

80. ...se existimat ....caritate servientem felicem. 7.3.356,357. Also note the same expression in: "he who presides over such places, who serves his brethren, in what are called monasteries."*En in ps* 99.11. In the *Ordo Monasterii* 7, the superior takes care of any need that might arise at table, facilitating the monk's maintenance of silence and their attention to the reading which accompanies the meal. We recall the term for monk discussed in the General Introduction, as "one who serves" or "servant of God."

81. The latter may be the Pachomian monasteries which the young Augustine describes in his early treatise which we have already mentioned. He is responding to the Manicheans, showing that the Christians too have their ascetics, the "fathers" who live in Christian monasteries: "These fathers are not only more saintly in their conduct, but also distinguished for divine learning and of high character in every way; and without pride they superintend those whom they call their children, having themselves great authority in giving orders and meeting with willing obedience from those under their charge." Hi vero patres non solum sanctissimi moribus sed etiam divina doctrina excellentissimi, omnibus rebus excelsi, nulla superbia consulunt iis quos filios appellant, magna sua in iubendo auctoritate, magna illorum in obtemperando voluntate. *De Moribus Ecclesiae Catholicae,* XXXI.67. CSEL 90 (128:17-20).

122 Augustine: Anger in Community / Notes

82. Vidi ego sanctorum diversorium Mediolani non paucorum hominum, quibus unus presbyter praeerat vir optimus et doctissimus. Romae etiam plura cognovi, in quibus singuli gravitate atque prudentia et divina scientia praepollentes certeris secum habitantibus praesunt Christiana caritate, sanctitate, libertate viventibus.... Neque hoc in viris tantum sed etiam in feminis; quibus item multis viduis et virginibus simul habitantibus et lana ac tela victum quaeritantibus praesunt singulae gravissimae ac probatissimae, non tantum in instituendis compenendisque moribus sed etiam instruendis mentibus peritae ac paratae. *Mor. Eccl.* XXXIII.70. CSEL 90 (132:16-21).

83. Bene autem sentio de fratribus meis, et semper bene credens ab hac inquisitione dissimulaui: quia et ista quaerere, quasi male sentire uidebatur mihi. Noueram enim, et noui omnes, qui mecum uiuerent, nosse propositum nostrum, nosse legem uitae nostrae. *Sermon* 355.2. Lambot, *Sermones Selecti,* (126: 7-11).

84. [I]ta non uult caritas quod uindicet inuenire. *Obj.* 1.

85. Gerald Bonner believes "Augustine may have lacked the dominating temperament [of St. Ambrose or St. Bernard]...he was not at his best in a hostile confrontation;" and that this contributed to the "mood of the Rule." See Gerald Bonner, *The Monastic Rules.* New York City Press, Hyde Park, New York, 2004: 90. There can be no doubt that Augustine's own personal way of governing is reflected in the *Rule*; subsequent religious who live under the influence of his *Rule* (including Benedictines) can only rejoice that community is far more his focus than authority.

86. [U]t quomodo ego tenuem paupertatulam meam uendidi et pauperibus erogaui, sic facerent et illi qui mecum esse uoluissent, ut de communi uiueremus; commune autem nobis esset magnum et uberrimum praedium ipse deus. *Sermon* 355.2. Lambot, *Sermones Selecti,* (125:25-28).

87. Cf. *Op. Mon.* 20.

88. [Q]uapropter si se omnis anima intellegat in hoc saeculo destitutam atque desola-tam....profecto quandam uiduitatem suam deo defensori assidua et inpensissima precatione commendat. *Ep.*130.XVI.30. CSEL 44 (75: 8-11).

89. This presumably refers to turning in winter clothing when given summer-wear and vice versa.

90. Non occulte accipiatur, sed sit in potestate praepositi, ut, in re communi redactum, cui necessarium fuerit, praebeatur. 5.3.257-260.

91. In the context of gifts donated to the Church, Augustine once remarked that such things as shipping companies are totally inappropriate! Cf. *Serm.* 355.5.

92. Ita sane, ut nullus sibi aliquid operetur, sed omnia opera uestra in commune fiant, maiore studio et frequentiori alacritate, quam si uobis singuli propria faceretis. Caritas enim, de qua scriptum est quod 'non quaerat quae sua sunt,' sic intelligitur, quia communia pro-priis, non propria communibus anteponit. Et ideo, quanto amplius rem communem quam propria uestra curaueritis, tanto uos amplius profecisse noueritis; ut in omnibus quibus utitur transitura necessitas, superimineat, quae permanet, caritas. 5.2.240-251.

93. ...quantum ad meum adtinet commodum, multo mallem per singulos dies certis horis, quantum in bene moderatis monasteriis constitutum est, aliquid manibus operari et certeras horas habere ad legendum et orandum aut aliquid de diuinis litteris agendum liberas. *Op. Mon.* XXVIIII.37. CSEL 41 (587:2-7).

94. Cf. Jerome, *Ep.* 22.34; Cassian, *Conf.* 18.7; Benedict, *Rule,* chapter 1.

95. [M]ultos hypocritas sub habitu monachorum usquequaque dispersit, circumeuntes prouincias, nusquam missos, nusquam fixos, nusquam stantes, nusquam sedentes. alii mem-bra martyrum, si tamen martyrum, uenditant; alii fimbrias et phylacteria sua magnificant; alii parentes uel consanguineos suos in illa uel in illa regione se audisse uiuere et ad eos pergere

mentiuntur. et omnes petunt, omnes exigunt aut sumptus lucrosae egestatis aut simulatae pretium sanctitatis. *Op. Mon.* XXVIII.36. CSEL 41 (585: 15-22).

96. See van der Meer, 82-83, 88.

97. [S]olent enim ire hac illac, nusquam habentes sedes; et facere quae nostis. *En. in ps.* 132.3.17-18. CCL 40 (1928).

98. [S]ed non periit fraternitas pia, propter eos qui profitentur quod non sunt. *En. in ps.* 132.4.2-3. CCL 40 (1928).

99. Ne expauescatis quando ibi inueniuntur reprobi; nam et latent quidam, qui non inueniuntur nisi in fine. *Ibid.* lines 17-19. Augustine is referring to the reprobates in the monasteries, but his words would apply equally well to all three categories.

100. Ament se, naues in portu bene sibi applicentur, non sibi collidantur. *En. in ps.* 99.10.24-25. CCL 39 (1399).

101. Cautus ero, nullum malum admittam....cum paucis bonis bene mihi erit. *En. in ps.* 99.11.3,5-6. CCL 39 (1399).

102. Vbi cognoscis quem forte uis excludere? Vt cognoscatur malus, intus probandus est. Ibid. lines 6-7.

103. Dicis enim, et nosti inspicere. Omnes nudis cordibus ad te ueniunt? Qui intraturi sunt, ipsi se non nouerunt; quanto minus tu? Multi enim sibi promiserunt quod impleturi essent illam uitam sanctam....missi sunt in fornacem, et crepuerunt. Quomodo ergo cognoscis eum qui sibi ipse adhuc ignotus est? Ibid. lines 10-13, 15-16.

104. Excludes malos fratres a conuentu bonorum? De corde tuo, quisquis ista dicis, omnes malas cogitationes, si potes, exclude: non intret in cor tuum uel suggestio mala. Non consentio, inquis. Sed intrauit tamen, ut suggereret. Nam omnes munita corda habere uolumus, ut nihil intret quod male suggeratur. Vnde autem intret, quis nouit? Ibid. lines 16-22 (199-1400).

105. Quis me huc quaerebat? Ego putabam quia caritas est hic. *En. in ps.* 99.12.54-55. CCL 39 (1401).

106. [T]amen propter humanorum animorum ignota et incerta rectissime apostolus admonet, ut non ante tempus quicquam iudicemus, donec ueniat dominus et inluminet abscondita tenebrarum et manifestet cogitationes cordis. *Ep.* 130.II.4. CSEL 44 (44:15- 45:1).

107. [T]amen nec sibi quisque ita notus est, ut sit de sua crastina conuersatione securus. *Ep.* 130.II.4. CSEL 44 (44).

108. Augustine uses the singular: quietus, placatus, humilis, tolerans, pro murmure precem fundit. *En. in ps.* 132.12.11-12. CCL 40 (1934).

109. Nam in quibus non est perfecta caritas Christi, et cum in uno sint, odiosi sunt, molesti sunt, turbulenti sunt, anxietate sua turbant ceteros, et quaerunt quid de illis dicant; quomodo in iunctura inquietum iumentum non solum non trahit, sed et frangit calcibus quod iunctum est. *En. in ps.* 132.12.5-10. CCL 40 (1934).

110. [I]n omnibus motibus uestris nihil fiant....sed quod uestram decet sanctitatem. 4.3.126-128.

111. Behind Augustine's metaphor of clothing is 1 Pt 5:5: clothe yourselves with humility....

112. Si autem hinc inter uos contentiones et murmura oriuntur, cum queritur aliquis deterius se accepisse quam prius habuerat et indignum se esse qui ita uestiatur, sicut alius frater eius uestiebatur, hinc uos probate quantum uobis desit in illo interiore sancto habitu cordis, qui pro habitu corporis litigatis. 5.1.228-235.

113. [S]ine murmure seruiant fratribus suis. 5.9.296.

114. This is Augustine's famous definition of peace which occurs in *The City of God* 19.13.1. Although related to his broader understanding of community, and rich in its varied aspects, a study of Augustine's concept of peace would take us too far afield in this thesis. I refer the reader to Augustine's own words in *The City of God* and the article "Peace" by Donald Burt, O.S.A. in *Augustine Through the Ages: An Encyclopedia*, ed. Allan D. Fitzgerald., O.S.A., William B. Eerdmans Publishing Company, Grand Rapids, MI. 1999: 629-632.

115. Cf. Lawless, "The Rule of Saint Augustine as a Mirror of Perfection," *Angelicum* 58 (1981): 467.

116. The reader will recall that *contentio* is the same word used in Rom 13:13: *non in contentione et aemulatione....*

117. Cum acceditis ad mensam, donec inde surgatis, quod uobis secundum consuetudinem legitur, sine tumultu et contentionibus audite. 3.2.80-82.

118. Qui infirmi sunt ex pristina consuetudine, si aliter tractantur in uictu, non debet aliis molestum esse nec iniustum uideri, quos facit alia consuetudo fortiores. 3.3.85-88.

119. *Ira* is used twice and *irascor* once in chapter six of the *Rule*.

120. Lites aut nullas habeatis, aut quam celerrime finiatis. 6.1.303-304.

121. See *The Rule of Saint Augustine: an Essay in Understanding*, by Sister Agatha Mary, S.P.B. Augustinian Press, Villanova PA, 1992: 255ff.

122. Luc Verheijen believes that this exegesis of Mt 7:3-5 helps to establish the Augustinian authorship of the *Rule* and to date it to c.397. See his: "The Straw, the Beam the Tusculan Disputations and the Rule of Saint Augustine–On a Surprising Augustinian Exegesis." *Augustinian Studies* 2 (1971): 35-36. Augustine first applied the imagery of the straw and the beam (or: splinter/*festuca* and timber/*trabes*) to quick anger and inveterate hatred in his *De sermone Domini in monte* around 394 and then continued to use the imagery another eight times in his writings or sermons. Ibid. 36, 22.

123. From 1 John 3:15: he who hates his brother is a murderer. The fuller quotation from the *Rule* reads: ne ira crescat in odium et trabem faciat de festuca, et animam faciat homicidam. 6.1.305-307.

124. Cf.: Quicumque c onuicio, vel maledicto, vel etiam criminis obiectu, alterum laesit.... Proinde uobis a verbis durioribus parcite. 6.2.310-311, 328.

125. "Be more earnest to dwell in concord than to vanquish each other in controversy." [M]aiorem date operam concordandis uobis quam redarguendis. *Ep.* 210.2. CSEL 44 (355:22-23).

126. [S]icut acetum corrumpit uas, si diutius ibi fuerit, sic ira corrumpit cor, si in alium diem durauerit *Ep.* 210.2. CSEL 44 (355:23-25).

127. This letter has had a long textual history. The first part, 211.1-4 is now known as the *Obiugatio*, or *Reprimand to Quarreling Nuns*. The second part, 211.5-16 is the feminine version of the Rule. For the history of the texts, see Lawless, *Augustine of Hippo and his Monastic Rule*, 152-154.

128. What his position was, is not clear: he may have held the position of a spiritual director, or perhaps he was some kind of liaison with the outside world, especially as regards things ecclesiastical.

129. The reader will recall the incident recounted earlier in this work regarding the Fussalians whom the bishop also avoided meeting. Although the nuns' anger is not directed at Augustine, as was the Fussalians', nevertheless both incidents reveal Augustine's reluctance to engage in an emotional conflict. These observations would confirm Bonner's statement cited in n. 85.

130. Cf.: orate ne intretis in temptationem, ne iterum in contentiones, aemulationes, animositates, dissensiones, detractiones, seditiones, susurrationes. *Ep.* 211.3. CSEL 44 (358:4-7).

131. Cf. Joseph M. Hallman, *The Descent of God: Divine Suffering in History and Theology,* Fortress Press, Philadelphia, 1991. A section devoted to Augustine deals with the subject of the divine immutability vis-á-vis certain emotions such as anger, jealousy, and repentance which are attributed to God in the biblical narrative (pp. 105-123). The author feels that Augustine, while upholding the Platonic view of God as immutable, continued to use the scriptural imagery for effect, but purged the emotion attributed to God (such as anger) of any negativity, thus implying a positive value to the emotion.

132. Sr. Agatha Mary deals extensively with the question of the *minoribus* in pages 272-278.

133. We recall the analogous situation between a master and a slave where Augustine advises the master to repent before God and punish his own heart. "And although it may not be fitting that he should say to the servant 'give me pardon,' yet he should speak to him soothingly. To speak to him with kindness, that is to beg his forgiveness." The fuller citation reads: Quid ergo? Ante oculos dei paeniteat eum, ante oculos dei puniat cor suum, et si non potest seruo dicere quia non oportet: Da mihi ueniam, blande illum alloquatur. Blanda enim appellatio, ueniae est postulatio. *Sermon* 211.4. PL 38 col. 1056.

134. In the *Rule* this is expressed as: cum dilectione hominum et odio uitiorum: "with love for the person and hatred for sin." 4.10.209.

135. Stephen "raged in word but loved in heart": saeuiebat ore, corde diligebat. *En. in ps.* 132.8.12. CCL 40 (1932).

136. *Vita* 22.6-7. See page 82 for citation.

137. Quam si ferre recusauerit, etiam si ipse non abscesserit, de uestra societate proiciatur. 4.9.200-202.

138. Non enim et hoc fit crudeliter, sed misericorditer, ne *contagione pestifera* plurimos perdat. 4.9.203-204. Medical terminology applied to the spiritual life is common among spiritual writers in the early Church. It entered the tradition through Stoicism which employed it analogously in the description of the diseases and treatment of the soul.

139. This first occurrence is found in the verses which begin this section: "Either have no quarrels or put an end to them as quickly as possible" (6.1.304). The Latin is cited in n. 120.

140. "An unwillingness to take responsibility for one's bad temper and to apologize for it when necessary is symptomatic of an unwillingness to be responsible for oneself in general, and it is this attitude which calls in question a person's fitness for life in the monastery." Sr. Agatha Mary, 269-270.

141. "When we say, 'Forgive us our debts, as we forgive our debtors,' we remind ourselves of both what we are to pray for and what we are to do to be worthy to receive it." [C]um dicimus: Dimitte nobis debita nostra, sicut et nos dimittimus debitoribus nostris, nos admonemus, et quid petamus et quid faciamus, ut accipere mereamur. *Ep.*130.XI.21 CSEL 44 (64:3-6). The daily recitation of this verse is compared to a "daily baptism" in *Sermon* 213.9. Besides the *Rule's* double citation of the verse from the Lord's prayer: "forgive us our debts as we forgive our debtors," Augustine quotes it "no less than 183 times elsewhere. The bishop of Hippo regards mutual forgiveness as the fundamental axis of Christian life." Lawless, "The Rule ...as a Mirror of Perfection": 468.

142. Lawless: "pardon doit être prompt, sincère et inconditionnel." The author also notes that: "dans ce problème de la réconciliation humaine et divine, la force du lien á Dieu est telle que le chrétien, dans une certaine manière d'agir, prive Dieu de liberté s'il refuse

d'accorder le pardon." Lawless, " "Le Pardon Mutuel dans la Compréhension augustinienne du Notre Père (Mt 6,12)." *Connaissance Péres de l'Église* 75: *La Pénitence.* Éditions Nouvelle Cité (1999). Quotations are from pages 48 and 50.

143. Donantes iniurias, sicut et deus in Christo donavit nobis. Cf. Eph 4:32 and Col 3:13, quoted in *Ep.* 48.3.3-4.

144. [E]t quam libens atque placatus bona desideria impleat eorum, a quibus aliena peccata nouit ignosci. *Ep.*130.VIII.15. CSEL 44 (57:13-15).

145. Nam in discordia non benedicis Dominum. *En. in ps.* 132.13.4. CCL 40 (1935).

146. "[P]erdonare e perdonarsi è la vita stessa dei cristiani." Vittorino Grossi, "Introduzione" to *Sant'Agostino: La riconciliazione cristiana*, Città Nuova Editrice, Rome (1983): 43. The "power of the keys," both in its sacramental form stemming from Christ's bestowal of the gift of forgiving sins upon Peter and in its more universal form in which the whole Church participates, is a theme of importance to Augustine and closely aligned with reconciliation. The latter use is the topic of the doctoral dissertation of Joseph Carola, S.J. *Solvitis et Vos: The Laity and their Exercise of the Power of the Keys according to Saint Augustine of Hippo.* Augustinianum, 2001. The essential Christian element of forgiveness is brought out by Verheijen who compares these lines from the *Rule*: "An individual who absolutely refuses to ask pardon, or does so without meaning it, is entirely out of place in the monastery, even if he is not dismissed," with Sermon 211.10 which refers to those who refuse to end animosities as unworthy of the name Christian. Verheijen, "Les Sermons..." de Saint Augustin pour le carême (205-211) et sa motivation de la vie 'ascetique.'" *Nouvelle Approche* I: 185.

147. Zumkeller takes "your" (*uestras*) to refer to those who are having the disagreement; the difference in pronouns (they and you), however, indicate to me that Augustine is making the distinction between the community he is addressing in the *Rule* and two hypothetical disputers. Adolar Zumkeller, *Augustine's Rule*, Augustinian Press, Villanova, PA (1987): 107.

148. E.g. in the phrase "...what does God prepare for those who bear with one another? ...quid praeparat sustinentibus se. *Ep.* 210.16-17(354). Cf. Augustine's depiction of monasteries as places where "all love, all forebear one another mutually:"...omnes se diligunt, omnes inuicem se sustinent. *En. in ps.* 99.12.47. CCL 39 (1401).

149. E.g.: *Ep.* 48 where Abbot Eudoxius is told to do all things for the glory of God, including:...sufferentes tribulationem et ante omnia uos ipsos inuicem in dilectionem–quid enim sufferat, qui fratrem non suffert? *Ep.* 48.3. CSEL 34² (139:6-8). Also note that Christ's words: "In this will one know that you are my disciples, if you love one another" (Jn 13:34) contains the responsibility to bear one's another's burdens. Cf. *De diversis quaesitiones* 71.1.

150. Christum autem diligendo, facile sustinemus infirmitatem alterius, etiam quem nondum propter bona sua diligimus. Cogitamus enim quia ille quem diligimus, Dominus propter eum mortuus est. *De diversis quaesitionibus* 71.7; PL 40 col. 83.

151. Cf.: Circa omnes seipsum bonorum operum praebeat exemplum, corripiat inquietos, consoletur pusillanimes, suscipiat infirmos, patiens sit ad omnes. 7.3.360-362.

152. [E]o robustior es ad ceteros sustenendos, quo iam non habes quod in te alii sustineant. *En. in ps.* 99.9.11-12. CCL 39 (1398).

153. [S]ed diversa tempora et diversa genera infirmitatis faciunt ut onera nostra portare invicem valeamus. Verbi gratia, iram fratris tui tunc portabis, cum tu adversus eum non irasceris; ut rursus eo tempore quo te ira praeoccupaverit, ille te lenitate et tranquillitate sua supportet. *Div. quaes.* 71.2. PL 40 col. 81.

154. Ut ergo cuncta ista seruentur et, si quid seruatum non fuerit, non neglegenter prae-tereatur, sed emendandum corrigendumque curetur ad praepositum praecipue pertinebit. 7.2.347-351.

155. Ghislain Lafont draws attention to certain oddities in Augustine's presentation including the differences between the Gospel's "communitarian climate" and the Bishop's "penal procedure" in: "Fraternal Correction in the Augustinian Community." *Word & Spirit* 9 (1987): 87-91.

156. [C]um dilectione hominum et odio uitiorum. 4.10.209.

157. [Q]uis enim facile inuenitur, qui uelit reprehendi? *Ep.* 210.2. CSEL 44 (355:1-2).

158. Verheijen discusses fraternal correction as a form of friendship and says that Augustine "is a convinced defender of 'friendly correction'." "The Staw..." 27-28. The rela-tion between *correctio* and *correptio* (correction and reprimand) is reviewed by Vitorino Grossi in "Correction," *Augustine Through the Ages*, 242-244. The author believes that *correctio* is better translated as "reproach" than "correction."

159. Cf: "...fraternal correction is a sound and necessary instrument for renewal and reform." Lawless, "Enduring Values...": 71.

160. [S]olet enim fieri et frequenter accidit, ut ad horam contristetur, cum reprehendi-tur, et resistat et contendat et tamen postea consideret secum in silentio, ubi nemo est nisi deus et ipse nec timet displicere hominibus, quia corripitur, sed timet displicere deo, quia non corrigitur, et deinceps non faciat illud, quod iuste reprehensus est, et, quantum odit peccatum suum, tantum diligat fratrem, quem sensit hostem peccati sui. *Ep.* 210.2. CSEL 44 (355:5-12).

161. Quid est, quod haec rerum pars alternat defectu et profectu, offensionibus et con-ciliationibus? An is est modus earum.... *Conf.* 8.8.40-41. CCL 27 (118).

162. [U]bique maius gaudium molestia maiore praeceditur. *Conf.* 8.8.37-38. CCL 27 (118).

163. Haec ergo agite–et deus pacis erit uobiscum. *Ep.* 210.2. CSEL 44 (355:25) and cf. Phil. 4:9

164. "On this cross, indeed, the Christian ought to hang continually throughout the whole of life, which is spent in the midst of trials and temptations.... This cross, I repeat, is not just meant for forty days, but for the whole of life." In hac quidem cruce, per totam istam vitam, quae in mediis tentationibus ducitur, perpetuo debet pendere christianus.... [C]rux, inquam, ista non quadraginta dierum est, sed totius hujus vitae. *Sermon* 205.1 (PL 38 col. 1039). Benedict will echo Augustine's sentiments in his chapter on the observance of Lent: "...at all times the life of a monk ought to possess a Lenten observance." [O]mni tempore vita monachi quadragesimae debet observationem habere." *Rule of Benedict* 49.1.

Numerical citations standing alone in this section will henceforth refer to the *Sermons.* English translations are those of Edmund Hill, O.P. *Sermons*, vol.1-10. *The Works of Saint Augustine. A translation of the 21ˢᵗ Century.* Ed. John E. Rotelle, O.S.A. New City Press. Brooklyn, NY (1990-95).

165. Lent as a special season for all Christians to renew their Christian life and to do penance, not only those who had committed major sins but everyone, as a celebration of the salvation won by Christ–are themes taken up by Allan Fitzgerald in "Pénitence et Carême." *Connaissance des Péres de L'Église* 75: *La Penitence.* Éditions Nouvelle Cité, Sept. 1999.

166. [T]e quaerit Deus magis quam munus tuum.... Plus quaerit Christus quem redemit sanguine suo, quam quod tu invenisti in horreo tuo. 82.5. PL 38 col. 508.

167. [U]t oratio secura procedat: nec offendat, aut palpitet, aut sub conscientiae stimulis obmutescat, cum ad eum locum venerit, ubi dicendum est, *Dimitte nobis debita nostra, sicut et nos dimittimus debitoribus nostris.* 208.2. PL 38 col. 1046. A question remains whether

the bishop alone said the Our Father or whether it was recited by the congregation as well. *Sermon* 58.12 (dated 410-412) indicates that they only hear it recited (cf. n.12), while *Sermon* 49.8 (dated 420) strongly implies that they are saying it. Are these signs of a liturgical development?

168. Again backed by scripture: Eph 4:26.

169. Sed in cujus pectore adhuc usque permansit [ira], pellat eam saltem jam proximus dies Dominicae passionis, qui non est iratus interfectoribus suis, pro quibus in ligno pendens et precem fudit et sanguinem. 208.2. PL 38 col. 1045.

170. For example: 206.1-3, 207.1-3 and 210.4-5,9 mention all three exercises, and alms and fasting are both mentioned in 205.2.

171. Prae caeteris, fratres, a litibus et discordiis jejunate. 205.3. PL 38 col. 1040. This is a concrete illustration of Augustine's emphasis on interiority.

172. "It's human to get angry–and if only we could avoid that too–it's human to get angry..." Humanum est irasci: et utinam nec hoc possemus. Humanum est irasci.... 211.1. PL 38 col. 1054. And cf: *Be angry*, like human beings, if it gets the better of you.... *Irascimini* quasi homines, si vincimini; 58.8. PL 38 col. 397. We will return to this latter passage below.

173. "To be indignant with the sinner with a view to his correction...is an emotion, as far as I can see, no sane judgment could reprove." Irasci enim peccanti, ut corrigatur;...nescio utrum quisquam sana consideratione reprehendat. *De civitas dei* 9.5. PL 41 col. 260.

174. Non potes illam [iram] interimere, potes illam reprimere. 315.10. PL 38 col. 1431.

175. Denique in disciplina nostra non tam quaeritur utrum pius animus irascatur sed quare irascatur. *De civ. dei* 9.5. PL 41 col. 260. These words occur in the midst of a discussion on the passions in which the Bishop of Hippo, aligning himself with Cicero's thought, regards an emotion such as compassion as a good. Augustine straddles the issue when the discussion turns to God and the angels; he would like to see an analogous sense of compassion even in them (and allowing a kind of fear in the angels as well when they are rightfully fearful of someone else's danger), while insisting that they (both God and the angels) are "not subject to our passions." Ibid.

176. Intus enim sibi ipse inimicus est, qui odit alterum. Sed quia non sentit quid sibi mali faciat, in alterum saevit, eo periculosius vivens, quo non sentit quid secum mali agit; quia et saeviendo sensum perdidit. 82.3. PL 38 col. 507.

177. Quid autem stultius, quam inimicum forinsecus devitare, et multo pejorem in praecordiis intimis retinere? 208.2. PL 38 col. 1045.

178. A vicious side of hatred that often accompanies anger is "lust for revenge" (*libido vindictae* 58.8).

179. The full text reads: Non exspectemus vindicari, fratres. Quid est, vindicari, nisi malo alieno pasci? Scio quotidie venire homines, genua figere, frontem terrae concutere, aliquando vultum suum lacrymis rigare; et in ista tanta humilitate ac perturbatione dicere: Domine, vindica me, occide inimicum meum. Plane ora, ut occidat inimicum tuum, et salvet fratrem tuum: occidat inimicitias, salvet naturam. Sic ora, ut vindicet te Deus: pereat qui te persequebatur, sed maneat qui tibi reddatur. 211.6. PL 38 col. 1057-58. I have simplified Hill's translation of the first line which seems to be unnecessarily cumbersome in this instance: "Don't let's expect to be avenged...."

180. Cf: Qui odit fratrem suum, ambulat, exit, intrat, procedit, nullis catenis oneratus, nullo carcere inclusus: reatu tamen ligatus est. Noli illum putare sine carcere esse: carcer ejus, cor ejus est. 211.2. PL 38 col. 1055.

181. The references are chronologically diverse and may indicate that Augustine had encountered this phenomenon in individuals a number of times during his life. It seems to have struck him as particularly absurd. See *Sermons* 82.1 (dated 408 A.D.), 58.8 (dated 410-412), 114A.6 (dated 428-9), and 387 (undated: this sermon is a pastiche of Augustine's words, attributed by Morin to St. Caesarius).

182. [I]ra inveterata fit odium, festuca nutrita fit trabes. 49.7. PL 38 col. 324. Also cf. 387.2, 82.1-2 and the following note. Although he does not acknowledge the source, Augustine took his definition of hatred (odium est ira inveterata) from Cicero's *Tusculanae* IV.9.21, who in turn received it from the Stoic tradition. It is found in a biography of the Stoic Zeno. Verheijen, "The Straw..." 24. Also see above, p.98, n.122.

183. The full sentence: Quod e rat ira, cum esset nova, odium factum est; quia in vetustatem conversum est. Ira festuca est, odium trabes est. 58.8. PL 38 col. 397. The translator is Edmund Hill as mentioned in n. 164.

184. Quid est odium? Ira inveterata. Ira inveterata si facta est iam odium dicitur. 58.8. PL 38 col. 397. The term *inveterata* conjured up for Augustine not only something old, but also hard. See Verheijen, "The Straw..." 21. He makes a similar point elsewhere: "La haine ressemble donc á une poutre. Plus elle devient vieille, plus elle devient dure." Verheijen: "Les Sermons..." 177.

185. We recall Augustine's sentiments at the time of Bishop Megalius' death.: "[Hatred] sneaks up on us since no one who is angry thinks that his anger is unjust. For, when it takes root in that way, anger becomes hatred while the sweetness added as if from righteous resentment holds it longer in the cask until the whole becomes sour and spoils the cask." *Ep.* 38.2. [S]ubrepit autem, dum nulli i rascenti ira sua uidetur iniusta. Ita enim inueterescens ira fit odium, dum quasi iusti doloris admixta dulcedo diutius eam in uase detinet, donec totum acescat uasque corrumpat. CSEL 34.² (l65: 20-23).

186. The distinction is also seen in the desire a person has for another's good or ill: "It is quite possible that in becoming angry with a person you actually wish for his amendment; however, if you hate a person, you cannot wish to change him for the better." Fieri autem potest ut si irascaris homini, velis eum corrigi; si autem oderis hominem, non potes eum velle corrigere. *De sermone Domini in monte*19.63. PL 34 col. 1298. I am indebted to Verheijen for this reference; "The Straw..." 19.

187. [U]t aliquando magis odisse convincatur, si non irascitur. 82.2. PL 38 col. 506.

188. Qui sum ego, qui in hominem exsero comminationes? Morior forte antequam vindicer. Et cum anhelans, ira inflammatus, et sitiens vindictam, exiero de corpore, non me suscipit ille qui noluit vindicari: non me suscipit ille qui dixit, *Date, et dabitur vobis; dimittite, et dimittetur vobis* (Luc. VI, 37, 38). Ergo compescam me ab iracundia mea, et redibo ad quietem cordis mei. 63.2. PL 38 col. 424. The sermon is a commentary on the storm at sea in Mt 8:23-27. As Christ calmed the waves, so he too calms our anger and other passions. The second line might also be translated: I might die before I am vindicated.

189. Etenim omnis homo, quem poenitet, sibi irascitur: poenitentiae iram exercet in se. 296.12 (296.10 in PL) col. 1358; and cf. 179A.7.

190. Omnis enim paenitens irascitur sibi: nam, quia irascitur, punit se.... Certe omnia haec indicia sunt hominis saevientis in se, et irascentis sibi.112A.5 MA I (258:15-16, 19-20.); see also113.2 and 315.9. The gestures of the penitent include: tearing the hair, wrapping oneself in sackcloth, and beating the breast.

191. Videte, fratres mei; videte, filii mei; videte filii Dei; videte, quia dico vobis. Pugnate cum corde vestro, quantum potestis. Et si videritis iram vestram stare adversus vos, rogate contra illam Deum: faciat te Deus victorem tui; faciat te Deus victorem, non inimici

forinsecus tui, sed intrinsecus animi tui. Aderit enim et faciet. Plus vult ut hoc ab illo petamus, quam pluviam. 57.13. PL 38 col. 392.

192. The fuller passage is worthy of citation: [T]antum dominata est iracundia, quantum potuit, ut non solum tumultuaretur cor, sed et convicia et crimina vomeret lingua. Non vides quo te impulit? non vides quo te praecipitavit? Tandem corrige, dic, Male feci, peccavi. Non enim morieris, si dixeris. 17.6.PL 38 col. 127.

193. Homines autem faciles sunt ad irrogandas injurias, et difficiles ad concordiam requirendam. Pete, inquit, veniam ab homine quem offendisti, ab homine quem laesisti. Respondet: Non me humiliabo. Vel Deum tuum audi, si fratrem tuum contemnis: *Qui se humiliat, exaltabitur* (Luc XIV.11). Non vis te humiliare qui cecidisti? Multum interest inter se humiliantem et inter jacentem. Jam jaces, et humiliare te non vis? Bene diceres, Nolo descendere; si noluisses ruere. 82.6. PL 38 col. 508. I removed the biblical citation from the Hill translation above (Mt 18:4), leaving that of PL which is the accurate one.

194. Qui se concordiae recolit neglectorem, excutiat expergiscendo torporem: qui se cupit esse sui debitoris exactorem, Dei se cogitet debitorem: qui erubescit petere ut sibi frater ignoscat, vincat per bonum timorem malum pudorem: ut noxiis inimicitiis finitis, ut eis mortuis, vos vivatis. 209.1. PL 38 col. 1046.

195. The full citation reads: Dimitte mihi quod in te peccavi: si dixisti ex toto corde, si vera humilitate, non ficta charitate, quomodo Deus videt in corde unde dixisti, sed ille noluit tibi dimittere, noli esse sollicitus. Servi estis ambo, habetis Dominum: conservo tuo debes, noluit tibi dimittere; interpella Dominum amborum. 211.4. PL 38 col. 1055-56.

196. Blanda enim appellatio, veniae est postulatio. 211.4. PL 38 col. 1056. A like case was that of the superior mentioned above (p. 101) who fears that he or she may have used *verba dura* in correcting, but does not wish to apologize for fear of undermining his or her authority.

197. A pastiche of lines from 58.7-8: Dimittite omnia de cordibus vestris....Si ergo irasceris; ne occidat sol iste in corde tuo super iracundiam tuam.... Ergo dimittite: dimittite ex corde. 58.7-8. PL 38 col. 396-397.

198. The fuller quotation reads: Si pecuniam piget erogare indigenti, eroga veniam paenitenti. 114A.5 MA I (235: 24-25).

199. This is the essence of a feigned dialogue Augustine has with a person who doesn't want to forgive: "I won't forgive him," you say. "He's done me such harm, he's crossed me and opposed me so much." You're treating yourself much worse. "I won't forgive him." "I beg you, pardon him, forgive him." "But he isn't begging me." "You do his begging for him." Non ignosco, inquit; multum me laesit, multum mihi adversarius fuit. Peior tibi es. Non ignosco. Rogo te, ignosce, dimitte. Sed non me rogat. Tu pro illo roga. 179A.7. MA I (679: 24-26). Hill has translated "inquit" as "you say" for the sake of consistency with the rest of the dialogue.

200. Cf: [C]onsiderate, charissimi, utrum christianus dicendus sit, qui saltem his diebus inimicitias non vult finire, quas nunquam debuit exercere. 210.12. PL 38 col. 1054.

201. Cf: Debent inter vos esse alii pacifici, qui illum objurgent, ut a te prius veniam petat: tu tantum paratus esto ignoscere, prorsus paratus esto ex corde dimittere. 211.5. PL 38 col. 1057.

202. Si paratus es dimittere, jam dimisisti. 211.5. PL 38 col. 1057.

203. That is: ....do not wish to free your brother from sin? Sermon 211.3.

204. For more on this topic, see the already cited: *Solvitis et Vos: The Laity and their Exercise of the Power of the Keys according to Saint Augustine of Hippo* by Joseph A. F. Carola.

205. Permane amicus amborum.... Mala si quae audis ab altero de altero, noli prodere alteri.... Audisti ab irato verbum, a dolente, a succensente; moriatur in te. Quare proditur, quare profertur? Non enim si in te fuerit, disrumpet te. 49.6 PL 38 col. 323.

CONCLUDING REMARKS

The portraits of the four faces of anger which we have surveyed have turned out to possess many of the same features; yet each displays as well his own particular visage to the world. Seneca, coming from a tradition different from our Christian authors, is the most distinct. His absolute condemnation of anger sets him apart from the others, as does his underlying assumption that the goal of virtue lies solely in personal fulfillment through a life of discipline. But there are areas as well which overlap with the values of our three Christian authors; for example, Seneca's teaching that imperfection is the norm in the world goes far in lessening a person's frustration and brings with it as well an attitude of forgiveness which in turn leads to the inner peace of mind and soul which is his aim. Another vital area of overlap is the role that thoughts play in curing a person from anger: for Seneca, thoughts are controlled by a proper view of reality including the insight that the real enemy is the vice hidden in the soul. And finally, a quality which endears him to all, Christian and non-Christian alike, is his ability to be radically self-honest.

Our Christian authors also have some features particular to themselves, due primarily to their common heritage in scripture, but also somewhat dependent on their common classical education. All three agree that the scriptural depiction of God as angry is a projection of human emotions onto God for the sake of conveying an abstract truth, such as divine justice, in concrete language familiar to the readers. Important to grasp is that their reluctance to ascribe anger to God is not because anger is sometimes evil but because it is human. They are all also in agreement that anger is an essential constituent of human nature, being at root a neutral power (faculty) which becomes good or evil according to the use made of it. And as such, it is in each person's power to turn this irascible force on itself when it raises its head in a harmful way. Evagrius and Cassian also speak of turning it against the devil to offset the latter's temptations.

Note that these authors never present the use of anger against ourselves or the demons as if it were an option, or as if it were only for those who are exposed to violent temptations and therefore need to use some kind of counter violence in order to overcome evil. Anger is not an option, it is a necessity, albeit used correctly. The ancient masters taught their fellow brothers and sisters to stand up courageously and fight against their own habits of sin and to withstand the attacks inflicted from the underworld. The Lord himself said: "The kingdom of heaven has suffered violence and the violent take it by force" (Mt 11:12). Anger is thus a God-given power within each human being to be used to vanquish the forces of evil whenever they suggest a thought or action contrary to the will of God. Jesus' own words: "Get behind me, Satan!" (Mt 16:23) were no doubt spoken with that irascible force which brooked no compromise. That same incentive power inflamed into zeal compelled him to drive the buyers and sellers out the temple (Jn 2:17). But zeal, like its less ardent type–anger–may be exercised in two directions: its positive thrust moves a a person towards greatness, its bitter counterpart forever feeds the fires of hell.[1]

Most importantly, our Christian authors see that anger can never be legitimately used against another human being. The underlying reason is the bond which exists among all Christians and to a lesser degree among all the human race because of the salvific work of Christ. The relationship of love owed to everyone which is central to the Christian faith has created new patterns of relating based on Christ's teaching that love of God and neighbor now replaces the former "an eye for an eye and a tooth for a tooth" (Mt 5:38). Acts leading to separation from our brothers or sisters incur a like estrangement from God, expressed succinctly in the Lord's prayer. Therefore, all three authors advocate a loving and harmonious relationship with every human being as the norm based on humility and reconciliation if anger does occur. The intensity of their teaching on common relationships differs however. Evagrius, our semi-anchorite, is concerned with relationships which the desert monks have one on one, emphasizing the role which discernment of thoughts have in converting anger into gentleness. Cassian the cenobite is more community minded, but even he speaks in terms of personal spiritual advancement through combating anger as one of the eight deadly sins. This is however balanced by the juxtaposition of two issues, anger and friendship, in the same treatise. As I argued above, both friendship and anger have an impact on community as a whole and this concept undergirds the whole treatise, even when it is not explicit. The most community oriented of the three by far is Augustine whose concept of community as members united in Christ, sharing "one heart and one soul" undergirds nearly everything that he says, whether the other members are fellow monks in the monastery at Hippo or brothers or sisters in the Bishop's congregation. Although he echoes his three predecessors that anger in a soul harms primarily the person who harbors it, his main purpose is to show that anger destroys community whenever its object is another human being. His global vision of each person as a single entity of that larger Body of Christ, the Church, raises one to view the panoramic expansion of love and thereby the potentially wide destructive power of anger. Both idealistic and realistic, Augustine leaves us with a contemplative view of love and anger which is both comforting and challenging.

The issue of influence, except for Evagrius on Cassian–amply noted above, is more difficult to establish. The Stoic approach to anger would certainly have been known to all three of our Christian authors from their classical education with or without a direct reading of Seneca's *De ira*. Augustine displays no evidence of contact with Evagrius' writings in translation or through Cassian's works. The probability greatly lessens when we realize that Cassian wrote after 418, and therefore after nearly all the works of Augustine which we have considered in this undertaking. Conversely, Augustine's influence on his younger contemporary, Cassian–acknowledged elsewhere[2]–is not evident in our study. Rather, the lack of direct influence of our three Christian authors on each other, combined with similarities in thought and pursuit–notably their unflinching agreement that anger against another human person is never justified–bring ever more into relief the scriptures and their monastic experience as fundamental sources of inspiration. All those dedicated to the pursuit of holiness today would do well to heed the divine injunction with like zeal.

> *But I say to you that every one who is angry with his brother shall be liable to judgment; whoever insults his brother shall be liable to the council, and whoever says, "You fool!" shall be liable to the hell of fire (Mt 5:22).*

Notes

1. Speaking of the two-pronged potential of anger, Fr. Simon Tugwell, O.P. writes: "It is the power that smashes through limitations, leading us either to become visionaries or to become vandals." *Magnificat*, Editor-in-Chief: Peter John Cameron, O.P., Yonkers, NY. Vol. 11, No. 13 (February 2010) 390.

On the two types of zeal, St. Benedict teaches: "Just as there is a wicked zeal of bitterness which separates from God and leads to hell, so there is a good zeal which separates from evil and leads to God and everlasting life." *Rule of Benedict* 72.1-2.

2. "Cassian's relationship to Augustine was rather more rich than is generally acknowledged." Boniface Ramsey, O.P. "John Cassian: Student of Augustine." CSQ 28 (1998): 5-15, 199-200. Citation is from p.15. Cf. also George Lawless, O.S.A. "John Cassian: The Conferences." A book review of Boniface Ramsey's translation of *The Conferences* [translated in 1997]. *Augustinian Studies* 31/1 (2000): 119-128.

APPENDICES

I. Personal Portrait

The oldest extant depiction of the saint dates to 150 years after Augustine's death.[1] It conforms to the evidence that we know of him: namely, that he wore his hair very short, was clean shaven, had sharp features, and wore the monastic *birrus* which seems to have been a short, dark choir mantle open in the front with a strap, over a basic tunic. The *cuculla* is a later development of the same garment. There does not seem to be a hood at this period. Augustine dressed simply, like the rest of his monastic clergy. He avoided carelessness and elegance in his attire. Regarding personal hygiene, he always felt that people who seek sanctity to the neglect of their persons are just dirty fellows. He felt too that ragged clothing was often a deceit, hiding a hypocrite.[2] As for his health, he tended to have a weak constitution. He abhorred travel by sea since he suffered from sea-sickness, and although he often had to travel to Carthage, he never went by boat; instead he traveled over land, even when he was old.

II. Topography

The most important city of Roman Africa was Carthage, with its half million inhabitants. Augustine lived there as a young adult for many years and so the familiar city was a second home to him. Nevertheless, Augustine hated to be away from his beloved Hippo Regius, which was in its own right one of the more important cities of North Africa after Carthage. Lying about 125 miles to the west of Carthage, Hippo was also a seaport town with a population of about 30-40,000. Africa was the granary–the bread basket–of Rome and the empire, and Hippo was an important port for exporting the grain going to Italy and elsewhere. Yet for all its prosperity and importance, it was still only a provincial town. It was very much like any Roman town of its day with its usual market, forum, theater, and two baths which were often used for lectures. It also had exclusive seaside villas and a strong city wall which enabled it to defend itself for fourteen months, when in 430 A.D. it was besieged by the Vandals. In the countryside there were several small chapels and *martyria*, and at least one pilgrim hostel.

III. Ruins of Augustine's church complex[3]

Archeological evidence from nearly 90 years ago[4] has turned up a Christian "island" within the city walls of Hippo not far from the seashore. In relationship to the rest of the town, this area lies a half mile from "downtown" in the direction of the harbor, between the forum and one of the baths. The complex is shaped like an irregular polygon, enclosed by a wall and consists of several buildings including a large church which very likely is the *basilica major*, "the Great Church," also called the "basilica of peace." If so, then this island is the ecclesiastical complex where Augustine the bishop, lived, prayed, carried on his episcopal duties and wrote his great works. The church is not large, about 60 by 147 feet including the apse, and has several rooms connected to it on the east side, one of which may have been the *martyrium* which housed the relics of St. Stephen. To the northeast and also joined to the church is another complex which would have served well as a clerical residence for the bishop and his clergy. Literary evidence mentions other buildings in the ecclesiastical complex including a *secretarium* containing the archives, reception rooms, and a hostel (completed in early 426). One of these buildings must also have housed Augustine's fine library. Van der Meer also mentions some small rooms with a garden which may have been part of Augustine's "garden monastery" for his lay monks.[5]

Literary evidence also mentions a monastery of nuns in Hippo whose superior was Augustine's older sister. We do not know her name; she seems to have died around 420. The exact whereabouts of the nuns' monastery remains uncertain.[6] According to Van der Meer, there were over a hundred nuns in the monastery of Hippo, as well as at the monastery in Tagaste, which seems not to have been unusual.[7]

The ecclesial compound contains another church, to the west of and smaller than the "Great Church" which is possibly the older Leontian basilica–dedicated to St. Leontius, a former bishop of Hippo and possibly a martyr–which literary evidence also places in the town. On one occasion, when Augustine was preaching in this older basilica, the noise inside a nearby Donatist church could be heard from inside the Catholic basilica.[8] The two buildings must have been quite close indeed. The ruins of yet another church outside the compound to the northeast raises the possibility–however remote–that the older church to the west of the Great Church is the older Leontian basilica. However, since the precise location of neither church–St. Leontius or the Donatist church–is known, nothing definite can be said about this second church in the compound.

The town of Hippo continued to exist after the Vandals seized the town in 431 and retained a bishop up to the time of Islam. A small Christian community continued up to the eleventh century, after which the inhabitants moved farther northwards to the site of the present day Annaba, in modern Algiers, abandoning the old city to decay and demise. Annaba has a church to St. Augustine which was constructed in 1890. Augustine's tomb is in Pavia.

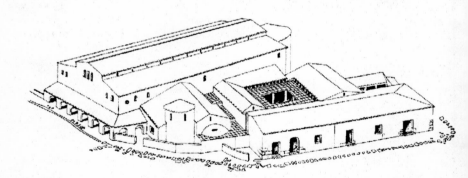

Plan A: A reconstruction of St. Augustine's church at Hippo. To the right of the Church are probably the episcopal quarters, which would have included the clerical monastery as well as rooms designated for diocesan business.

Plan B: This map of the Christian "island" of Hippo is based on the ruins which can still be seen today. The "Great Church" where St. Augustine preached is easily identifiable; the probable episcopal rooms are located in the NE corner of the map. The location of the "Garden Monastery" is unknown, but may have been in the area marked "C" south of the smaller church (B) in the diagram.

IV. Some Important Monastic Writings

De moribus ecclesiae catholicae 1.13.65ff: an early treatise begun in Rome and very likely finished in Tagaste in which Augustine makes mention of the monks of the Catholic Church. Even here the ideal of Acts 4:32: living with one heart and one soul, dispossessed of all is central to his monastic ideal.

Ordo Monasterii: this work remains something of a mystery, both in authorship and place of origin.[9] Probably known at Vivarium (same sequence of psalms), it was used along with the *Praeceptum* by Caesarius of Arles. Alypius is thought by Verheijen to be the author (he did visit Jerome in Bethlehem and 2 of the 3 psalms are the same as that of the East), but this information could have come via Milan or Rome. Augustine's authorship cannot be ruled out. Was it perhaps his first rule for the Tagaste monastery?

Praeceptum: the *Rule*, probably written around 397 for the lay monks when Augustine left them to reside in the bishop's residence. It would then be an aid for the "brothers" after losing Augustine's charismatic leadership in the house. Augustine does not refer to the text as a "rule" but as a *libellus*, a little book. The number of scriptural quotations or illusions makes it clear that they are not so much a "set of laws to be observed but, rather, gospel values to be incarnated."[10] The *Praeceptum* uses *famulus dei* (twice) and *frater* (seven times), one of which is a citation from scripture. It is somewhat of an anomaly that Augustine uses *monasterium* (nine times) without identifying its members as *monachus/i*.[11]

Obiurgatio or *Reprimand to Quarrelling Nuns (Ep.* 211.1-4): There was actually a third monastery at Hippo or its environs, i.e. one for nuns with Augustine's sister as the superior. A few years after her death, there was some dissatisfaction with her successor, a certain Felicitas, and some of the nuns insisted upon her removal. This letter is Augustine's reply. Unfortunately, we do not know much about the nuns. For work, they copied books, spun and wove and may have had a home for orphans.[12] The cloister was not as strict as it was for Caesarius' nuns; nonetheless they did not leave the monastery without good reason. A reference to "flocks of processing and chanting nuns" as part of the honors shown a bishop may imply that the nuns sometimes welcomed visiting bishops with choral music.[13]

Ep. 211.5-16: Appended to *Letter* 211 at some point in the manuscript history, this second section, known separately as the *Rule for Nuns* is virtually identical with the *Praeceptum,* except for obvious changes in grammatical gender, and stripped of interpolations which conservative textual criticism disallows.[14] Augustine doubtless meant his *Rule* to be used by both lay monasteries; even the nuns are permitted to go to the public baths, as long as at least three go together (whereas "two or three" is stipulated for the men). Cf. *Rule* 5.7 and *Ep.* 211.13.

Ep. 48 *to Eudoxius:* Augustine asks this abbot of an island monastery near Sardinia for prayers and begs him and his monks not to be selfish if the Church should need them for ministry.

De opere monachorum: Some monks in Aurelius' diocese of Carthage were refusing to work, saying that the scriptural verse: "Do not take care for tomorrow...." (Mt 6:34) was a counsel which they wished to take literally. Augustine appeals to them to obey the same scripture they want leisure to read, because St. Paul said that one who does not work should not eat. Christ's words were meant only for those who cannot work, such as the sick, or for those employed with preaching and ministry, as were the Apostles. Monastic life must not turn into an excuse for indolence. There are false monks out there, do not fall into this trap and become another scandal in the Church. Besides, one can always keep praying while one is working.

Sermones 355-356: These deal with a scandal among his own clergy. A monk, a widower, died leaving a will when he was supposed to have dispossessed himself of everything when he entered the clerical monastery. Augustine's honesty in dealing with the issue before his congregation offers a lesson in humility and openness.

Confessions 8: Description of his own conversion, after having heard of the narrative of Antony's renunciation and subsequent life in the desert.

Enarratio in psalmos 132: This sermon defends the term "monks," which was in common use but not scriptural in its origins. Augustine links *monachus* to the Greek, *monos,* and then to this psalm which praises those who constitute themselves as a single reality: *unum.* Those who are truly "one" are not those who live alone, but those who live in holy comm*unity* with others bound together by the love of the Holy Spirit.

En. in ps. 99: A somewhat humorous and patently realistic description of life in community, which is compared to boats anchored in a harbor and rubbing up against each other!

V. Structure of Community in Augustine's *Rule*

(Although the points below do not follow a rigid pattern in the Rule, *nevertheless enough of the general structure is in place to warrant this approach:)*

    I. What "makes" Community according to the *Rule*
        1. *Love and Harmony*
            a. honor God mutually in each other (1.8)
            b. harmony of voice and heart (2.3)
            c. service to the community:
                – officials (5.6-8, 5.10-11)
            d. – superiors (5.4, 5.7, 7.1-3)
        2. *Everything in common*
            – God (Cf. 1.2 *in deum*: when you have nothing else, you possess God more
                fully)
            – prayer (2.1)
            – work (5.2)
            – things (5.1)
    II. What "breaks down" Community according to the *Rule*
        1. seeking love/affection outside the community (4)
        2. murmuring (5.1)
        3. anger/quarrels (6.1-2)
        4. contumacy (4.9)
    III. Repairing the "Damage" (Restoring Harmony) according to the Rule
        1. forgiveness (6.2)
        2. patience endurance (7.3)
        3. correction (7.2-4, 4.10)

VI. Afterlife of Augustine's Rule

The *Rule* would subsequently influence the following early monastic legislators:
Fulgentius of Ruspe (462-c.527)
Eugippius of Lucullanum (c. 455-535)
Caesarius of Arles (c. 470-542)
Benedict (480-c.547)
Leander of Seville (c. 545-c.600)
Isidore of Seville (c.560-636)

It was not used exclusively by any of the above, but in conjunction with other monastic Rules and texts. Not until the 9th - 11th c. does the *Rule* of Augustine appear as a Rule of life valid in itself, by different groups. Eventually more than a hundred different groups would adopt it as their Rule of life.[15] Augustine's influence on Benedict–of special interest to this writer–is mostly evident in the horizontal dimension of community life which the great Patriarch incorporated into the last chapters of his *Rule*. One wonders if the *Rule of Benedict* would have had the influence it has had without those important Augustinian additions.

VII. An Outline of Cassian's *Conference* 16 On Friendship

Introduction: Different kinds of human bonds
A. Non-enduring
  a. similar interests, etc. 2.1
  b. natural bonds of family, etc. 2.2
  c. bond formed by magic 28
B. Enduring: founded on virtue 3.1 not destroyed by different desires 3.2
  1. What breaks it down:
    a. is weakened if the same zeal does not exist 3.2
    b. does not work among the spiritually weak 3.3
  2. What cements it: characteristics of true friendship 3.4
    – one mind and one will: Cf. Acts 4:32 (death to one's own will)
    a. one chosen orientation
    b. one desire
    c. one willing
    d. one not willing 3.5
    – common behavior rather than common location makes for unity
      (difference of wills destroys peace)

I TRUE FRIENDSHIP 6.1
  A. Rules for true friendship (6.1-2)
    1. contempt for worldly possessions (People are more important than things)
    2. Restrain self-will
    3. All things are subordinated to the good of love and peace
    4. Never to be angered for any reason
    5. If a brother is angry, have the desire to calm him
    6. Reflect daily on death
      – one who lacks these injects the poison of annoyance into the heart of his
        friends and separate hearts who love one another.

B. Commentary on the above rules 6.3
   1. Possessions: remove the source of conflict; Acts 4:32 (6.4)
   2. Self-will: remove it: Jn 6:38
   3. Good of peace more precious than self-will 6.5
   4. No just reason for anger; and anger destroys prayer. Mt 5:23 Go first to
      your brother... 6.6
   5. One must go graciously and be reconciled before the sun goes down; Eph 4:26.
      It is not a matter of your anger only, but your brother's too. You will be
      punished for not doing your part to be reconciled. 6.7
   6. The thought of death assuages the annoyance at one's brother. 6.8
C. Summary: there are two choices: love or rage. One should do everything to promote
   love and peace and do everything to avoid rage which leads to destruction. Cassian
   here links possessions and self will to two kinds of attachment: to carnal (tangible)
   things and to spiritual perceptions (under which hides pride and self-will).
D. Virtues opposed to the vices:
      Humility: humble thoughts and harmonious will 9
         Do not trust your own judgment (devil gets in here)
         Reveal your thoughts 11
         Desire to be of the same mind
         Consider others to be superior to yourself (Phil 2:1-3) 11.2
         Accept advice from others (cf. Paul → Jerusalem) 12
      Love: to be shown to all (believers and unbelievers) 13
         Difference between agape and affection 14.2
         Scripture backing for his approach; general vs particular 14
   E. Conflict:
      1. Wrong Ways to react: Anger is very subtle and can be disguised as some-
         thing good 15
         a. false spiritual demeanor: (singing psalms)
            vice: stubbornness, pride, spiritual self-righteousness (we are "just")
            remedy: be considerate and humble
            – we cannot hide behind "everything is okay on my side," if the brother
            is annoyed, we cannot deny responsibility for our brother's annoyance
            16.1 God will not accept our gifts. If we are ashamed to be humbled, we
            disdain Christ's commandment. 16.2
         b. those who are too easily hurt and then refuse to accept apologies. This is
            just as blameworthy as the original remark, especially when they refuse to
            endure something from a brother (they more readily forgive a pagan than
            a monk!) 17.1-2
         c. bitter silence or a derisory gesture of disdain. Silence is here used as a
            gesture that arouses anger (18.3). This is feigned patience, a mockery of
            the virtue of patience and it is spiteful. We are not without blame, rather
            we are blameworthy before God, since it provokes others to even more
            anger. Remedy: to understand that virtue is not a matter of acting in a
            particular way but of having a particular *intention*. 18.2 Such a person
            deceives no one but himself. 18.5
         d. those who fast when they get annoyed! (19.1) A show of virtue hides their
            real feelings: anger spurs them to do what they cannot do usually, giving
            them extra energy. The root is the vice of pride, and their fast is a sacrilege
            because their fast is actually increasing their sin. 19.2

e. those who provoke others to rage with a nasty word and then feign a counterfeit patience (20). The Gospel is about peace and concord and soothing feelings, not about provoking another in any way. This can look like patience but we have to look at the intention and the spirit of the person to see if it really is virtue; is the behavior bearing fruit in mildness and patience or in rage and impatience? 21.

– Jesus is our model of patience and mildness (22)– an outward and an inner attitude (intention) of humility and submission: remain calm. Real mildness conquers rage (22.2) Feigned mildness (with a proud spirit) arouses anger in another and in oneself.

Virtue: submission of will requires strength in action; patience/endurance shows spiritual health.

Conclusion: One weak person never puts up with another weak person. Weak: one who sows discord, but will not put up with the slightest mistreatment. Therefore, re: friendship: strong and stable love cannot exist except among those of the same virtue and chosen orientation. 24

– What is to be done about the weak? 25
– They should change or depart: someone else's magnanimity is no excuse for continuing their behavior 26.1

2. Right ways for friends to respond. If anyone is aroused to anger:
   A. Preserve the exterior calm (of the lips) and the interior (heart)   26.2
   B. Concentrate on the soon-to-be amity.
   C. Restrain yourself, smother the negative feelings 27.1 and 27.5
   D. Receive the adverse waves in the broad harbor of love:
      forbearance and patience, enlarge the mind and dissipate anger.
   E. Submit to the treatment, realizing that we are worthy of mistreatment 27.3
      [idea of self] Submission is not the same as walking away. Flight inflames rather than diminishes anger (27.4); submission is wisdom

Conclusion: harmony and indivisible fellowship exists only among men of fault-less behavior who share the same virtue and chosen orientation. 28.1

Notes: Appendices

1. The portrait is a fresco in the Papal Library of the Lateran, dating to circa 600 A.D.
2. Van der Meer, 211 and 235.
3. I have relied for this description on Serge Lancel, 235-245.
4. Excavations began in 1924.
5. Van der Meer, 20f.
6. Van der Meer (p. 20) places the Hippo nuns inside the ecclesial compound "close to the bishop's residence," while Lancel more cautiously follows Verheijen in stating that the location remains uncertain. Lancel, 224.
7. Van der Meer, 217.

8. *Ep*.29.11. The letter is describing the practice of celebrating the anniversary of Leontius with a drinking party in the church. Augustine, decrying such a practice, relates to Alypius his success in convincing the Catholic congregation to break from this depraved tradition on this particular day, even while they could hear the Donatists carrying on in their church. [I]n haereticorum basilica audiebamus ab eis solita conuiuia celebrata, cum adhuc etiam eo ipso tempore, quo a nobis ista gerebantur, illi in poculis perdurarent. CSEL 34.1 (121: 23-26).

9. Lawless, *Monastic Rule*, 167-171.

10. Martin, *Our Restless Heart*, 70.

11. I owe this observation to Fr. George Lawless, O.S.A. communicated verbally to the author.

12. Cf. *Ep*. 98.6.

13. Ep. 23.3.

14. Lawless, *Monastic Rule*, 138-139.

15. Lawless, "Regula": *An Encyclopedia*, 709.

BIBLIOGRAPHY

FOR SENECA:

Primary Sources:

Cicero. *Tusculan Disputations.* Latin with English transl. by J.E. King. Harvard University Press, Loeb edition. Cambridge MA, reprint 2001.

Seneca. *De ira.* Latin with Eng. transl. in *Seneca: Moral Essays I.* Transl. John W. Basore. Harvard University Press, Loeb edition. Cambridge MA, (reprint 1998): 253-355.

_____. *De tranquillitate animi.* Latin with Eng. transl. in *Seneca: Moral Essays II.* Transl. John W. Basore. Harvard University Press, Loeb edition. Cambridge MA, (reprint 2001): 202-285.

Jerome. *De viris inlustribus.* Eng. tr. E. Richardson. *Library of the Nicene and Post-Nicene Fathers* 3, ser.2 (1892): 359-384.

Secondary Sources:

Anderson, William S. "Anger in Juvenal and Seneca." *Classical Philology* 19, No. 3: 127-196. University of California Press, Berkeley and Los Angeles, 1964.

Braund, Susanna and Glenn W. Most. *Ancient Anger: Perspectives from Homer to Galen.* Cambridge University Press, Cambridge England, 2003 (Reprint, 2004).

Brunschwig, Jacques and Martha C. Nussbaum, eds. *Passions and Perceptions.* Cambridge University Press, Cambridge, 1993.

Cooper, John M. and J.F. Procopé. *Seneca: Moral and Political Essays.* Cambridge University Press, Cambridge, 1995.

Fillion-Lahille, Janine. *Le De ira de Sénèque et La philosophie stoïcienne des passions .* Études et Commentaires 94. Klincksieck Publishers, Paris, 1984.

Harris, William V. *Restraining Rage: The Ideology of Anger Control in Classical Antiquity.* Harvard University Press, Cambridge MA and London England, 2001.

Inwood, Brad. *Ethics and Human Action in Early Stoicism.* Clarendon Press, Oxford, 1985.

_____. *Reading Seneca: Stoic Philosophy at Rome.* Clarendon Press, Oxford, 2005.

Motto, Anna Lydia. *Seneca.* Twayne Publishers, Inc. New York, 1973.

Nussbaum, Martha C. *The Therapy of Desire*: Theory and Practice in Hellenistic Ethics. Princeton University Press, Princeton, NJ, 1994.

Rist, John M. "Seneca and Stoic Orthodoxy." *Aufstieg und Niedergang des Römischen Welt,* vol.2.36.3. Berlin (1989): 1993-2012.

Sorabji, Richard. *Emotion and Peace of Mind: From Stoic Agitation to Christian Temptation.* Oxford University Press, Oxford, 2000.

Sørensen, Villy. *Seneca: the humanist at the court of Nero.* Canongate Publishers, Ltd and the University of Chicago Press, Chicago, 1984. (Originally published title: Seneca. Humanisten ved Neros Hof. Gyldendal Publ., Netherlands 1976.)

Sevenster, J.N. *Paul and Seneca.* E.J. Brill, Leiden, 1961.

Stevens, John A. "Preliminary Impulse in Stoic Psychology." *Ancient Philosophy* 20 (2000): 139-168.

Rist, John M. "Seneca and Stoic Orthodoxy." *Aufstieg und Niedergang des Römischen Welt,* vol.2. Walter de Gruyter Publishers, Berlin-New York (1989): 1993-2112.

Timothy, H.B. *The Tenets of Stoicism: Assembled from the works of L. Annaeus Seneca.* Adolf M Hakkert Publishers, Amsterdam, 1973.

FOR EVAGRIUS PONTICUS:

Primary Sources:

Aristotle. *Nichomachean Ethics* . *The Basic Works of Aristotle*. Ed. Richard McKeon. Random House, NY, 1941.

Antony of Egypt. *Epistles*. Eng.tr. Derwas J. Chitty: *The Letters of Saint Antony the Great*, SLG Press, Oxford, 1995.

Athanasius' *Life of Antony*. Ed. J.-P. Migne. PG 26 col. 835-976 (1887). Eng. Tr. with Introduction by Robert C. Gregg. *Athanasius: The Life of Antony and the Letter of Marcellinus*. The Classics of Western Spirituality. Paulist Press. Ramsey, NJ, 1980.

Basil. *Ascetical Works. The Fathers of the Church* 9. Transl. by Sr M. Monica Wagner, csc. The Catholic University of America Press. Washington, DC, 1962.

Benedict. *Rule of Saint Benedict*. Transl. by Luke Dysinger, O.S.B. Source Books, Trabuco Canyon, CA, 1997.

Evagrius. For the Greek of all the texts used in this thesis, see www.ldysinger.com/Evagrius, compiled by Luke Dysinger, O.S.B.

_____. *On Asceticism and Stillness, On the Evil Thoughts* (called here: *On Discrimination*), and *On Prayer*. Transl. G.E.H. Palmer, et al. *The Philocalia*, vol. 1. Faber and Faber Ltd. London (1983): 31-71.

_____. *The Praktikos & Chapters on Prayer*. Transl. John Eudes Bamberger. *Cistercian Publications* 4. Kalamazoo, MI, 1981.

_____. *The Mind's Long Journey to the Trinity: The* Ad Monachos *of Evagrius Ponticus*. Transl. with an Introduction by Jeremy Driscoll, O.S.B. The Liturgical Press. Collegeville, MN, 1993.

Gregory the Great. *Dialogues*. English translation by Odo Zimmermann, O.S.B and Benedict R. Avery, O.S.B. *Life and Miracles of St. Benedict*. The Liturgical Press. Collegeville, MN (no date).

Jerome. *Commentary on Matthew*. PL 26, col. 15-218 (1845).

_____. *Commentary on Ezechiel* PL 25, col. 15-490 (1845).

_____. *Epistles*. PL 22, col. 325-1212 (1845).

Nemesius of Emesa. *De Natura Hominis*. Ed. Moreno Morani. BSB. B.G. Teubner, 1987. Eng. Transl. *On the Nature of Man*, 35, Library of Christian Classics 4. Westminster Press, Philadelphia, 1955.

Origen. *Traité des Principes* III, *Sources Chrétiennes* 268. Les Éditions du Cerf. Paris. 1980. Eng. tr: *On First Principles*. ed. G.W. Butterworth. Peter Smith Publishers. Gloucester MA, 1973.

Palladius. *The Lausiac History. Ancient Christian Writers* 34. Westminster. MD, 1965.

Prudentius. *Psychomachia*. Loeb Classical Library, Tr. H.J. Thomson. Harvard University Press. Cambridge, MA, 1969.

Secondary Sources:

Allen, Diogenes. "Ascetical Theology and the Eight Deadly Thoughts."*Evangelical Journal* 13 (1995) 15-21.

Bamberger, John Eudes, O.C.S.O.: *"Desert Calm:* Evagrius Ponticus: The Theologian as Spiritual Guide." *Cistercian Studies Quarterly* 27 no. 3 (1992) 185-198.

Bunge, Gabriel. "The 'Spiritual Prayer': On the Trinitarian Mysticism of Evagrius of Pontus." Monastic Studies 17 (1986) 191-208.

_____. *Vino dei Draghi e Pane degli Angeli: L 'insegnamento di Evagrio Pontico sull'ira e la mitezza.* Edizioni Qiqajon. Comunitá di Bose.

Casiday, A.M. *Evagrius Ponticus.* Routledge, New York, 2006. This work contains primary texts translated by the author as well as secondary material.

DelCogliano, Mark. "Situating Sarapion's Sorrow: The Anthropomorphite Controversy as the Historical and Theological Context of Cassian's Tenth Conference on Pure Prayer," *CSQ* 38.4 (2003): 377-421.

Driscoll, Jeremy, O.S.B. "Listlessness in *The Mirror for Monks* of Evagrius Ponticus. *Cistercian Studies* 24 (1989): 206-214.

_____. "A Key for reading the *Ad Monachos* of Evagrius Ponticus." *Augustinianum* 30 (1990) 361-392.

_____. "Gentleness in the *Ad Monachos* of Evagrius Ponticus." *Studia Monastica* (1990) 295-321.

_____. *The 'Ad Monachos' of Evagrius Ponticus: Its Structure and a Select Commentary.* Studia Anselmiana 104. Rome, 1991.

Dysinger, Luke, O.S.B. *Psalmody and Prayer in the Writings of Evagrius Ponticus.* Oxford Theological Monographs, Oxford University Press, 2005.

Gould, Graham. *The Desert Fathers on Monastic Community.* Clarendon Press, Oxford, 1993.

_____. "An Ancient Monastic Writing: Giving advice to Spiritual Directors. (Evagrius of Pontus, *On Teachers and Disciples)." Hallel* 22 (1997): 96-103.

Layton, Richard. *"Propatheia:* Origen and Didymus on the Origin of the Passions," *Vigiliae Christianae* 54.3 (2000): 262-282.

_____. "From 'Holy Passion' to Sinful Emotion." *In Lordly Eloquence: Essays on Patristic Exegesis in Honor of Robert Louis Wilkin.* Eerdman's Publishing Company, Grand Rapids, MI, 2002.

Misiarczyk, L.: "Smutek i zlosc w nauce duchowej Ewagriusza z Pontu [Grief and anger in the spiritual teaching of Evagrius Ponticus]." *Studa Plockie* 30 (2002): 83–96.

Sinkewicz, Robert E. Evagrius of Pontus: The Greek Ascetic Corpus. Oxford Early Christian Studies, Oxford University Press, 2003.

Stewart, Columba. "Imageless Prayer and the Theological Vision of Evagrius Ponticus." *Journal of Early Christian Studies* 9.2 (2001): 173-204.

Veilleux, Armand. *La Vie de Saint Pachôme*, Spiritualite Orientale 38, Abbaye de Bellefontaine. 1984.

Ware, Kalistos. "The Passions: Enemy or Friend?" *In Communion* 17, Fall 1999.

FOR CASSIAN:

Primary sources:

Cassian, John. *De Institutis Coenobiorum.* Ed. Michael Petschenig, supplemented by Gottfried Kreuz. *Corpus scriptorum ecclesiasticorum latinorum* XVII, Vienna, 2004. English: *The Monastic Institutes.* Transl. by Jerome Bertram. The Saint Austin Press, London, 1999.

_____. *Collationes.* Ed. Michael Petschenig, supplemented by Gottfried Kreuz. *Corpus scriptorum ecclesiasticorum latinorum* XIII, Vienna, 2004. English: *The Conferences.* Transl. by Boniface Ramsey, O.P. Paulist Press, New York, NY/Mahway, NJ, 1997.

_____. *On the Incarnation.* Transl. Edgar C.S. Gibson. *Post-Nicene Fathers* (series 2), vol. 11. Hendrickson Publishers, Peabody, MA, reprint 1994.

Secondary sources:

DelCogliano, Mark. "Situating Sarapion's Sorrow: The Anthropomorphite Controversy as the Historical and Theological Context of Cassian's Tenth Conference on Pure Prayer," *CSQ* 38.4 (2003): 377-421.

Fiske, A., R.C.S.J. "Cassian and Monastic Friendship," *American Benedictine Review* 12 (1961): 190-205.

Funk, Mary Margaret. *A Mind at Peace : The Lessons of John Cassian and the Desert Fathers.* Lion Publishing plc. Oxford, England, 1999. A reprint of *Thoughts Matter.* The Continuum Publishing Company, New York, NY 1998.

Konstan, David. "The History of Christian Friendship," *Journal of Early Christian Studies* 4.1 (1996): 87-113.

Hunter, David. "The Resistance to the Virginal Ideal in Late-Fourth-Century Rome; the Case of Jovinian." *Theological Studies* 48 (1987): 45-64.

Lawless, George. "John Cassian: The Conferences." *Augustinian Studies* 31/1 (2000): 119-128.

Leyser, Conrad. *Authority and Asceticism from Augustine to Gregory the Great.* Clarendon Press. Oxford, 2000.

McGuire, Brian Patrick. *Friendship & Community: the Monastic Experience.* Cistercian Publications, Inc. Kalamazoo, MI, 1988.

Ramsey, Boniface, O.P. "John Cassian: Student of Augustine." *CSQ* 28 (1998): 5-15, 199-200.

Steward, Columba. *Cassian the Monk.* Oxford Studies in Historical Theology . Oxford University Press, Oxford, 1998.

FOR AUGUSTINE:

Primary Sources:

_____. *De moribus ecclesiae catholicae.* PL 32 col. 1310-1383 (1845). Eng. translation: *On the Morals of the Catholic Church.* The Nicene and Post-Nicene Fathers. First Series Vol. 4. Reprinted by Eerdmans Publishing Co, Grand Rapids MI (1989): 69-89.

_____. *De diversis quaesitionibus LXXXIII.* PL 40 (1845). Eng. translation by David L. Mosher in Eighty-Three Different Questions. FC 70. The Catholic University of America Press, Washington DC, 1982.

_____. *De opere monachorum.* CSEL 41 (1900). Eng. translation by H. Browne, *Of the Work of Monks,* in the Post-Nicene Fathers 3, series 1: 503-524. Reprinted by Eerdmans Publishing Co, Grand Rapids MI, 1989.

_____. *Ordo Monasterii* and the *Praeceptum.* Text and translation with Introduction in *Augustine of Hippo and his Monastic Rule,* by George Lawless, O.S.A. Clarendon Press, Oxford, 1987.

_____. *Epistulae.* Ed. Al. Goldbacher CSEL 34.1-2 (1895, 1898), CSEL 44 (1904), CSEL 57 (1911). Vienna. *Letter* 211.1-4 (*Obiurgatio*) and *Letter* 211.5-16 (*Regularis informatio* or *Rule for Nuns*) may also be found in *Augustine of Hippo and his Monastic Rule,* by George Lawless, O.S.A. Clarendon Press, Oxford, (1987): 104-109, 110-118. Eng. translation by Ronald Teske, S.J. in *Letters of Augustine* I-III (1-210). New City Press. Hyde Park, NY, 2001-2004.

_____. *Epistolae ex duobus codicibus nuper in lucem prolatae.* CSEL 88. Ed. Johannes Divjak. Vienna, 1981. Eng. translation by Robert B. Eno in *The Augustine Letters* 1*-29*. FC 81. The Catholic University of America Press, Washington DC, 1989.

_____. *Confessiones.* PL 32 col. 659-868 (1845). Eng. translation. Maria Bolding, O.S.B. New City Press. Hyde Park, NY, 1997.

_____. *Enarrationes in psalmos.* Corpus Christianorum 38-40. Brepols Publishers. Turnholt. 1956. Eng. transl. by Maria Bolding, O.S.B. in *Expositions on the Psalms* vol. 1-6 (Psalms 1-120) New City Press, NY (2000-2003). Also a complete translation may be found in: *A Library of the Fathers of the Holy Catholic Church.* Ed. by E.B. Pusey. Oxford, 1847-1857.

_____. *Sermones.* PL 38 (1841). English translation by Edmund Hill, O.P. *Sermons.* New City Press. Hyde Park, NY, 1995-2000. Sermones 355-356 were also edited by D.C. Lambot O.S.B. in *Sermones Selecti duodeviginti.* Brussels, 1950.

Secondary Sources:

Agatha Mary, S.P.B., Sister. *The Rule of Saint Augustine: an Essay in Understanding.* Augustinian Press, Villanova PA, 1992.

Asiedu, Felix Baffour Asare. "Paul and Augustine's Retrospective Self: The Relevance of *Epistula* XXII." *Revue des Études Augustiniennes,* 47 (2000): 145-164.

Bavel, T.J. "'Ante omnia' et 'in Deum' dans 'Regula Sancti Augustini.'" *Vigiliae Christianae,* 12 (1958): 157-165.

Beduhn, Jason David. "Augustine Accused: Megalius, Manichaeism, and the Inception of the *Confessions.*" *Journal of Early Christian Studies* 17.1 (2009): 85-124.

Bonner, Gerald. *The Monastic Rules.* New York City Press. Hyde Park, New York, 2004.

Brown, Peter. *Augustine of Hippo: A Biography.* Dorset Press. New York, 1967.

Burt, Donald O.S.A. "Peace" in *Augustine Through the Ages: An Encyclopedia,* ed. Allan D. Fitzgerald., O.S.A., William B. Eerdmans Publishing Company. Grand Rapids, MI (1999): 629-632.

Carola, Joseph A.F., S.J. *Solvitis et Vos: The Laity and their Exercise of the Power of the Keys according to Saint Augustine of Hippo.* Doctoral Dissertation submitted to the Augustinianum, Rome, 2001.

Fitzgerald, Allan. "Pénitence et Carême." *Connaissance des Peres de l'Église* 75: *La Péni-tence*. Éditions Nouvelle Cité. Roma, 1977.

Grossi, Vittorino. "Introduzione" to *Sant'Agostino: La riconciliazione cristiana*. Cittá Nuova Editrice, Rome (1983): 9-56.

_____. "Correction," *Augustine Through the Ages: An Encyclopedia*, ed. Allan D. Fitz-gerald, O.S.A., William B. Eerdmans Publishing Company. Grand Rapids, MI (1999): 242-244.

Lafont, Ghislain, O.S.B. "Fraternal Correction in the Augustinian Community." *Word & Spirit* 9 (1987): 87-91.

Lancel, Serge. *St Augustine*, Librairie Arthème Fayard, 1999. Eng. transl. Antonia Nevill, SCM Press. Canterbury, 2002.

Lawless, O.S.A. George. "The Rule of Saint Augustine as a Mirror of Perfection," *Angelicum* 58 (1981): 460- 474.

_____. "Psalm 132 and Augustine's Monastic Ideal," *Angelicum* 59 (1982): 526-539.

_____. "Enduring Values of the Rule of Saint Augustine," *Angelicum* 59 (1982): 59-78.

_____. "The Monastery as Model of the Church: Augustine's *Commentary* on Psalm 132." *Angelicum* 60 (1983): 258-274.

_____. *Augustine of Hippo and his Monastic Rule*. Clarendon Press, Oxford, 1987.

_____. "Le Pardon Mutuel dans la Compréhension augustinienne du Notre Père (Mt 6,12)." *Connaissance Péres de l'Église* 75: *La Pénitence*. Éditions Nouvelle Cité. (1999): 47-50.

_____. "Augustine's Decentring of Asceticism" in *Augustine and His Critics, Essays in Honor of Gerald Bonner*. Routledge, Taylor Francis Group. London and New York (2000): 142-163.

_____. "John Cassian: The Conferences." A book review of Boniface Ramsey's transla-tion of *The Conferences* [translated in 1997]. *Augustinian Studies* 31/1 (2000): 119-128.

Leyser, Conrad. *Authority and Asceticism from Augustine to Gregory the Great*. Clarendon Press. Oxford, 2000.

Marec, Erwan. *Monuments Chrétiens D'Hippone: ville épiscopale de Saint Augustin*. Arts et Métiers Graphiques, Paris, 1958.

Martin, Thomas. *Our Restless Heart: The Augustinian Tradition*. Orbis Books. Maryknoll, NY, 2003.

Van der Meer, Frederick. *Augustine the Bishop*, Eng. transl. Brian Battershaw and G.R. Lamb. Sheed and Ward, London and New York, 1961.

Verheijen, Luc, O.S.A. *La règle de saint Augustin* II. *Recherches historiques*. Études augus-tiniennes, Paris, 1967.

_____. "The Straw, the Beam the Tusculan Disputations and the Rule of Saint Augustine – On a Surprising Augustinian Exegesis." *Augustinian Studies* 2 (1971): 17-36.

_____. *Nouvelle Approche de la Règle de Saint Augustin* I. Vie Monastique Spiritualité. Begrolles-en-Mauges, 1980.

_____. "Les Sermons de Saint Augustin pour le carême (205-211) et sa motivation de la vie 'ascetique.'" Chap. 8 of *Nouvelle Approche de la Règle de Saint Augustin* I. Vie Monastique Spiritualité. Published by the Abbaye de Bellefontaine, Begrolles-en-Mauges, (1980): 153-200 or 357-404.

Zumkeller, Adolar, O.S.A. *Augustine's Rule*. Tr. Matthew J. O'Connell; ed. John E. Rotelle, O.S.A. Augustinian Press, Villanova, PA, 1987.

INDEX

incentive power 22, 24-25, 38, 39, 134
indignation 24-25, 28, 34, 42 n.20, 43
  n.33, 54, 112
insult/s 4, 64, 68, 98, 103, 135
impurity 25, 41 n.11 (see also: lust)
ignorance 7, 12, 23, 44 n.37
irascibility 14 n.15, 17 n.50, 24, 28, 31,
  34-36, 44 n.37, 45 n.61
irascible 24-27, 30-31, 34-35, 37,
  43 n.35, 45 n.49, 68 n.9, 133-34
irritation 7, 63

Januarius 90, 100, 108
jealousy 1, 76, 79, 81, 99, 125 n.131
Jerome 22-23, 41 nn.11 and 14, 42
  nn.17 and 20, 70 n.46, 122 n.94
Jesus 62, 64 (see also: Christ)
John the Baptist 40 n.3
John (the Evangelist) 62, 70 n.46
John Chrysostom 40 n.4, 50

Leo (Pope) 121 n.46
  light 12, 28, 31, 38-39, 44 nn.37 and
  43, 45 nn.54 and 55, 47 n.82, 78
logismoi/logismos 22-24, 26, 32, 41
  nn.11 and 12, 42 nn.15 and 17, 50-51,
  69 n.23
love 5-6, 22, 30, 34, 37, 43 n.26, 45
  n.58, 46 n.75, 47 n.84, 50, 58-62, 64-
  65, 67, 68 n.10, 69 n.29, 70 n.46, 71
  n.55, 75-79, 84-9, 91, 93-97, 99, 101-
  102, 105-8, 110, 112, 114, 120 n.65,
  121 n.69, 125 nn.134 and 135, 126
  n.148, 134, cf. 17 n.42 (self-love)
lust 22, 24, 30, 32, 36, 51, 128 n.178
  (see also: impurity)

Makarios, 43 n.23
Manichee 77
  Manichean/s 117 n.20, 119 n.49, 121
    n.81
  Manicheanism 79, 118 n.29
Martin (St) 81
meekness 34, 37, 39, 46 n.71-2, 47
  n.81, 77
Megalius 74-75, 78-80, 118 nn.25-6
  and nn.28-30, 129 n.185
Melania 22, 40 n.8
mercy 31, 35, 38-39, 81, 102, 104, 115

Milan 73-76, 88
mildness 64 (see also: gentle/ness)
monastery 29, 49-50, 57, 69 n.30
  Augustine's *clerical* monastery 74,
    81-83, 100, 119 n.35
  Augustine's *garden* monastery 74,
    80-83, 90, 101, 119 n.37
  nuns' monastery 74-75, 99, 108

Moses 37-38, 47 n.79
murmurring 94, 96-98
music 36, 46 n.65, 87

Nebridius 119 n.6
Nero 1, 9, 14 n.15, 17 n.47
nous 25, 27, 31-38, 35, 42 n.22, 43 n.35,
  45 n.54, 46 n.78
nuns (see monastery: nuns' monastery)
  cf. 50: monastery of Cassian's sister

obedience 105, 121 n.81
orgē 24
orientation 58, 60, 64, 66, 69 n.35
  (see also: purpose)
Origen 21-23, 40 n.4, 41 n.11, 42 n.17,
  42 n.20, 50, 53
Origenist/s 50, 68

Pachomius/Pachomian 21, 49, 66, 121
  n.81
Palladius 40 n.8, 45 n.57
pardon 12, 79, 101, 103-104, 111, 113-
  16, 125 n.133, 126 n.145, 130 n.199
  (see also: forgive)
passion/s 2-6, 14 n.6, 15 nn.21, 23 and
  25, 18 nn.55 and 60, 21-24, 27-32,
  35-37, 39, 40 n.4, 41 n.11, 42 nn.16
  and 20, 44 n.45, 46 nn.65 and 68, 47
  n.80, 51, 53-54, 101, 116, 128 n.175
  129 n.188
  pre-passion 3 (see: first movements)
  passionlessness (or: passionless state)
    23, 27, 43 n.35, 47 n.80
    (see also: *apatheia*)
pathos/pathē 2
patience 26, 34, 37, 46 n.64, 61, 64-66,
  76-77, 106
patient 24, 34, 37
  patient endurance 103, 105

156 Index

Paul (St.) 14 n.1, 21, 41 n.12, 52, 54-
55, 71 n.53, 75, 77-78, 91, 97, 117
n.12, 120 n.65
peace 8, 11, 13, 24, 29, 53, 58-61,
63-65, 68 n.10, 71 n.55, 80, 97,
99-100, 103-8, 124 n.114, 133
peaceful 3, 23, 50
penance 77, 102, 113, 127 n.165
Peter (St.) 126 n.146
Plato/nic 2-3, 14 n.11, 15 n.18, 16 n.32,
39 n.1, 52, 125 n.131
Platonists 68 n.9

Possidius 73, 83, 119 n.8, 118 n.26,
119nn.35 and 49
poverty 74, 83-85, 89-91, 100
(see also: dispossession)
praktikē 38, 40
pray/er(s) 24, 28-37, 39, 43 nn.23 and
30; 44 nn.41, 43, 45, and 46;
45 nn.49, 52 and 55; 46 nn.67-68;
50, 52-53, 56-57, 61, 63, 74-75, 79,
81, 83, 85-87, 89-90, 92, 94, 103-
105, 109-111, 115, 119 n.42, 125
n.141, 134
pure prayer 29-31, 43 n.30, 44
n.46, 53, 68 n.15
pride 23-24, 27, 31, 35, 45 n.47, 46
n.63, 51, 61, 63-65, 76, 83, 101, 115,
121 n.81
Profuturus 79
psalm/s /psalmody 29, 31, 34, 36, 41
n.9, 43 n.24, 46 n.64, 46 n.65, 63
purity of heart 38, 40 n.4
pure prayer (see prayer: pure prayer)
purpose (vocation/orientation) 58, 66-
67, 86, 89, 91-2, 96, 102
(see also: orientation)

quarrel/ing 40 n.2, 67, 78, 98-100, 108,
110-11, 113, 125 n.139
quiet/ly 9, 13, 22, 29-31, 43 n.26, 77,
80, 93-94

rage/d 47 nn.78 and 84, 64, 79-80, 101,
110, 113, 118 n.30, 125 n.135
rational 8, 25-26, 65, 68 n.9
irrational 32, 42 n.16

reason/ing 2-3, 4-6, 8-9, 11, 13 n.1,
14 n.9, 15 nn.22-3, 18 n.53, 22, 28,
41 n.12, 43 n.26
reconcile/d 28, 33, 56-57, 63, 70 n.43,
100, 109, 114
reconciliation 32-4, 45 n.59, 56-57, 65,
69 n.27, 98, 102-105, 108, 115, 126
n.146, 134
refectory 81-82, 97
reform 9-10, 16 n.31, 75, 107, 127 n.159
remedy 3, 9, 11-13, 17 n.48 and 50,
19 n.68, 24, 27, 31-32, 34-37, 42 n.22,
44 nn.42 and 65; 45 n.59; 63, 76
repent 38, 101, 113
repentance 5, 113, 125 nn.131 and 133
resent/resentment/s 11, 24, 28-29, 31, 37,
39, 45 n.49, 80, 99, 111-13, 129
n.185
resentful 31, 34
respect/ed 9, 37, 44 n.46, 46 n.63, 53,
75, 80, 86, 88, 97, 101
restrain/t 5, 9, 12-13, 17 n.52, 31, 45
n.50, 59-60, 65, 88, 101, 106, 110,
113
retaliate 27, 34
retaliation 35, 104, 106, 113
revenge 4, 6, 8, 10, 28, 34, 111, 113,
128 n.178
(see also: avenge, vengeance)
Rome 1, 49-50, 80, 88
Rufinus 22, 40 n.8, 41 n.11

sadness/dejection 23, 28, 42 n.15, 51,
63, 68 n.6
Satan 61, 134
(see also: demon, devil)
self-knowledge 10, 11
Seneca (outside of chapter 1) 22, 33, 41
n.11, 49, 54, 69 n.23, 133, 135
service 82-83, 86-89, 97, 119 n.35
skill(s) 9, 11-12, 17 n.52, 64
slander/er 74, 79
silence 28, 31, 46 n.7, 63, 107, 121
nn.32 and 42, 123 n.80, cf. 81 and
115 (silently), cf. 64 (silent)
Socrates 1, 11, 14 n.2
solitude 28, 33-34, 52, 56, 81, 93, 119
n.42

ABOUT THE AUTHOR

Sister Gertrude Gillette, O.S.B. received her Ph.D. from The Catholic University of America in Early Christian Studies (Patristics). She did post-graduate work in Rome, earning an S.T.B. from The Angelicum and an S.T.L. with a Specialization in Monastic Studies from the Benedictine Collegio Sant'Anselmo. She is currently an Associate Professor of Theology at Ave Maria University, Ave Maria, Florida and the superior of a house of Benedictine Sisters.